LAWYERING AN UNCERTAIN CAUSE

LAWYERING AN UNCERTAIN CAUSE
Immigration Advocacy and Chinese Youth in the U.S.

MICHELE STATZ

Vanderbilt University Press
Nashville

Library of Congress Cataloging-in-Publication Data
LC control number 2017042894
LC classification number KF337.5 I45 .S73 2018
Dewey classification number 342.7308/3
LC record available at *lccn.loc.gov/2017042894*

ISBN 978-0-8265-2208-5 (cloth)
ISBN 978-0-8265-2209-2 (paperback)
ISBN 978-0-8265-2210-8 (ebook)

For my parents

CONTENTS

ACRONYMS

BIA   Board of Immigration Appeals

BID   Best Interests Determination

CAT   United Nations Convention Against Torture

CAPTA   Child Abuse Prevention Treatment Act

CBP   US Customs and Border Patrol

CNCS   Corporation for National and Community Service

CPC   Country of Particular Concern

CRC   Convention on the Rights of the Child

DACA   Deferred Action for Childhood Arrivals

DCFS   Department of Child and Family Services

DHS   Department of Homeland Security

DOJ   Department of Justice

DUCS   ORR's Division of Unaccompanied Children's Services

EOIR   Executive Office for Immigration Review

ESL   English as a Second Language

GAL   Guardian ad Litem

HHS   Department of Health and Human Services

ICE   US Immigration and Customs Enforcement

IJ   Immigration Judge

INA   Immigration and Nationality Act

INS   US Immigration and Naturalization Service

LPR   Lawful Permanent Resident

NGO   Non-governmental Organization

ORR   Office of Refugee Resettlement

SIJ	Special Immigrant Juvenile Status
SNAP	Supplemental Nutrition Assistance Program
SSI	Supplemental Security Income
TANF	Temporary Assistance for Needy Families
TVPRA	William Wilberforce Trafficking Victims Protection Reauthorization Act
UAC	Unaccompanied Alien Child
UDHR	Universal Declaration of Human Rights
UCA	Unaccompanied Children's Alliance
UMP	Undocumented Migration Project
UNODC	United Nations Office on Drugs and Crime
USCIS	US Citizenship and Immigration Services
VAWA	Violence Against Women Act
VTVPA	Victims of Trafficking and Violence Prevention Act
WIC	Women, Infants, and Children

ACKNOWLEDGMENTS

This book only exists because of the extraordinary generosity and insights of others.

I am grateful to everyone who participated in my research. These individuals entrusted me with their personal hopes and professional frustrations, as well as with their complex and often very intimate life stories. They also shared their time, networks, and knowledge. With humility and deep respect, I have done my best to weave together these expert perspectives. I owe special thanks in particular to Young Sullivan, John Sullivan, Hannah Sibiski, Maria Woltjen, Jajah Wu, and those friends (and friends of friends) who provided shelter, food, and helpful directions on so many research stops.

At the University of Washington, I had the incredible gift of attentive, stimulating, and truly caring mentors. My warmest thanks to Arzoo Osanloo, who in the spirit of her father's academic pursuits always "left the lights on" for me. It remains my heartfelt goal to do the same for my students. I similarly had the good fortune to have Roberto Gonzales's wise perspective and unwavering support. My appreciation extends to George Lovell, who introduced me to and exemplifies the dynamic and truly collegial world of law and society studies. And finally, I offer my deepest thanks to Steve Harrell. I am a better anthropologist because of his careful attention, high standards, and trustworthy mentorship. This book is written to him.

I am steadfastly grateful for Shanna Scherbinske, Kenny Robinson, Stephanie Maher, Marlaine Figueroa Gray, Jennifer Carroll, and Anne Greenleaf. Special thanks are due Steve Herbert, who has always been a source of trusted counsel, and Mimi Kahn, who always made us feel like family. My life and work have been enriched by the d'Ambruoso family, the Sanfords, the beautiful women of the Double P, Josh Clark, Amy Burke, Kari Smalkoski, Lisa Pruitt, Kathy Letourneau, and Pastor Betty Landis and the good people of St. Paul's. My deep appreciation extends to Lauren

Heidbrink, a trusted collaborator and friend. At the University of Minnesota Medical School, Duluth campus, I thank Paula Termuhlen, Angie Slattery, and Mustafa al'Absi for their good energy and support. My editor at the Vanderbilt University Press, Beth Kressel-Itkin, guided this work to production with a sincere commitment and immense care. Two anonymous reviewers, as well as Lauren Heidbrink and Kate Kirchman, offered enthusiastic and keen insights that profoundly enhanced this book. Any mistakes or oversights are mine alone.

This project received generous financial support from the US National Science Foundation's Law and Social Sciences and Cultural Anthropology Programs, the American Association of University Women, and the Department of Anthropology and the Graduate School at the University of Washington. It also benefited greatly from the helpful insights of those at the Chicago Area Law and Society Writing Seminar at the American Bar Foundation and from workshops hosted by the Association for Political and Legal Anthropology, the Law and Society Association, and the West Coast Law and Society Retreat. Some of the material in Chapter 3 appeared in an article in *Political and Legal Anthropology Review*.

Finally, my thanks to my family. I am grateful to Steve and Mahnaz Warner for their warmth and good humor. My sister, Jennifer, has always guided me with her trustworthy perspective and love. The kindness and confidence of Kathleen and William Statz led me to this journey and carried me through it. As a parent, I will feel lucky if I can match even a fraction of their love and selflessness.

This book could not exist without Bijan Warner, who more than anyone has exemplified the courageous, joyful, and necessary pursuit of knowledge. Since our drive from Chicago to Seattle in 2008, he has been my wise counsel and a source of laughter, music, strength, and growth. He is my truest friend.

This book is also for Zona. I love you.

PREFACE
"The future doesn't come to me"

The future doesn't come to me." I listened as Ruolan described her life in China and some of her reasons for leaving. Now twenty-two, Ruolan had migrated alone and clandestinely to the United States from Fujian Province, on China's southeast coast, when she was sixteen. Like the other Fujianese youth I spoke with for my research, she had been apprehended upon arrival and identified as an Unaccompanied Alien Child, or UAC. She was put in a federal detention center and placed in removal proceedings, also like the others.

When we met, Ruolan worked in a Chinese restaurant in a small town in Wisconsin. This was her odd day off, so we met together at a nearby café to talk. As with most of my fieldwork sites, the space outside our window was an unexpected yet in many ways commonplace intersection of experience: Amish and Latinx[1] community members examined dishes at a garage sale across the highway. Tourists drove past in luxury cars on their way to an outdoor theater performance. Above the café's parking lot a billboard read, *God says . . . He loves us all!* and beyond it, long rows of corn flashed green and grey in the midday sun.

As we sat together, Ruolan talked expertly about the birth-planning policy in China and about changing norms of childhood and parental responsibility. She told me about growing wealth and internal migration and property values and educational policies. Switching often between Chinese and English, she described how her hometown had experienced neither the flush of development nor the effects of many state programs; still, she added, it had changed. "You used to have everything you want, everything you need, [like] everyone else in your village. But now, you know, you can't even buy a house because the growth of the city, the growth of the economy, land becomes more expensive . . ." She looked out the window and shrugged.

"The future doesn't come to me," Ruolan stated, and from her presence in Wisconsin one could perhaps extend the sequence: *so I have to go and get it.*

Like Ruolan, the other Fujianese youth who participated in my research offered distinct and distinctly expert understandings of transnational mobility. Their reflections accordingly reveal that what is often briskly categorized as "Fujianese migration" is at once individual and relative. It is differentiated by political and economic policies, regional histories, intersecting and often conflicting intergenerational expectations, and deeply felt experiences of marginalization. A young person's sense of "having to" migrate may further arise from individual responsibilities, persistent ambitions, hidden suffering, the lure and familiarity of established migration networks, and more. Indeed, there is always more, particularly as youths' multiple journeys—across the United States, into adulthood, within the workplace—unfold.

Yet amid these shifting unknowns, the implied *so I have to go and get it* raises subtler questions that this book takes up, questions that almost exclusively matter in, and to, legal advocacy efforts. What does it mean for a young person to *have to* migrate? What does it mean *to* a young person? How can an immigration attorney sufficiently elicit and re-present the *having to*—the intricate realities detailed above—through the language of the law? Is it possible? And at what cost? As practitioners and scholars of law already know, how the question of "having to" is answered is often the lynchpin of a successful legal case, one in which a child's migration journey is understood as a matter of abandonment, neglect, or trafficking. Yet as I demonstrate here, these questions prove critical to another and less considered dimension of lawyering.

In this book, which I overview in greater detail in the following chapter, I focus on cause lawyering on behalf of Fujianese youth in removal proceedings. Most of the lawyers who participated in this research direct or work for nonprofit immigrant advocacy organizations, and as cause lawyers, they assert a professional and personal commitment to Fujianese youth amid constraining and contradictory rights frameworks, bureaucratic practices, and immigration policies. This context is, of course, common to legal advocacy on behalf of unaccompanied youth more generally. So too is what sustains many advocates throughout such urgency and incongruity, namely a moral ideology of childhood as an inherently vulnerable and dependent space.

Still, the cause at hand is relatively niche. Fujianese youth represent only a fraction of the overall number of youth designated unaccompanied in the US. They are further set apart by their relatively older age (fifteen to seventeen), the absence of a generalizable, explicitly tragic migration narrative, and the shadowy, Orientalist stereotypes their presence invokes, stereotypes that of course undergird the United States' earliest exclusionary immigration policies. As I demonstrate, however, it is precisely the unique uncertainty of this particular cause that unsettles the broader presumptions of power, age, and race that guide advocacy on behalf of unaccompanied minors more generally, not just Fujianese youth. Spanning outward, this uncertainty compels a reconsideration of the institutional practices, laws, client strategies, and moral commitments that in many ways demand these framings, and that likewise render attorneys themselves uniquely vulnerable. Uncertainty also occurs as young clients contend with smuggling debts, insecure employment, and restricted rights and protections outside the legal realm, a reality that destabilizes prevailing notions of legal "success."

In this book, I do not answer the question of why Fujianese youth migrate. Rather, I contextualize the uneven geographies of a small number of young Fujianese migrants at a certain point in time. This inconclusiveness is perhaps unsatisfying, but it importantly underscores the "deeply ambivalent and uncertain" ways in which young people imagine and live transnational mobility (Yarris 2014, 288). It also shows why the questions—Did Ruolan *have to* migrate? What, or who, compelled her migration?—ultimately matter more than their answers. The inextricable conditions of "having to" migrate, and perhaps of "choosing to" pursue one's own future, raise a host of uncertainties around age, volition, coercion, professional responsibility, and best interests. They also prefigure the intimate and unexplored choices that young migrants and, just as significantly, their *legal advocates* make about, around, and sometimes in spite of one another. Rather than answer the question, I offer this book as a response—an attempt to contextualize and make space for the complex uncertainties at the heart of lawyering youth mobility.

1   *"I didn't think it was in her best interest"*

PROTECTION FROM WHAT?

In 2012, I attended "On Their Own: Protecting the Rights of Immigrant Children" in Washington, DC. The conference was publicized as an opportunity for government representatives and legal advocates to examine the policies affecting UAC—individuals under age eighteen with no lawful immigration status and without a parent or guardian available to provide care and physical custody in the US.[1] The event additionally promised immigration attorneys a chance to "learn more about legal issues facing immigrant children . . . and brainstorm new ideas on ways to further the protection of unaccompanied immigrant children in the United States."[2] As someone interested in the legal experiences of young Chinese migrants designated "unaccompanied," I was eager to learn more about the actors and practices they would encounter in the US. Instead, I found a space rife with tension, urgency, conviction, and ambiguity.

The first day's proceedings were held at the headquarters of the Organization of American States in Washington, DC, a historic building that inside boasted curving marble staircases, fountains, and palm trees. In the main hall, the audience sat below long windows framed by heavy curtains. We craned our heads toward the stage, where throughout the day dignitaries and liaisons from various US agencies spoke flanked by colorful bunches of flags. With a few exceptions, including myself as a researcher and a small group of social workers,[3] the audience was composed of attorneys who were employed by or were directors of immigrant advocacy organizations around the US.

In this book, I recognize these attorneys as *cause lawyers*, individuals who use legal skills to pursue political or moral commitments. Importantly, these commitments include but also transcend direct client service, as through policy-making efforts (Scheingold and Sarat 2004). Encompassing advocacy that employs legally based "rights" strategies with broadly based "needs" strategies to "do good" (Menkel-Meadow 1998, 37), cause lawyering is a broadly inclusive and, accordingly, often contested term. It is also a frustrating enterprise, one in which attorneys negotiate a shifting constellation of bureaucratic contradictions, diverse political and juridical contexts, institutional inefficiencies, and, as my data demonstrate, a cause that is often less clearly defined than expected or needed.

While all attendees were ostensibly at the "On Their Own" conference with a common purpose, it was not long before I began to encounter a steadily murmured—and sometimes uncomfortably unconcealed—grumbling from those attorneys around me. The discontent ranged from organizational politics to the perception that plenary speakers were "toeing the party line," as one attorney complained. During a presentation on different forms of legal relief, another lawyer leaned toward me and whispered, "The strategies the folks from New York suggested would never work in Chicago." She shook her head. "This isn't helpful."

Walking into the humid air at the day's close, I was perhaps most unsettled by what seemed an *absence* of purpose in so "well-intentioned" an event. Instead of providing timely, policy-advancing information, representatives from Immigration and Customs Enforcement (ICE), the Department of Homeland Security (DHS), and the Office of Refugee Resettlement (ORR) presented incomplete data and skirted audience questions—many of which were admittedly only thinly veiled attacks—with a rehearsed vagueness. Likewise, the attorneys in the audience offered a different sort of ambiguity. Where I had expected a more altruistic focus, a more demonstrable concern for young migrants, the principal sentiments I observed were impatience, frustration, and even hostility directed against state actors and, sometimes, one another.

The next day of the conference, participants—the majority of whom were young to middle-aged women—sat together at round tables, drinking coffee and listening intently. Many typed or jotted down notes, and it wasn't unusual for someone in the crowd to raise her hand and interrupt a speaker. This was clearly a small world. Panelists and audience members addressed one another comfortably by first name. As I would discover, this familiarity often extended to one another's employment history, involvement with notable cases, law-school education, and acceptable or threatening affiliation with other organizations. "Our work does become a turf issue," a conference attendee told me later. "It's always a turf thing." It's worth noting, of course, that this was very much an *elite* and *urban* turf thing.

Grateful for my anonymity at the "On Their Own" conference, I listened carefully to the strategies and information attorneys shared:

> I always like to talk about my "10k kid," a client who had ten kilos of marijuana on him. If you're successful with a client like this, they get URM [Unaccompanied Refugee Minor] and stay in Seattle or go to Michigan. But it was really frustrating to deal with ORR, with case workers who didn't understand.

> Some of our families [the families of young clients] have never accessed these educational services, and they're not very good advocates for themselves.

> There was a case in New Jersey where the judge ruled that the child wasn't abandoned or neglected in Guatemala, because it's okay for youth to be working in Guatemala at age twelve. But no judge in the US should be assessing the standards in a foreign country . . . this was child labor! But the judge saw it as okay.

> I was supposed to advocate for her expressed legal interest—it was a girl who wanted voluntary departure. But I didn't. I didn't think it was in her best interest to go back to her country.

Though routine to the immigration attorneys in the room, these statements baffled me, revealing and casting doubt on the easy assumptions I held about legal advocacy and immigration relief. Why did no one discuss rights, only "best interests?" Why were clients' parents and home countries discussed in such patronizing and disparaging ways? Why was so little attention paid to youth from regions other than Central America, even among the attorneys I knew portrayed Chinese youth as their niche? More profoundly, what was the point of immigration relief? What about *other* rights and protections? The questions I formulated in this space largely propelled my research. They remain forefront to this book, an inquiry into professional demands, personal motivations, and an arguably impossible interpretation of legal success.

EVALUATING "SUCCESS"

Jarring as it was, the "On Their Own" conference succinctly foreshadowed the complex conditions and contingencies that motivate cause lawyers as much as the cause itself does. The particular cause I explore in this book is popularly understood as *the provision of free legal advocacy to unaccompanied Chinese children who are held in federal facilities and called into removal proceedings alone.*[4] Though the number of Chinese youth designated unaccompanied in the US is relatively small, their experiences are worth understanding for their own sake, as well as for what they uniquely demonstrate about the limits and consequences of legal advocates' moral commitments.

Each year, approximately fifteen hundred Chinese youth (typically ages fifteen to seventeen) migrate alone and clandestinely to the US.[5] The majority of these young people arrive from Fujian Province and, more specifically, from the region surrounding the provincial capital of Fuzhou.[6] While I often heard it characterized as a "small, poor province" by attorneys, Fujian has a population of approximately thirty-seven million and is one of China's wealthier provinces.[7] This is largely owing to its location: situated on China's southeast coast, Fujian is an attractive site for national development and international investment. This location matters for another reason, namely as regards Fujian's unique and widely recognized history of emigration among China's provinces.

I explore the broader political and socioeconomic context of Fujianese migration in more detail in Chapter 3. For now, I wish to briefly note the transnational negotiations youth themselves recognize as important. The clandestine migration of these individuals to the US is an increasingly complex and sophisticated process, one by which people and enormous sums of money—fees average $80,000 USD—are moved by "snakehead" (*she tou*) smuggling networks through multiple nations. As youth recounted, these journeys are influenced by local norms and family expectations, national policies and overseas connections, intimate sorrows, and rumored incentives. Weighing so many structural and subjective factors, many youth perceive migration as the best, or only, way to advance themselves and their families socioeconomically.

Such complex and uncertain motives present a distinct challenge to cause lawyers who must appeal to political and legal discourses that differentiate between "migrant workers" and "refugees" and between "economic" and "forced" migration (Willen 2015). As older and potentially voluntarily displaced migrants, Fujianese youth often appear to fit more squarely in the "migrant worker" and "economic" categories. Yet, of course, the notion of choice—i.e., whether or not someone *chooses* to migrate—is hardly such a neat dichotomy. Rather, it is a persistently complex and contested dimension of migration (Yarris and Casteneda 2015). To position someone as a voluntary "economic migrant" elides the intricate realities of structural violence and economic inequality (Quesada 2009); the role of immigration policy in creating and reinforcing a distinction between agency and force (Yarris and Casteneda 2015); states' responses to migration as reflective of geopolitical interests (Coutin 2011; Horton 2004); and the vulnerability that humanitarianism demands against the backdrop of the deportation regime (De Genova and Peutz 2010; Statz 2018; Ticktin 2011).

At the same time, such necessary insights on the nuanced deficiency of the "economic migrant" categorization may have little salience with immigration cause lawyers. This largely owes to the demands of legal and bureaucratic frameworks but also, as this study demonstrates, to the arguably more motivating, and in a sense also demanded, moral ideologies of childhood and dependence that many attorneys espouse. Recognizing how these forces are distinct from—and effectively distance lawyers from—pragmatic questions about formalized entitlements, social and political access, and the violence of human rights protections (Dawes 1999; Willen 2012) is a central goal of this book.

As my data suggest, the young people in this study are often portrayed by legal advocates as vulnerable children *even as* they simultaneously manage kin and peer networks, employment, legal pursuits, and transitions to adulthood via technological and physical mobility (Liu 2011; Mummert 2009). Relatedly, the intimate and intergenerational networks that facilitate a young person's migration over time are often denied or pathologized in the legal realm (Heidbrink and Statz 2017; Young 2004). This is significant, for to recognize the opposite of these framings, namely the agency and the active transnational connectedness of young migrants, is to subtly upend juridical notions of "unaccompanied"—a category that is elsewhere rightly challenged as inconsistently premised on cultural constructions of care and family and on the fiscal and political interests of the US state (Heidbrink 2014).[8] With all this in mind, the cause becomes somewhat less sure.

I explore this uncertainty by focusing in particular on rights, responsibilities, and expectations. I consider rights as they relate to age, best interests, citizenship and labor, and culture as practice and explanation (Kuper 1999; Osanloo 2009). I examine the ways in which lawyers' sense of their professional and moral responsibilities defines and perpetuates a certain type of cause and, I argue, a certain type of client. I concurrently recognize young people's ongoing contributions to household economies and transnational migration networks—responsibilities that are significantly managed through and from the legal realm. Finally, I document the expectations that youth and attorneys hold for one another, promises guided by disparate understandings of age, efficacy, and success.

Accordingly, my research draws on such diverse bodies of scholarship as socio-legal studies, the anthropology of law, the anthropology of youth, China studies scholarship, and migration studies. Predictably, my research also relies on the Cause Lawyering Project. Largely attributed to and shaped by the work of Austin Sarat and Stuart Scheingold, the project produced a range of literature dealing with the significance, influence and contested parameters of cause lawyering. From it, I recognize the attorneys at the center of my study as cause lawyers—individuals who self-consciously commit themselves and their skills to a political cause and for whom lawyering is not value-neutral (Sarat and Scheingold 1998; see also Luban 1988).

RIGHTS

Chinese youths' legality is predicated on a powerful, contradictory definition of rights. Having compromised her or his own citizenship by leaving China unauthorized, a Chinese youth who is apprehended in the US is at once positioned between two opposed rights practices. Because she or he is typically under age eighteen, the state acts as a discretionary guardian, providing the young person food and shelter as inalienable rights. At the same time, having not ratified the Convention on the Rights of the Child and thus not required to provide youth with comprehensive guardianship or legal representation (Bhabha 2009), the state normalizes the youth's detention and weakened ability to claim citizenship rights.

It is the *stateless* individual, here the unaccompanied minor, who exposes the limits of these supranational "inalienable" rights. The young person's presence doesn't break the presumed continuity between human and citizen, nativity and nationality (Agamben 1998). Instead, it evidences a "continuum" of citizenship—one in which youth experience different degrees of member-ship that distinguish undocumented immigrants, legal residents, and citizens (Calavita 2005; Ngai 2004; Schuck 1998). Though no longer experiencing the socioeconomic and emotional constraints of deportability (Gonzales and Chavez 2012; Willen 2007), youth on one end of the continuum—those who have lawful permanent residency or even citizenship—still embody "illegal life" in regard to their labor. That cause lawyers do little to acknowl-edge or address this reality implicitly challenges the holistic nature of the cause at hand.

In this context of rights and regulation, attorneys who assume the cause of representing youth without court-appointed representation must make an unaccompanied youth "legible" before the law (Scott 1998). To under-stand this process, I ask: how and why do cause lawyers, for whom law-yering is a "deeply moral or political activity" (Scheingold and Sarat 2004, 2), frame the cultural and economic realities of their Chinese clients to guarantee them some measure of legal relief? My research suggests that as lawyers advocate for what they perceive to be in a youth's best interests—avoiding repatriation—the persuasiveness of these claims is contingent on the defendant's age and the "narrowed" narrative told about her or him in court (Mather and Yngvesson 1980–1981; Statz 2016b). In other words, legal status largely depends on the extent to which a Chinese youth is portrayed as a rights-worthy *child* from a patriarchal culture and authoritarian state who did not consent to her migration journey, as opposed to a much less defensible or pitiable economic migrant. It is chiefly through this conflation of cultural identity with age and nation-state that attorneys appeal to a reality of rights that constrains them as well as their clients.

RESPONSIBILITY

To most of the cause lawyers I interviewed, these tactics are successful; they secure legal status.[9] They also permit attorneys to contend with the contradic-tory nature of unaccompanied youths' rights, and with the limited number of legal protections available to them, and to maintain "principled" altruistic goals and responsibilities (Menkel-Meadow 1998). I argue, however, that these strategies simultaneously deny youths' voices and the agentive roles they take in their migration journeys and transnational community contexts (Dreby 2007; Rae-Espinoza 2016; Yarris 2014). They may also compromise youths' own long-term financial commitments and personal responsibilities (Heidbrink and Statz 2017). Significantly, attorneys' understanding of "best interests" in these practices appears rooted in a Western, legally dominant view of childhood, one that presumes an apolitical, sacrilized child; families', schools', and professionals' responsibility for children; and "a general presumption against [youths'] paid labor" (Appell 2009, 709; Nieuwenhuys 1996). Perhaps unsurprisingly, these ideas conflict directly with many of the reflections that Chinese youth shared with me.

To illuminate this dissonance, I deliberately document the practices and aims of attorneys alongside—and sometimes against—the agency and age-specific positionalities of young Chinese migrants in removal proceedings. Without diminishing a young person's tenuous legal status or her unique social and emotional needs (Atkins et al. 2008; Goździak 2008), my research engages young people's expert understandings of legality and inequality (Ozer 2016; Stepick and Dutton Stepick 2002) and, throughout, acknowledges that identities are "forged in relation to law, in accommodation and in resistance to it" (Coombe 1995, 795).

How a young person who is designated unaccompanied internalizes and responds to the law emerges on multiple levels. For one, her or his autonomous and unauthorized presence in the US implicitly challenges conceptualizations of children as exclusively dependent (Coutin 2005). Following that "passive states . . . are not seen as lacking in intentionality" (Das 1989, 273), in my work I pay particular attention to interactions between persons conceived as "active" legal agents, such as attorneys and judges, and youth themselves. Challenging the presumption of youths' passivity or dependency, I also focus on the deliberate decisions youth make—often alone—in the course of their legal journeys, thereby underscoring their "overtly agentful" roles (Coe et al. 2011). Finally, I examine the "spatialized networks of practice" (Jeffrey and Dyson 2008) by which youth develop new forms of social mobility. These networks, often forged with other youth in ORR detention centers or with unapprehended acquaintances through various technologies, allow youth to attend to personal and economic responsibilities even before legal status has been secured.

EXPECTATIONS

Complicating the "narrowed" migration accounts that attorneys present in removal proceedings, relevant research situates Fujianese migration trends in Chinese state reform policies and economic development, and in established migration networks in the US (K. Chin 1999; Kwong 1997). The picture of migration is further complicated by Julie Chu (2006), who argues that Fujian Province has a distinct "politics of destination" by which the expectations of "emplaced" Fujianese—those who have not yet migrated—are remade in relationship with others' actual (or showy displays of) transnational migration (see also Massey 1993). Taken together, this scholarship creates a more detailed picture of the economic and socio-cultural motivations for Fujianese migration. At the same time, it grants little specific attention to youth. While other recent anthropological research examines how youth in China navigate and reconfigure networks of family, finance, and tradition in domestic settings (Fong 2004; Ikels 2004; Ngai 2004), still no one has asked how young Chinese uniquely negotiate quickly changing filial and economic obligations in and beyond the unfamiliar spaces of US law and regulation.

No longer a "dependent" charge of the state, a Fujianese youth becomes (or resumes being) an independent, transnational economic actor once legal relief is secured. Even with a successful legal claim, however, young people often reassume tremendous economic obligations connected to smuggling fees. While cause lawyers are certainly aware of this reality, it remains at odds with the expectations they express for their clients, namely that youth will go to school, learn English, and otherwise lead lives appropriate to their age and legal status in the US.

To shed light on this tension, my work examines the experiences and expectations of youth who have obtained legal status, recognizing youths' "semi-autonomy" post-release (Jeffrey and Dyson 2008) as evidenced in the identities they maintain or make for themselves as family members, consumers, and individuals who perform valuable work. Here, I engage the literature on "new destinations," or communities in the South and Midwest that in recent years have experienced the highest relative immigrant population growth in the US (Marrow 2011; Portes and Rumbaut 2006). Because primarily Mexicans and Central and South Americans have driven this process, new destinations scholarship tends to focus on Latinx communities (see Donato, Stainback, and Bankston 2005; Fennelly 2008; Lichter and Johnson 2009; Massey and Capoferro 2008). While the youth in this study are not nearly as concentrated or visible as their Latinx counterparts, they pursue or are directed to "new destinations" for a similar reason, namely that labor-market opportunities in these areas are more attractive than saturated immigrant niches in gateway cities (Light 2006). Accordingly, their experiences in these spaces deserve attention—as do attorneys'.

As an understudied contrast to cause lawyering in immigrant gateways, attorneys in new destinations practice a unique form of localized and long-term advocacy on behalf of unaccompanied minors. Also evident, and perhaps correspondingly, is a compelling *lack* of an explicit professional "cause." As I demonstrate, the shifting demographic and socioeconomic context of new destinations facilitates novel ways by which both lawyers and Chinese youth forge professional relationships, legal identities, and "insider" experiences of belonging.

TIMING AND FORMS OF LEGAL RELIEF

The goal of this book is to rigorously engage the uncertainty that exists in the intricate, constrained, and often rushed entanglements of legal advocacy. Of course, to describe this uncertain space is to unnaturally pause something that is fundamentally premised on conflicting interpretations of mobility. There is the geographic mobility of young Fujianese migrants, of course, as well as the momentum youth sustain across legal and employment trajectories, transitions to adulthood, and transnational social hierarchies. There is also the urgent movement of cause lawyers, both as they physically traverse the distances between immigration court, legal offices, and detention centers— distances that are arguably even more consequential for new destination attorneys—and as they navigate the persistent unfolding of administrative demands and institutional documentation.

These mobilities are both hindered and further intensified by changes in federal and state policy and by public perceptions of migration. Given the rate of such changes, it is important to note that although I began preliminary research in 2009, I am finalizing this manuscript in 2017. To state that the physical, legal, and emotional geographies of transnational migration have changed in those eight years is axiomatic. There are rising numbers of refugees worldwide; changing geographies of international migration; rapid internal displacement of people by conflict, violence, and natural disasters; an increase in migrant fatalities; new and renewed questions about immigrant integration and human rights; and an ever-increasing structural reliance on migrant labor and the exponential growth of remittances. As I write, there are more than 244 million international migrants, a 41 percent increase since 2000. Of this population, an estimated 53 million individuals are under age twenty-five.[10]

In some ways, the United States' reaction to these immense shifts has not changed but become more grievously amplified. There is now, as there was when I began this research, a swelling backlog of immigration cases. There is an increase in immigration enforcement and in the number of arbitrary raids and crackdowns. There is the aggressive criminalization of immigrants in everyday life and the accelerated marginalization of executive immigration actions—actions Chief Judge Roger Gregory recently characterized as "[dripping] with religious intolerance, animus, and discrimination."[11] Amid the alarm and mistrust this context rightly incites, it is worth noting that the explicitly discriminatory structure of these immigration controls is not new. Indeed, the anti-immigrant political rhetoric, nativism, and racialized economic fears we observe today are largely what undergirded the 1882 passage of the Chinese Exclusion Act, the US' first major law to restrict immigration (Ruskola 2013; Statz 2016b). In subtle and not-so-subtle ways, exclusion laws remain the model for immigration regulation in the US, where gatekeeping has taken on a variety of guises including national origins quotas,[12] preference categories based on family reunification and professional skills,[13] and so many militarized operations at the US-Mexico border[14] (Lee 2003).

As it specifically pertains to apprehended young migrants and likewise engages with the bureaucratization of their custody, immigration law is notoriously Kafkaesque (Bhabha and Schmidt 2006; Terrio 2015). In what follows, I provide a brief overview of the legal and institutional channels that cause lawyers and young migrants most commonly engaged during the course of my research.

In the United States, many unauthorized and detained migrant youth are either deported or reunified with family members.[15] When these options are not or cannot be selected, as is often the case with Fujianese youth designated

UAC,[16] three forms of legal relief are evaluated: asylum, the T visa, and Special Immigrant Juvenile (SIJ) status.

With asylum perceived as a problematic or suspect choice,[17] many cause lawyers evaluate the T visa, a nonimmigrant-status visa for victims of trafficking.[18] A number of the lawyers I interviewed regard the T visa as a particularly salient option for young Fujianese clients. Still, it may be difficult to demonstrate that a Fujianese youth was trafficked and is thus eligible for a T visa, as many youth argue they were complicit in their migration journeys and thereby demonstrate consent to being smuggled. Of course, "consent" is itself a socially and legally constructed term.

This leaves Special Immigrant Juvenile status (SIJ). A hybrid remedy, SIJ is significantly the only provision in US immigration law that considers the best interests of the child and is thus, theoretically, an opportunity for the young person's voice to be heard in immigration proceedings. Yet in practice, as I discuss below, SIJ proves consistent with immigration law's conceptions of children as exclusively dependent, unable to be responsible for migration decisions, and without the same access and rights as adults (Heidbrink 2014, 100).

The criteria for SIJ eligibility are as follows: the applicant must be unmarried and under age twenty-one; a state juvenile court must find that reunification with one or both of the youth's parents is not viable because of abuse, abandonment, neglect, or similar basis found under state law; a state juvenile court must find that it would not be in the child's best interests to return to her or his country of origin; and a state juvenile court must declare the child dependent on the court or place the child under the custody of an individual, entity, agency, or department of a state.[19] Like other humanitarian immigration benefits, SIJ status is granted on a discretionary basis. A lawyer must demonstrate that her or his client not only qualifies for the relief from a rules standpoint but also deserves status from a social and moral standpoint (Morando Lakhani 2013). In this case, deservedness hinges on corresponding cultural perceptions of age and vulnerability.

Moreover, SIJ proves a form of "protection" that is in many ways consistently exclusionary. A person who has LPR through SIJ status is no longer considered the child of her or his parents for immigration purposes, even if parental rights were not terminated. As a result, the recipient is not able to use the lawful status attained through SIJ as a means to obtain lawful status for her or his parents.[20] Significantly, this bar applies to both parents, even if SIJ status was obtained because of abuse, neglect, or abandonment by only one parent.[21]

These, then, are the forms of legal relief this research engages—but again, engages *at the time in which I conducted research*. As I write this section, the words of an attorney I interviewed nearly four years ago come to mind easily, and with renewed relevance. "For me, it's [about] time," Roberta stated. Referencing the rapid increase in migrant youth apprehensions at the US-Mexico border (see Chapter 7) and so many shifting bureaucratic obstacles, she added, "It's kind of the quality versus quantity argument. Anytime that quantity increases, and especially so dramatically, there's always an inevitable sacrifice of quality. . . . There's just so much: It's like you're running, running, running, and then boom. Wall. So you divert and . . . ," she smacked her palm against the desk, "another wall. So you just keep going, you know? There's just door after door after door."

When we spoke in 2013, there was no way Roberta or I could anticipate the complex ways in which the pace and unpredictability of her work would be exacerbated. Yet the things that continue to persist, and what I believe are worth documenting amid these changes, are the responsibility, insecurity, contradiction, and care still motivating the mobility of youth and attorneys—the steady center of an uncertain cause.

A NOTE ON BEST INTERESTS

While this is not a study of best interests per se, the concept is powerfully implicated in the context detailed above. Despite being a fundamental principle in US domestic child welfare law and the Convention on the Rights of the Child, there is no statutory best interests standard for youth in removal proceedings. As a result, complex questions of family, safety, and well-being may not be considered, or not consistently considered, when decisions are made regarding a young person's case (see, e.g., Thronson 2005; Zatz and Rodriguez 2015).

A moment that helps explain this arbitrariness is the 1966 Iowa Supreme Court decision in *Painter v. Bannister*, a custody dispute between Harold Painter and the maternal grandparents of his son Mark, with whom Mark had lived for the year following his mother's death in a car accident. There were no traditional grounds on which to deny Painter's custody, but the court, prioritizing whoever the child had "bonded" with, in this case his grandparents, and likewise opining Painter as "unconventional" and "Bohemian," ruled that it was in Mark's best interests to stay with his grandparents. They could offer him "greater stability and security" than could his father. Where *Painter v. Bannister* meaningfully extends to this project is in Martin Guggenheim's analysis of the case: "Once the best interests test became standard . . . there were no guideposts for assessing best interests. . . . [*Painter v. Bannister* shows] that one's views of a child's best interests are contingent upon the decisionmakers' beliefs and values and that it is impossible to separate their views from those beliefs and values" (2005, 39–40).

US child welfare and family law has since *Painter v. Bannister* endeavored to clarify the best-interests standard, identifying it as a *process* that is child centered and allows the child's voice to be heard and as a *standard* that considers the "safety, permanency, and well-being of the child" (see Carr 2009). In the context of youth mobility, however, best interests still prove subjective and largely aspirational. The notion of "best interests" emerged naturally over the course of nearly every open-ended interview I conducted with cause lawyers, but *when* best interests matter, *whose* best interests matter, and *who* determines a young person's best interests were questions that presented no consistent answer.

Some attorneys referenced the best-interests standard put forth in the UN Convention on the Rights of the Child as guiding or necessitating advocacy—yet significantly, the US has not ratified the Convention. It is now the only nation not to do so. Others mentioned US immigration law, where SIJ status is one provision to explicitly include the child's best interests. Of course, while many argue that the US has a moral imperative to consider the best interests of young migrants no matter the protection or classification, the state's application of the concept proves inconsistent.[22] And finally, while in theory permitting the young migrant's voice, a youths' best interests are in practice typically determined by the "expertise" of a state juvenile court or the adult professionals who serve on Best Interest Determination (BID) panels. Following Guggenheim, amid absent or contradictory guideposts, the individuals who take on the role of determining "what's best" for young migrants largely rely on beliefs and values that fail to integrate or may even reject the interests young migrants themselves articulate. This misalignment and its unconsidered consequences is a prominent thread throughout this book.

BOOK OVERVIEW

Lawyering an Uncertain Cause is divided into six substantive chapters. In Chapter 2 I consider the relevance and restrictions of immigration policy, the scales of bureaucracy, the time and funding that attorneys must navigate, and the personal successes and disappointments that motivate—and often delineate—specific advocacy efforts. Chapter 2 thus provides a more comprehensive consideration of the legal context, ideologies, and strategies that, foreshadowing Chapter 3, necessitate and contribute to placing Fujianese youth "in the right box."

To understand the physical and very personal reach of migration, Chapter 3 examines the ways in which the youth at the center of this study situate their migration stories within a broader regional history and a complex present in the US. This chapter provides a detailed overview of Fujianese migration alongside youths' nuanced reflections on their own experiences and valued and/or resented identities. I argue that Fujianese youth are in a sense like Fujian Province itself, what Julie Chu describes as the "leading and lagging edge of China" (2010, 25). This chapter returns to and complicates my earlier discussion of autonomy, migration, and age, and it begins to illuminate the limited and consequential nature of attorneys' strategic reframing of youths' relationships, obligations, and identities.

Chapter 4 describes the collision of complex histories, motivations, and strategies (i.e., the dynamics explored in Chapters 2 and 3) that occurs in the specific context of removal proceedings. Drawing on observations in immigration courtrooms, interviews with youth and attorneys, relevant case law, and social-science literature, this chapter examines attorneys' evaluation and bifurcation of otherwise intricate tensions. It traces cause lawyers' arguably necessitated reduction of family, age, and culture to simple either/or calculations—parents as bad/not that bad; youth as agents/victims; youth as alone/in a relationship—and their confident selection, or production, of an unequivocal moral narrative. This chapter highlights powerful undercurrents of American exceptionalism and constructions of professionalism and expert knowledge, and it forewarns of the confining and consequential nature of attorneys' strategies. It concludes by suggesting that the attorneys in this study are aware of the fraught nature of legal advocacy and rely largely on what I call "The Spectacular Case" to legitimate their work to themselves and others.

Chapter 5 examines the structure, utilization, and value of "The Spectacular Case" in more detail. It considers one Fujianese youth's unusually dramatic legal and personal journey through a variety of lenses, including interviews I conducted with the young man, his adoptive parents, and members of his legal team; legal documents pertaining to his case; depictions of his migration journey in nonprofit fundraising and publicity campaigns; and ongoing references to his story in public-media presentations on unaccompanied youth or immigration reform. My aim in this chapter is to counter attorneys' suspicion of Fujianese youth as "using the system" by carefully outlining the ways in which youths' stories are themselves "used" or commodified by attorneys to gain positive press, garner funding, and mitigate or atone for the strategies some attorneys privately question and grieve.

Chapter 6 completes my analysis by considering the lives of those Fujianese youth who have obtained legal status. Drawing together the professional restrictions cause lawyers describe in Chapter 2 and the unique structure and fragmentation of Chinese enclaves in Chapter 3 (including suspicion of Fujianese youth), Chapter 6 offers a final instance of "limited relief." It considers lawyers' and Chinese communities' inability or reluctance to extend advocacy efforts to Fujianese youths' labor rights or access to health care, mental-health services, and education, particularly in less traditional contexts of reception. This chapter serves as a broader reflection on lawyers' inconsistent views of age, citizenship and responsibility, and (now clearly provisional) "best interests."

In Chapter 7, I present some final reflections on the cause and anthropology's engagement with it. As I discuss, the cause lawyering my work explores is inherently contradictory, ambivalent, well intentioned, and vulnerable. So too is the youth mobility that legal advocates represent. Retracing the contours of a cause, this chapter underscores the *potential* inherent in such incongruence and uncertainty.

ON RESEARCH AND RISK

That this book is about uncertainty is perhaps rooted in the largely unexpected path to its inception. I began this research after a number of years spent living in western China and studying Mandarin and Tibetan there and in the US. My interest was environmental anthropology, and I planned to document grassland restoration efforts across A-mdo communities on the Tibetan Plateau. This unexpectedly changed when I learned about the Unaccompanied Children's Alliance (UCA),[23] a nonprofit organization in Chicago. UCA's mission was to work on behalf of youth in ORR detention centers and removal proceedings through advocacy and policy reform. At the time, it was composed of attorneys, a social worker, support staff, and a number of law-student volunteers, though it has since expanded.

I was introduced to UCA by a friend who had volunteered with the organization. The majority of the youth she had worked with were Central American, she told me, but UCA also advocated on behalf of young migrants from across the globe, including China. I was surprised. I had worked in immigrant and refugee services before, but this was the first I had heard of Chinese youth in federal detention centers. Already planning to be in Chicago for the summer, I reached out to UCA to see if they needed volunteers. The organization's director responded to my email enthusiastically: as someone who could speak Mandarin, I would be unique among UCA's staff and pool of volunteers, the majority of whom spoke Spanish.

I only volunteered with UCA for the summer, but those few months introduced me to a form of advocacy I found both admirable and perplexing, and to an experience of Chinese mobility I felt compelled and well positioned to explore. With a persistent and even urgent curiosity, I changed my research plans. I returned to Chicago for preliminary fieldwork in 2010. There, I volunteered with a young Fujianese man in a federal detention center, visiting him once a week and accompanying him to immigration court as I had with other Fujianese youth the summer before. I also spent more time at the UCA offices. With the staff's understanding and consent that I was there as a researcher to familiarize myself with their work, I participated in UCA's everyday activities, helping organize and manage data on young clients, observing BID panels, and sitting in on meetings with relevant stakeholders. During this time I also conducted formal, semi-structured interviews in person with UCA staff and volunteers, other immigration attorneys, and law professors in Chicago, and telephonically with many of the cause lawyers across the US with whom the organization consulted.

Later that summer, I traveled to the US-Mexico border to briefly participate in the Undocumented Migration Project (UMP).[24] There, I observed Operation Streamline[25] court proceedings in Tucson and visited shelters for deported migrants in Nogales, Mexico. This was an important and often devastating experience. At a more personal level, it was also revelatory. I realized that the true "puzzle" of my research originated—or at least operated—back in the UCA offices: what I observed and felt there, including the warmth and productivity of the individuals around me, the frenetic nature of their work, and the palpable sense of frustration and compulsion, largely motivated this study.

I continued to familiarize myself with global youth mobility. This included sustained observations in Executive Office for Immigration Review

(EOIR) courtrooms in Seattle and Tacoma, interviews with Customs and Border Protection officials at the US-Canada border, attendance at local anti-trafficking task force meetings, and visits to migrant youth shelter facilities in Seattle. With my experiences at UCA as a baseline, I began to see how the institutional management of young migrants shifted from place to place and how local politics, economies, and histories shaped the forms it took.

While these regional differences interested me, I remained most concerned with the intentions and efforts of attorneys and youth—endeavors that extended to the future in impact and to the past in commitment and that spanned and animated national advocacy networks and labor trajectories. I wondered: What demands and motivations influenced immigration cause lawyers? How might an attorney's goals and self-identity affect the life, labor, and success of a young client? Asking the inverse was equally meaningful and perhaps more destabilizing: What demands and motivations influenced these youth? How might a young person's power-filled goals and self-identity affect the life, labor, and success of her or his *attorney*?

These are uncomfortable questions for everyone, including myself. As I explain in the preface, I do not aim to, nor can I, answer why Fujianese youth "have to" migrate. I likewise recognize that putting forth a generalizable and plainly tragic account of "Fujianese youth migration" would be safer, both symbolically and in fact. As a writer, I have felt profoundly conflicted over what and how much of youths' reflections to include in this book. Betraying any pretext of "anthropological objectivity," I admittedly *liked* the young people who spoke with me. I enjoyed and respected their good humor and hip haircuts, their savvy understandings of Greyhound bus routes and social media, the quick connections they made with other global youth, the pride with which they recounted paying down smuggling fees and sending home remittances. I also recognize the risk in highlighting (let alone even featuring) in print the independent achievements these youth described. I fear that what I documented might be read with a cursory and cynical *See?* by individuals who maintain different understandings and agendas toward unauthorized migration. Surely these and other Fujianese youth don't *deserve* some form of protection, the reasoning goes—they are not desperate, helpless children. In this book, they even laugh.

Of course, the successes I mention here are but one—and one positive—dimension of complex, shifting transitional lives and transitions to adulthood. During research interviews, I steadily reminded participants that the questions I asked didn't have to be answered or could be answered off the record. Some young people selected the latter option, asking that I pause my voice recorder while they detailed aspects of their migration journeys, family lives, or legal experiences that visibly anguished and often confused them. I was surprised and humbled to be entrusted with these emotions. Years later, I remain troubled that young Fujianese migrants likely continue to navigate such grief, stress, and loneliness, and largely in isolation. If others were made aware of these realities, would it change youths' experience? I'm not sure. I continue to hold what they shared in deep confidence.

I also recognize that much of what I do and do not include in this book could affect the work of the cause lawyers who participated in this research and whose realistic yet tireless conviction I admire. This is a subtler but still real concern. As I mention above, a less uncertain and arguably more tragic account of Fujianese migration may be safer—and also in many ways helpful, serving as a citable resource for legal advocates who struggle to fit ambivalent narratives into narrowly defined legal categories. Of course, acknowledging this as *helpful* in turn spotlights, and may be read as destabilizing, the sincerity or legitimacy of legal advocates' aims. What to make of work on behalf of youth who are not always that vulnerable—at least not in the ways the law and public discourse expect and in the ways attorneys themselves promote? How authentic is the cause when the youth at its center implicitly complicate and at times overtly resist it? How confident is the advocacy that insistently searches for facts beyond, or despite, what clients offer?

I reflected on these questions a great deal before writing. While I offer no simple solution, I ultimately understand this as a study of the circulation and unconsidered effects of narrowed migration narratives. To meaningfully illuminate the legal categories and moral ideologies that contribute to this reduction of narrative—and in many ways, rights—my response must be *full*, embracing and elucidating an uncertain and often uncomfortable cause. I don't think this is a particularly novel approach. In many ways, it simply follows what my research participants have already done.

I feel profoundly compelled to share what I documented, largely because every person I spoke with, attorneys and youth alike, was unfailingly helpful, articulate, at times deeply frustrated, and ultimately expert. I was consistently startled by how forthcoming these individuals were, and by the honesty and urgency with which they shared the complex and at times confounding realities of their work and lives. Following Jason De Leon and Michael Wells

(2015), I believe anthropologists owe it to our research participants and the public to match that level of openness, to persistently consider the nuanced and often difficult worlds our interlocutors inhabit. I have attempted to do so with great sensitivity and care, bringing together voices and experiences that matter quite a lot to one another but do not always meet in a sustained or mutual way. There is a lot of suspicion around legal advocacy on behalf of undocumented youth. If I have done my best, this work assuages some of the suspicions *within* it.

FIELDWORK WITH YOUTH

My aim in recognizing the power of youth—and in particular, their power in and beyond the attorney-client relationship—was two-fold. First, it was important to me to reduce the estranging effects of much child-focused scholarship by considering how young migrants' lives intersect with attorneys' social and professional worlds, rather than focusing on the differences between "adult" and "child" (Cheney 2007). Second, and relatedly, even a casual reader will likely note that the "children" in this study are individuals whose experiences, skills, and achievements signal a transition to adulthood or "emerging adulthood" (Arnett 2000; Rumbaut 2005). The active and accepted dismissal of this fact by cause lawyers indicated a critical elision, one that necessitated further inquiry. To this end, I sought to illuminate the broader context of a young person's migration journey, family, and employment. The result, I imagined as I prepared for sustained research, would be a youth-centered ethnography.

That this document does *not* exclusively center on youth is significant. Indeed, I believe it at once indicates the "invisibility" of a certain population of youth as well as its agentive mobility. It likewise demonstrates the ways in which these young people are linked to and often restricted by larger structures that define the parameters of their legal experiences in the US (see Gleeson and Gonzales 2012; Laerke 1998), such as the institutional management of unaccompanied minors, which also affected the initial parameters of my fieldwork.

I expected to begin my research in federal detention centers, what ORR euphemistically terms "UAC care provider facilities" or "shelter care" (see Heidbrink 2014; Terrio 2014). Here, young people move through a form of surveilled and segregated everyday life, one in which activities such as class, mealtime, recreation, sleep, and health appointments are largely constrained to the immediate facility. This is also where attorneys and paralegals offer "Know Your Rights" presentations and conduct legal intakes with newly detained youth to gauge whether they might qualify for legal relief. The detention center is accordingly a key space for the initial elicitation or "scripting" of a legal narrative. Yet as I observed in my earlier visits as a volunteer, it is also a dialogical site (Bakhtin 1981; see also Osanloo 2009), one in which unaccompanied Fujianese youth interpret and exchange information about their legal identities with other Central and South American, West African, and, at the time, South Asian youth.

I was naïve. In 2003, the care and custody of unaccompanied minors was officially transferred from ICE, a subsidiary of DHS, to ORR, which is under the umbrella of the Department of Health and Human Services (HHS). The shift initiated a considerable conflict of interest and agenda: ORR is tasked with "caring" for apprehended youth, yet it must still regularly collaborate with ICE, which is mandated to *remove* unauthorized migrants.[26] As Lauren Heidbrink (2014, 11) argues, the transition from ICE to ORR has led to an institutional bias in which the security and safety concerns of the nation outweigh the safety and welfare concerns of this population.[27] The heightened control of ORR shelters extends as well to researchers; these spaces are notoriously difficult to access (Terrio 2015), and there is little transparency regarding the data ORR presumably collects on youth.[28]

Eleven months after submitting the necessary institutional-review paperwork to conduct research in an ORR-contracted shelter, I received a call: did I still want to conduct research? The woman on the phone was apologetic. "You can resubmit your paperwork," she said, "but I can't give you any guarantees." By this time, I had recalibrated and in some ways curtailed my research with youth. However disappointing, the institutional impasse was now data.

With research in federal shelters an unlikely possibility, I chose to center on the experiences of youth who had been released from shelter care and whose removal proceedings were ongoing or had concluded. I was deliberate in working only with youth who had been apprehended and designated UAC, not only because my research emphasized youths' *legal* journeys, but also for ethical reasons. When I spent time with research participants in the Chinese buffets where they worked, I often encountered coworkers who were eager to speak with me in Mandarin. Such exchanges were always friendly, yet because I suspected these individuals lacked documentation, I respectfully but deliberately kept our exchanges brief.[29] I feared my transparent but none-theless mystifying presence as a researcher could feel threatening to manage-ment fearful of government officials or ICE raids. I likewise did not want to risk the safety, job security, or status of unauthorized individuals working in what was likely an "invisible" workplace—a site where coworkers might be undocumented and/or below the legal working age and where employers may not comply with labor laws or safety regulations (see Chapter 7).

Of course, I also recognize the unintentional role my research could play in the lives of Fujianese youth designated unaccompanied, including those who have since arrived in the US, and the work of their attorneys. This project largely centers on the ways in which particular narratives of child-hood, family, and nation are used to advance legal claims, galvanize public support, and intimately sustain cause lawyers' ambitions. I am also aware that these narratives could be interpreted and contorted for other purposes, including to contradict or to undermine the legal claims of Fujianese youth in removal proceedings. Over the course of securing permissions to conduct research through my university's institutional review board, making adjust-ments to the project design, conducting fieldwork and data analysis, and writing and rewriting, I endeavored to take extra care in how I collected information and what I did with it. Mine was an inherently power-filled position that required great mindfulness and, at times, the wisdom of trusted colleagues and legal experts who assisted me in attending to critical questions that arose.

There were occasions when I felt the self-identified cynicism or exhaus-tion of an interlocutor, whether a young person or attorney, betrayed infor-mation that could affect the lives and work of their peers. Occasionally, I feared that my transparency about my own limitations as a researcher—including not having a JD or not being a young person, Chinese, or a young migrant—resulted in some informants assuming an almost avuncular role. This upended a power dynamic I had initially feared, specifically one in which I might take for granted that my livelihood did not depend on legal success. Yet it also introduced new questions about what to do with potentially malleable data put forth with a disarming casualness and how to engage interlocutors who rightfully maintained expert authority and privilege but often seemed indifferent to the bounds of confidentiality I so diligently maintained.

In all these instances, I returned to the ethical guidelines that directed my research,[30] asking participants if they understood and consented to this information being made public. Even though most of these individuals did consent, I have been especially careful with those data that I feel could exacerbate the already existing tensions between cause lawyers, the state, law enforcement, nongovernmental organizations, and young migrants who are simultaneously imagined as vulnerable and suspect. In this book I have maintained the integrity of participants' reflections by presenting their own words and demeanors. I have also been deliberate in including the most fully representative diversity of viewpoints I documented. Ultimately, I believe these unique, uncertain, and often contradictory positionalities will *themselves* challenge any attempts to use the data I collected to serve a particular agency's political or institutional agenda—perhaps most simply by disrupting the certainties on which agendas rely.

Unable to conduct research in shelter facilities and unwilling to work with unapprehended young people, I relied heavily on the contacts I gained during preliminary fieldwork. These included youth I knew through my volunteer experiences with UCA as well as young people who were referred to me by social workers or attorney contacts. In the end, twenty-five once-apprehended Fujianese youth officially designated "unaccompanied" participated in this project in some way, whether in extended informal conversations or in more formal, open-ended narrative interviews. These interviews were conducted at locations young people chose, typically a restaurant or coffee shop, and once in the basement of New York's Grand Central Terminal. Interviews usually lasted about an hour, though occasionally much longer. Because I often traveled cross-country to meet with young people, a formal interview was typically followed by more casual and sustained conversations throughout my visit—and with a few participants, periodic phone calls, text messages, and letters long after.

Though most of these individuals had been introduced to me through a trusted peer or adult, I was still deliberate in detailing the project beforehand and as we met together. I always described their role in my research, and I clarified that youth would not experience any tangible benefits from this study. My research would not help youth with their financial obligations, nor would it influence anyone's legal case. If anything, and very abstractly, it might someday help other young Fujianese migrants by making their achievements and challenges better understood. Yet even without clear compensation, the young people I spoke with were overwhelmingly interested in the project and eager to share their reflections about their migration journeys, families, communities, motivations, and experiences in the legal realm. A number of the individuals I spoke with exhibited a uniquely reflexive helpfulness and expertise as they recounted these things: "You should know about . . ." or "Has anyone mentioned . . . to you? No? Let me explain it . . ." In the confidence with which they identified and recounted the achievements, confusion, and intimate sorrows of migration, these youth interlocutors were meaningfully representative of the uneasy "cause" at hand.[31]

Between interviews and casual correspondence, I also accompanied a number of research participants to immigration court. Here I noted in particular the participation of youth, judges, and lawyers in hearings; the availability of translation services; and the ways in which youths' personas shifted in these spaces of institutional power and legal intervention. After proceedings were concluded, I recorded youths' reflections and their questions about the process. I also traveled with young people to those spaces they identified as important: workplaces, grocery stores, shopping malls, and restaurants. This portion of fieldwork familiarized me with the tacit realities of a young migrant's life—realities that are ostensibly "extra-legal" but nonetheless remain uniquely affected, and sometimes constrained, by legal advocacy. It also introduced me to the relevance and broader context of communities of reception and to the regionally specific challenges and benefits youth navigate in "new destinations."

The data I collected across these spaces were invaluable, but the logistical challenge of arranging research with young migrants proved equally meaningful. Formal interviews were often delayed, day after day, and sometimes until just before I needed to depart for home. Phone numbers changed. I expected to meet with one individual and was met by three. The youth in this project are *mobile*, a descriptor that extends beyond individual migration histories. As I detail in Chapter 6, Fujianese youth typically journey from detention centers to New York City, then to employment in "new destination" communities across the US. Most of the young people I interviewed stay at a workplace for a year or two, though sometimes just a few months. It may be unsafe or not lucrative. It may be too exhausting or too boring. The cycle continues.

While youth can't control the economic obligations urging and perpetuating this movement, they are largely responsible for the decision of when and where to move next. Thus, just as the inaccessibility of ORR detention centers represented meaningful data, so too did the sporadic silences between casual phone conversations, funny text messages, and research-related meetings with youth. I recognize these gaps as indicative of the full reality of youths' transnational lives—lives that include work, involvement in Chinese household economies, management of kin and social networks, and unique, geographically expansive pursuits in the US.

CREATING AND CRITIQUING A CAUSE: ATTORNEYS' REFLECTIONS

The data I collected from my fieldwork with youth create a compelling counter to the legal portrayal of unaccompanied minors as vulnerable and dependent children. Of course, this portrayal matters. Indeed, its production and dissemination is the current that prompted my initial curiosity as a volunteer and later wound through the data I collected during preliminary fieldwork. This current contained the uneasy quality of a "cause"—and to understand it, I needed to understand what, or who, was produced through its subjective jurisdiction.

Following Andrew Abbott (1988), I believe attorneys establish their professional expertise, obligation, and indispensability via "subjective jurisdiction," or the practice of defining a problem, reasoning about it, and taking action on it. As this book demonstrates, the mechanisms by which cause lawyers define and simplify the "cause" (unaccompanied Fujianese migration); reason about it (as a matter of deviant parents, coercive culture, and so on); and take action (by providing legal relief) not only produce and perpetuate a certain type of young migrant but also a certain type of lawyer. Put differently, in a profession that is itself uniquely vulnerable to bureaucratic constraints and political shifts, immigration cause lawyers attempt to mitigate a client's vulnerability just as they pragmatically and morally *require* it.

Knowing youths' life stories and the grounds for their migration journeys would help me understand the background of a "cause." To understand its impetus, however, I needed to speak with attorneys. I began in Chicago, where I conducted longer and more formal interviews with some of the individuals I met through preliminary fieldwork. This time, my questions were open-ended but still focused. I inquired into the process by which an attorney determines a young person's eligibility for legal relief; the relative significance of a client's economic obligation, family, age, and national and cultural background as a claim is developed; the benefits and drawbacks of the various and limited legal protections for a client and the client's family; the perceived consequences of attorneys' legal strategies; and attorneys' hopes and expectations for young clients. I also moved beyond practice to practice *site*, examining the ways in which organizational mandates, institutional structures, state and federal policies, local economies, histories, and demographics grounded and formed the "conditions of possibility" (Foucault 1994) for their work and likewise affected clients, volunteers, and researchers like myself. I also explored the opportunities attorneys had or forged—or sometimes disregarded—for creative partnerships and sustained, extensive advocacy.

In the end, I interviewed nearly one hundred attorneys for this project: eighty individuals during my fieldwork and fifteen during preliminary research. Because of the sustained nature of my fieldwork, I was able to conduct a number of follow-up interviews with attorneys to discuss questions that arose over the course of research or to review changes in immigration trends and policies. Many of my research interviews occurred in gateway cities like Chicago or New York, where lawyers practiced or directed large nonprofit organizations that serve immigrant youth. Other interviews took place in new destination communities in Alabama, Tennessee, Arkansas, Oklahoma, Missouri, Texas, and Wisconsin. There, I primarily met with lawyers who worked for regional branches of national nonprofits or directed small local nonprofits, though I also met with a few private practitioners who took on young migrants' cases pro bono. Interviews were generally conducted in lawyers' offices, though occasionally at nearby coffee shops, and they typically lasted between sixty and ninety minutes.

More than once did an attorney laughingly tell me, "You won't have any trouble getting a lawyer to talk for your research!" And while this ultimately proved true, there were of course individuals who were short on time, preoccupied, or prepared with what felt like stock introductions to child migration. No longer a newcomer to the phenomenon, I knew it was critical, if not occasionally uncomfortable, to evidence my familiarity with these issues and the relative depth and preparedness of my inquiry. Comfortably mentioning a practice advisory or a recent case elicited a visible shift in attorneys' demeanor; so also did admitting my limited knowledge of substantive immigration law and relevant administrative process. I was overwhelmingly met

with a level of openness, helpfulness, and candor I never could have anticipated. Accordingly, while this book is at times critical of attorneys' practices,
it is worth underscoring that elements of this critique were largely illuminated and shared by attorneys themselves.

In addition to practitioners, I also interviewed legal scholars and cli-
nicians at universities and bar associations across the US. Many of these
individuals were experts in immigration law, child welfare, or children's or
parents' rights—and as such were keen to discuss the theoretical context and
broader ramifications of the cause at hand. Lasting an hour or more, these
conversations often moved at what felt like break-neck speed. They were
unfailingly challenging and helpful.

Along with interviews, I observed attorneys in removal proceedings,
organizational fundraisers, media events, and conferences. Because this
project intersects with child welfare, I also attended relevant professional
gatherings like the annual National Child Welfare, Juvenile, and Family
Law Conference. I additionally collected and analyzed the practice advisories and policy reports research participants had published, as well as
the case documents a number of attorneys shared with me.[32] These documents represented a particularly illuminating if not daunting source of
data. For instance, the legal briefs and collected correspondence pertaining
to Young's case (Chapter 5) filled over eleven bankers' boxes. I performed
content analyses on all the documents I collected, coding for key terms
and seeking definitions for the many I didn't understand. Analyzing documents in this way allowed me to critically compare institutional and legal
discourses about Fujianese youth with the articulations of individual youth
and attorneys I acquired elsewhere.

With attorneys and young migrants at the center of my research, I
traced outward to the individuals who affect youths' legal and labor journeys in significant but often overlooked ways.[33] I visited Chinese service
organizations in gateway cities, as well as relevant public-assistance centers,
immigrant-advocacy nonprofits, and religious organizations in "new destination" communities. I was often given tours of these spaces, during which
I corresponded casually with staff members. I also conducted more formal
interviews with eighteen English as a Second Language (ESL) teachers, social
workers, and program directors in charge of employment or youth services at
nonprofit organizations across my many field sites. This portion of fieldwork
allowed me to better evaluate the rightful (or right-filled) provision of services

beyond the immigration context, like language training and job development, accessible health care, and housing and citizenship assistance.

STUDYING UP AND DOWN: ANTHROPOLOGY ACROSS AN UNCERTAIN CAUSE

In 1969, Laura Nader published "Up the Anthropologist: Perspectives Gained from Studying Up." In it, she called for anthropology to examine the experiences of the powerful and to conduct ethnographic studies of those institutions at the heart of capitalist stratification like banks, law firms, corporations, and government regulatory agencies. Doing so would shed light on processes of domination in US society, she wrote, and would help revitalize American democracy (see also Gusterson 1997).

The immigration cause lawyers at the center of this study would likely distinguish their work from what Nader identifies as "up." Indeed, these individuals often identify themselves and their cause as a moral fight *against* the bureaucratic, contradictory "controlling processes" (Nader 2010) that govern the management of young migrants in the US. Moreover, and more generally, cause lawyers' approach to legal advocacy is often a deliberate response to their observations and frustrations with dominant professional and social structures.

Yet from another perspective, these individuals are very much "up," both in regard to their young clients and to me. Just as my research was shaped and constrained by more powerful external institutions, such as the inaccessibility of ORR detention centers, so was it more intimately influenced by both the support and *expectations* of the attorneys with whom I conducted research. Having first entered this context as a volunteer, I struggled with and at times resisted what proved a necessary and occasionally distressing transition to "anthropologist."

When I initially conceived of this project, I aimed to advance relevant socio-legal theory and to contribute to more comprehensive legal advocacy efforts—efforts I admired but suspected were consequential in ways lawyers did not always anticipate. It was not long before I realized that a number of the cause lawyers I had met in Chicago approached my research—and anthropology more generally—with a pragmatism that proved instructive if not disappointing. Openly identified as the "China person"—presumably for my language capacities and academic credentials, as I am not Chinese—I was often asked to look over relevant policy reports that cause lawyers were developing on Fujianese migration and advocacy on behalf of Fujianese youth in removal proceedings. I took the task seriously, writing careful comments in the margins, adding historical context if requested, introducing more complex "push" and "pull" factors in overviews of youths' migration journeys. I also highlighted attorneys' utilization of relatively outmoded anthropological concepts and in place referenced more recent studies of Chinese kinship, political economy, and migration.

I was surprised when later editions of these reports omitted my contributions, or when attorney authors subsumed my comments with their own. It was quickly clear that this was about more than efficiency, ownership, and, as one attorney admitted, getting a report out before another agency did. It was also about what information mattered—or, more simply, what would win a case. I imagine this isn't particularly remarkable to the reader, but recall that cause lawyers ostensibly provide *more* than legal advocacy. My respect for attorneys' efforts to contribute to legislation and advance the "best interests" of youth made me reluctant to question the efficacy of efforts done in a rushed or haphazard way.

This and similar incidents early on in my fieldwork demanded that I rethink the role of my own expectations, and my ego, in this research. I *was* studying up. I might view cause lawyers' advocacy as constrained and often short-sighted—attributes a number of attorneys themselves recognized—but I could contribute neither legal expertise nor an explicit capacity to work in, and against, relevant networks of power. Attorneys already had these things. What immigration cause lawyers wanted from my research was different from what I aimed to contribute. I was a scholar whose presence validated policy reports and helped establish the holistic or "multidisciplinary" nature of advocacy, as through my potential participation in BID panels. Moreover, urged many participants, my research would be even more beneficial after I had published on this topic, wherein I could serve as an expert witness and testify about the "real" nature of Chinese culture and Chinese families.

I include these reflections not as a slighted anthropologist but because the expectations attorneys held for me *mattered*. In the end, the discomfort and disappointment they incited in me was freeing: no longer did I struggle to reconcile my own goals with what felt like an increasingly fraught cause. Instead, I came to view and value this project as a way to spark conversations with legal advocates about power and responsibility—the "democratizing project" to which Nader called anthropologists over forty years ago—and about what exists *beyond* the cause, namely the actual lived experiences, opportunities, and relationships young migrants themselves prioritize. By engaging legal advocacy both in relation to and through Fujianese youth, this book aims to open new ways of thinking about the contradictions that separate us from those on whose behalf we work (Behar 1992).

Of course, these young migrants signal the spaces where legal advocacy *and* anthropology fall short. As I detail in this book, attorneys have authority over Fujianese youth as necessary legal experts and as adults, authority that flows from and is bolstered by a set of institutional and ideological arrangements (Best 2007, 12). My role in these young people's lives was different: it was neither imposed nor essential. Indeed, I was most often recognized by youth as a student and sometimes as a friend or *jie jie*, older sister. Yet there was still an imbalance of power between me, an adult, upwardly mobile citizen, and youth who will in many ways remain "illegal" in certain spheres of life and labor (see Heidbrink 2014).

Furthermore, as an ethnographer, my work is largely to re-present the narratives I documented—a task that is in many ways not dissimilar to lawyering. While my approach is arguably more expansive, one in which I neither strategically elicit nor "script" youths' accounts for a preemptive claim or argument, I would be remiss if I did not acknowledge my collection of youths' individual experiences as data. Likewise, I recognize the power I hold as an interpreter and, thus, author of my observations and participants' reflections (Clifford 1988; see also Bamo, Harrell, and Lunzy 2007).

Without a set objective, such as establishing an individual's qualifications for legal relief, the narratives I present here are markedly less tragic or chaotic than those included in the legal reports, claims, advisories, and editorials I analyzed. This reflects my selection of participants (see Chapter 4) but also my flexibility as a non-lawyer. As a trusted "student," I could ask about young people's histories, legal experiences, and long-term plans, and I could invite reflections about obligation and family that when discussed with neutrality or even optimism might thwart a case. This freedom allowed me to complicate attorneys' practices through clients' perspectives, thereby lending weight to my broader argument.

Still, I recognize that my initial goal of contributing to advocacy efforts; my selections, omissions, and ultimate arrangement of youths' and attorneys' accounts; my epistemological or "expert" authority; my utilization of disciplinary and theoretical resources; and my ultimate crafting of a convincing narrative may at times look an awful lot like *lawyering*. Drawing on Yngvesson and Coutin (2008), I recognize that my prioritizing of evidence among potential interpretations, as well as the spaces and substitutions in my ethnography, are in a sense like legal fictions, fictions that enhance attempts to convey social truths.

I conclude, then, with an attorney's mention of these professional parallels. Perhaps more than anyone, Lisette succinctly described their profound significance:

Lisette: It's been great having Kyle as a [law] partner, because we've been great friends, but we've also been able to bounce ideas off each other all the time. He'll say, "No, don't do that. What about this?" And you have to go back and think, well, this is what the government might say—

Michele: So it's very creative.

Lisette: It can be. In some ways. In the nerdy kind of way. [She laughs.] But that's anthropology too, right? The way you write, the framework you put something into, it completely changes the thing. It's really freeing and also really scary, and a big responsibility.

I take this responsibility seriously, and I have endeavored to be careful and fair in my framing of all that follows, namely the nuanced and largely unconsidered vulnerabilities, responsibilities, and expectations that motivate young Chinese migrants *and* US legal advocates.

In so doing, my work simultaneously demonstrates where anthropology *diverges* from lawyering, namely in anthropology's abiding and in many ways demanded accommodation of ambiguity, doubt, and uncertain ends. This ethnographic project is often disorienting. And that, I believe, is also where it is likely most productive, compelling a deeper and perhaps even empathetic familiarity with the instability and doubt experienced by cause lawyers and their young Fujianese clients. By making space for these uncertainties, I attempt to counter the aforementioned "oppression of misunderstanding." Indeed, in confronting disorientation we may find its opposite—engagement with the world as it actually is (Greenhouse 2002, 28).

2   *The Cause in Theory and in Practice*

The lawyers at the center of this study work on behalf of and in relation to "a cause." How lawyers feel about this cause, what they do to legitimate it, and what happens when their efforts prove fraught with unexpected meanings and consequences are questions my research necessarily takes up. I also, and perhaps more unusually, explore the ways in which the cause itself affects and influences these lawyers (Barclay and Marshall 2005; Shdaimah 2005). Throughout, I identify attorneys as in dialogue with, and at times resistant to, the experiences, circumstances, and aspirations of their Fujianese clients (Shdaimah 2009; see also Shamir and Chinsky 1998). The result is a picture of uneasy vulnerabilities and uncertainty about professional responsibility, altruism, and self-affirmation. To make sense of this ambiguity, I rely largely on cause lawyering scholarship[1]—itself a fluid and oft-contested field (Hilbink 2004; see also Menkel-Meadow 1998; Scheingold and Sarat 2004).

An overview of this literature, what I turn to first in this chapter, helps situate the lawyers in my study along a "cause lawyering continuum." Yet my research also pushes against this body of work, most notably regarding how a Fujianese client's age affects a central feature of cause lawyering—namely attorneys sharing responsibility with their clients for the ends promoted in representation (Sarat and Scheingold 2005, 2). As I detail, lawyers prove unable to partner with their young Fujianese clients, not only because of the largely uncontested socio-legal category of "child" but also because the youth with whom they work identify as young adults. They do not "act like" children.

In this chapter I also consider the structural context of cause lawyering, attending in particular to limited forms of rights and relief, the nature of immigration court, and funding pressures and possibilities. Developing this context achieves a straightforward ethnographic goal: it helps explain the strategies that, in the words of one attorney, put young migrants "in the right box." "As a lawyer, you can't be unethical; you can't be dishonest," stated Russell, an immigration cause lawyer in Arkansas. Reflecting specifically on the unique challenges of working with Fujianese youth, Russell added, "But real-life situations have shades of grey. And so what the lawyers are doing, well, they're being deliberate. The law forces you—the law defines the box. The lawyering task is to put you in the right box."

This is a helpful interpretation, and I suspect many of the attorneys I interviewed for this research would agree with it. Still, just as the context that this chapter develops helps ground a key aspect of the immigration cause lawyering role—"to put [a client] in the right box"—so also does it demonstrate the insufficiency of Russell's explanation, particularly when considered in light of the cause. As so many attorneys shared, their work is more than putting someone in the right box. It is more meaningful, more complicated, and in many and significantly unexpected ways more tenuous than the work of other "non-cause" or conventional lawyers, those who utilize technical skills to achieve ends determined by the client, not the lawyer. As suggested in this chapter, the attorneys who work on behalf of youth they term vulnerable emerge as *themselves* vulnerable, both to what are perhaps predictable uncertainties—so many scales of bureaucracy, time, and funding, restrictive and quickly changing immigration policies—but also to less familiar or admitted realities regarding the age, motivations, and even approval of their "vulnerable" clients.

THE CAUSE LAWYERING CONTINUUM

For many immigration attorneys, the obligation to advocate on behalf of unaccompanied youth in removal proceedings is professional as well as moral. This moral commitment is arguably what establishes these individuals as cause lawyers and why I use the term to describe most of the attorneys in this study. Emerging from the "collective editorial project" (Hilbink 2004) of Austin Sarat and Stuart Scheingold, the cause lawyering literature explicitly considers the intersection of lawyering and moral activism. It examines those who deploy legal skills "to pursue ideological and redistributive projects . . . not as a matter of technical competence, but as a matter of personal engagement" (Sarat and Scheingold 2001, 13). Cause lawyers are characterized as working beyond their professional roles and duties (Luban 1988), combining litigation with political mobilization to serve objectives that often transcend service to clients (Sarat and Scheingold 2005). Their work tends to closely involve them with, and at times against, the state or other interests (McCann 1994; Sarat and Scheingold 1998).

In its conceptual openness, the cause lawyering typology invites and integrates the complex context, intimate motivations, and diverse practice sites of the attorneys in this study.[2] In turn, these attorneys reflect what scholars describe as a "continuum" of cause lawyering (Sarat and Scheingold 1998; Southworth 2005b). On one end of this continuum are lawyers who regard advocacy on behalf of causes as important but secondary to service to clients. This includes lawyers who spend the majority of their careers as commercial attorneys while also providing regular pro bono advocacy,[3] as well as lawyers who do not articulate any strong political commitments to their clients or their work but who take on occasional opportunities to "do good" (Barclay and Marshall 2005, 177). The definitional tension that emerges, namely between the *category* of cause lawyers and the attorneys who *actually participate* in cause lawyering (Barclay and Marshall 2005), is something this book steadily engages. It is perhaps most compellingly evidenced in Chapter 6, where a group of Texas-based attorneys who otherwise work in oil and gas litigation take on the case of an unaccompanied Chinese youth pro bono. As these attorneys' moral and professional commitment to their client grows, along with their knowledge and dismay about the US immigration system, an arguably "accidental" cause is transformed into an "intentional" one (Scheingold and Sarat 2004, 4). "If anything," noted one of these attorneys, evidencing the sort of political self-consciousness that often characterizes cause lawyering, "[this experience has] made me feel like there need to be firms with resources to go against the government." When the case concluded, this attorney returned to his regular practice yet still took on occasional pro bono work.

On the other end of the cause lawyering continuum are those lawyers who explicitly place causes ahead of clients and who make substantial sacrifices to pursue those ends. In other words, serving the client is but one component of serving the cause (Rhode 1982). This describes many of the attorneys featured in this book. These are individuals who are employed by or are directors of nonprofit immigrant advocacy organizations that variously identify "supporting," "promoting the best interests of," or "protecting the rights and safety of unaccompanied minors"—and at times somewhat secondarily, legal advocacy on behalf of unaccompanied minors—as their cause. Like others on this "end" of cause lawyering, these lawyers and the organizations for which they work further political goals through impact litigation[4] (Kawar 2015; Scheingold 2004); community activism and grass-roots organizing (Kilwein 1998; Menkel-Meadow 1998); and ideological commitment—commitment that is, significantly, not invulnerable to exhaustion or cynicism (Shamir and Chinski 1998).

Central to much of the literature on cause lawyering is the belief that attorneys partner with their clients to achieve shared goals (Sarat and Scheingold 1998). Here emerges a central tension in the cause of advocacy on behalf of migrant youth, as well as a shortcoming in this body of scholarship: the significance of a client's age and, correspondingly, her perceived autonomy in the attorney-client relationship. As many attorneys observed, advocacy on behalf of unaccompanied minors is both demanded and constrained. It is demanded in that undocumented youth have no guaranteed court-appointed representation, and constrained by the limited scope of legal protections available to unaccompanied youth.[5] It is further restricted, I argue, by lawyers' own "moral commitment" to working with a population that, despite being viewed and self-identifying as young adults elsewhere, is in the legal setting *children*.

WHEN THE CAUSE IS A CHILD: AGE, AGENCY, AND RIGHTS

That these clients may be both strategically and morally framed as children introduces a socio-legal construct of childhood with deep historic roots, one that powerfully figures into immigration cause lawyers' understanding of their professional roles toward, and the "appropriate" rights of, Fujianese youth. In my research, these rights were most prominently framed and prioritized as legal relief from deportation; access to legal representation and, significantly, to guardians; and the guaranteed protection of children's best interests. Evidencing what Kristen Cheney (2007) identifies as the distinction between the legal and moral rights of children, this framework puts forth a version of children's rights that, *while never fully specified*, remains inherently connected to consent (or lack thereof), dignity, and the legal provision of "protection" and "assistance." "What is categorically meant to be 'in a child's best interest,'" writes Cheney, "is really what adults deem to be best for maintaining social cohesion through *the constructed boundaries of childhood* as a particular stage of innocence and dependency" (2007, 14; emphasis added). To understand the cause that both motivates and frustrates the lawyers in this study, we must unsettle the constructed boundaries of childhood on which much of this cause rests.

To some extent, these socio-legal boundaries are located in Western political philosophy. While attorneys may accentuate or reject particular notions of childhood as strategic appeals to limited legal remedies, their practices—along with the broader tenor of the cause as "support," "protection," and "care"—also reveal a historic and power-filled dynamic that presumes youth have negotiable reason, agency, and, accordingly, freedom (see, e.g., Hobbes [1651] 2010; Jefferson [1788] 1954; Wollstonecraft [1792] 1975). John Locke's theory of property and Henry Maine's study of "status to contract" are particularly helpful in illuminating the contradictory nature of a cause as, or on behalf of, young migrants.

According to Locke, it is because of property, or "lives, liberties and estates" ([1689] 1988, 2:§123), that humans consent to the state of society, a concrete world in which individual political liberties are guaranteed by political arrangements (see also Macpherson 1962). In the state of society, the exercise of reason (*which only occurs with age*) qualifies an individual for the exercise of freedom. For Locke, it is the natural right of children to be cared for and protected: "its warrant is the temporally bounded state of natural incapacity which defines childhood" (Archard 2004, 10). As I demonstrate in this chapter, this presumed right of children to be protected—as opposed to a right to consent, which is powerfully connected to autonomy—underlies what can best be understood as the "gradations" of freedom permitted young migrants in the US.

Adding specificity to Locke's views on consent and age is the work of Henry Maine ([1861] 1969). Describing the shift that occurred in English and American law in the late eighteenth century, Maine identifies the legal definition of individual rights, duties, and relations as having shifted from "status" (e.g., primogeniture) to "contract." While the increased emphasis on political contract granted legal equality to many in the early nineteenth century, those "legally unequal" remained, including married women, slaves, and laborers for whom contractual relations were not permitted.

The prioritization of contract also raised new questions about age. If choice, not status, was politically privileged, then who could choose and under what circumstances? If consent was presumed at birth or soon after, could a person change her or his mind later, when she or he was more mature? And if anyone could consent, even a small child, then was consent rendered meaningless? It is perhaps no surprise that children come to be completely excluded from Maine's realm of "contract": "The child before years of discretion, the orphan under guardianship, the adjudged lunatic, have all their capacities and incapacities regulated by the Law of Persons. But why? . . . The great majority of Jurists are constant to the principle that the classes of persons just mentioned are subject to extrinsic control on the single ground that they *do not possess the faculty of forming a judgment on their own interests*" (Maine [1861] 1969, 181; emphasis added).

Like Locke, Maine emphasizes rationality, arguing that children cannot make contracts because they lack the ability to form their own judgments. Instead of being based on social order or the inheritance of property and title, the status Maine describes is dictated entirely by age. An "age of reason" was again the determinant of political legitimacy and the ability to consent (see also Brewer 2005).

FROM THEORY TO PRACTICE: USING, AND BEING USED BY, AGE

As my data demonstrate, Fujianese clients are at once too young and too old; their motives are both unfamiliar and uncomfortably clear. In this way, the presence of Fujianese youth helps illustrate—precisely by thwarting—the philosophical understandings that underlie attorneys' presumptions of children's dependence and limited capabilities and freedoms.

The cause lawyers I interviewed often contrasted their work on behalf of unaccompanied minors with past experiences representing adults—here, anyone age eighteen or older. "I love working with adults," one woman said, "because they're adult, they're grown up, they tell you, 'This is what I want, this is what I will pay you for, and if you achieve that, then I will be happy.' And then you don't think about it anymore. But with kids, it's different."

Similarly, another attorney stated, "With adults—you just don't argue. They tell you what they want, and you say, 'Do you understand the risks?' You know, you can't make decisions for them." Once the age of majority is reached, in other words, legal advocacy can be more straightforward. However subtle, the relief that attorneys expressed evidences a sort of moral reliance on professional codes and immigration statutes governing age. It simultaneously portrays advocacy on Fujianese minors' behalf as an imprecise and unruly task, a weighty endeavor of interpretation and responsibility.

It's worth noting, of course, that many of these young people *are* nearly adults in the legal sense. With a few exceptions, the majority of the Fujianese migrants I interviewed were age seventeen when apprehended. As a result, alongside the pressure attorneys experience with the impending "ageing out"[6] of their clients is a certain apprehension about the suspected "adult" motives of Fujianese youth. In our conversations, lawyers often admitted to feeling suspicious of Fujianese clients, complaining that their time and efforts had been abused by individuals "who just want to get out of detention and start working."

As we met for dinner one night in Chicago, I asked Joan, a young attorney, "How would you describe your work with Fujianese youth?"

She was quiet a moment, then said, "It's hard. I think they just bring morale down [for legal advocates] a lot faster than the other kids in shelter care. The Fujianese kids in the shelter now are older than they were a few years ago. They're all about to age out. . . . The other kids in shelter care act like kids—they're more emotional, they open up. It might have something to do with age, but Chinese kids are also more closed-off."

She took a drink of her beer and continued, "I had a recent [Fujianese] client who just made me feel so used. I visited her twice a week and even found a laptop she could use, since the shelter computers don't have Chinese capabilities. And then when she was released from shelter care and went to New York, she called me to get help with her legal documents. And she called me later—I mean, as soon as *that afternoon*—to see if I had done anything."

Joan shook her head and sighed heavily, her fingers toying with the label on the bottle. "What's worse," she said, "she and her family ended up deciding to go with *a private attorney*. After I did all that. She only told me about it when I called to see if she had received the documents I sent."

As Joan recounted this experience, it was clear that the actions of her client represented all that was wrong, or could be wrong, with Fujianese youth cases more generally. Though legally unable and often unwilling to regard these individuals as adults, attorneys like Joan nonetheless recognize their clients as older in age and in action. They don't "act like kids." They are independent and capable of determining legal strategies on their own. Joan's disenchantment and hurt also reveal much about what cause lawyers believe regarding the value of their own work and what they hope, and perhaps expect, from their clients in terms of vulnerability, appreciation, and commitment.

It is additionally significant, but not at all unusual, for Joan and others to contrast Fujianese youth with other apprehended and unaccompanied minors, the majority of whom migrate from Central America (Byrne and Miller 2012). Here, the "cause" of unaccompanied Fujianese youth is further complicated. When attorneys make their experiences representing Central American youth a reference point, the language, culture of origin, families, and goals of Fujianese youth appear even more dubious and obscure. No matter how "uncomfortably clear," their motives are simultaneously deplored as unfamiliar.

At the time of this research, most unaccompanied youth were arriving to the US from Honduras, Guatemala, and El Salvador. Accordingly, the legal advocates working on behalf of young migrants tended to speak Spanish or collaborate closely with Spanish-speaking colleagues. Many of the attorneys I interviewed contrasted their personal and professional familiarity with these populations with the discomfort they felt in working with Fujianese youth. Besides the obvious inconvenience of using a telephonic translator, broader cross-cultural barriers to communication were discussed with impatience, like Joan's mention of clients "being closed off."

"Our entire team speaks Spanish," said Elena, another Chicago-based lawyer. "And there's just a whole different style with Chinese. [You] can't make eye contact with them. It's hard to understand what their answers really mean . . . the Chinese kids are difficult." Occupying a particularly uneasy legal threshold, it is perhaps no wonder that Fujianese youth were so often depicted in conversations with attorneys as a maddening challenge. Represented as vulnerable and resented as autonomous, these young migrants are variously viewed through an ideological lens of childhood dependence, a racialized hierarchy of advocacy (Uehling 2008), and the stressful professional maneuvering necessitated by their own relatively "old" age.

"WHAT'S BEST FOR KIDS": THE UTILITY OF VULNERABLE CHILDREN

As Joan and others recounted, Fujianese youth act "like adults," making choices independent of their attorneys' plans and expectations. This independence is often disconcerting—and at times seems an affront—to the cause lawyers I interviewed. Still, it is important to highlight that the tension attorneys described involves more than a young person's legal age, economic goals, and country of origin. Returning to Locke and Maine, it also presents a pervasive ideological understanding of "children" and a corresponding conviction many of these cause lawyers hold, namely that attorneys and not their clients are responsible for young migrants' legal interests, personal well-being, and *choices*. This of course largely complicates the cause lawyering literature.

As I detail in Chapter 1, recent anthropological scholarship has meaningfully problematized the juridical category of "unaccompanied." Elsewhere, legal and policy reports have convincingly documented the inconsistent nature of DHS's determination of "unaccompanied" and, to a lesser extent, determinations of age (see Bhabha and Crock 2006; Haddal 2007; Nugent 2006). Still, most attorneys working on behalf of youth in removal proceedings comfortably and uncritically continue to utilize "UAC" language. In our conversations, few, if any, cause lawyers expressed concern about the state's and their own profession's reliance on the "child" category in particular. Indeed, in all my interviews with immigration attorneys, only one individual explicitly noted the conceptual varieties of age: "In working with children," Ife began, then corrected herself, "I suppose we would call them youth. Or young adults." Later in our conversation, Ife admitted that she herself had been an unaccompanied migrant, journeying as a young girl from West Africa to the US.

"Do you think this personal history affects your view of unaccompanied clients?" I asked.

"I'm not sure," she replied. "I don't feel like my clients are one dimensional or vulnerable. I see them as complex, dynamic. I'm open to that."

Ife's thoughtful perspective remained distinct. Nearly every other attorney I spoke with unhesitatingly employed the term "child" in courtrooms and in our less formal conversations. And in the policy reports and practice advisories these individuals published, "child" was often, and meaningfully, preceded by "*vulnerable.*"

This reflects what Greta Lynn Uehling calls "the economy of affect" surrounding unaccompanied children. "Precisely because of their vulnerability, they are especially malleable symbols, susceptible to being used for a variety of political purposes" (2008, 851–52). Consider these statements, each featured prominently on the websites of national advocacy organizations:

These are unusually vulnerable children. Many are fleeing violence, extreme poverty, abuse or abandonment in their home countries of Mexico and Central America. Some have been trafficked. . . . Regardless of why they come, they deserve basic protection as children and should not lack representation in a US court of law.[7]

These children often have nothing; no money, no support and no family, yet they come to America seeking its promises of a better life.[8]

HARROWING JOURNEYS CALL FOR HEROIC MEASURES. HELP US PUT CHILDREN'S BEST INTERESTS FIRST.[9]

When coupled with the spread of the "universal child" model put forth by international organizations, the popular imagery of disappearing, lost, or stolen childhoods perpetuates a compelling imaginary of the childhood domain as threatened or invaded by adult worlds (Stephens 1995, 9; see also Cheney 2007; Martinez and Renteln 2017). This imagery is rife in the preceding statements, where young migrants are generalized—and sensationalized—as "unusually vulnerable children" whose opportunities for "normal" childhood are threatened by violence, poverty, and families or home countries. Recall that these are organizational publicity efforts. Here, it is implicitly the "heroic" cause lawyer who can solve the problem of unaccompanied minors who "often have nothing" by providing legal representation and guarding the (however indeterminate) best interests of children.

Yet when we imagine Fujianese youth as also "too old," an attorney's political and professional relationship with her client emerges as markedly different from that put forth in fundraising campaigns or removal proceedings. Like "children," "youth" are often constructed as victims of circumstance and the manipulations of adults in power. At the same time, however, they are additionally perceived to be disruptive, destructive, and dangerous forces needing containment, those who "enter political spaces as saboteurs" (Durham 2000, 113). When their actions and inactions are discussed by attorneys beyond the legal realm, Fujianese minors are very much regarded as "youth":

They're sixteen! Of course they're irresponsible! By their nature they're irresponsible! If I go to a kid and say, "I got you a green card," they're like, "Eh." [laughs] You know, like that. Later on, they'll probably thank us. But at their age? They don't care.

Minor clients are difficult for us. Like all teenagers, they have strong opinions and don't always want to listen to advice or act in their own best interest. I was the same way.

As lawyers, we tend to sometimes not give our clients enough credit. I think our clients, for the most part, despite how difficult and how confusing immigration law is, our clients know in general what's going to get a judge on their side. . . . Most of them know to say migrating to the US wasn't their idea. I'm not ignorant of the fact that it helps their immigration case for them to not take agency or ownership over that decision. . . . But still, I think they're not old enough to make the decision [to migrate]. They're not old enough to take ownership over that decision.

Taken together, these reflections evidence the humor, cynicism, empathy, and ambivalence so present in this form of cause lawyering, along with—and often because of—the uncomfortable tension between the two categories of children and youth. Fujianese clients are irresponsible, like teenagers everywhere; they are independent, "like I was at that age"; they may know how to work the legal system, but they're still *not old enough* to control all aspects of their lives or stories. In this sense, Fujianese youth are only conditionally "youth." While almost amusingly untrustworthy and unwieldy when they act in "familiar" teenage ways, they are recast as victims—as children—in the legal realm, even as their autonomy unpredictably extends beyond the expected bounds of childhood and beyond the limits of US immigration law.

THE LEGAL RIGHTS AND SOCIAL ENTITLEMENTS OF "ARENDT'S CHILDREN"

As evidenced, many of the immigration attorneys in this study uphold a paternalistic stance toward unaccompanied youth. Yet while an attorney's professed role and relationship with a client may be guided in part by her or his perception of the client's young/vulnerable age, the form this advocacy takes is also influenced by the legal rights available to the client as an unaccompanied and undocumented youth. Following Jacqueline Bhabha (2009), this young person is one of "Arendt's children," a minor who is separated from her or his parents or customary guardians and who is either a noncitizen or the child of noncitizens.

It was Hannah Arendt, writes Bhabha, who recognized "the fundamental rights challenge of our age: supposedly 'inalienable' rights are unenforceable for individuals who 'lack . . . their own government'" (2009, 411; see also Ticktin 2006). Having compromised her or his own citizenship by leaving China unauthorized, an unaccompanied Chinese youth is one of Arendt's children—an individual whose "right to have rights" is tenuous at best. Twenty years after the near universal ratification of the 1989 UN Convention on the Rights of the Child, and several generations into an "age of rights" (Henken 1990), still no political consensus exists on the rights accorded to young migrants. Protection from violence and access to basic shelter, subsistence-level welfare programs, education, and health care are viewed as fundamental to a modern conception of rights. Yet in practice, argues Bhabha, these social entitlements are not officially confirmed (see also Statz 2018). As observed in the behavior of the many actors who manage unaccompanied minors in the US, including border patrol and immigration officials, these social rights can be easily curtailed or denied.

The negotiable nature of these presumably "inalienable" rights presents a unique challenge for cause lawyers and evidences their tenuousness. Consider, for instance, the significance of ORR, the official custodian of unaccompanied minors. While cause lawyers discuss ORR with frustration at professional gatherings, most are loath to overtly contest its practices—even ORR's funding and oversight of detention centers, many of which are significantly understaffed and fail to provide adequate social, educational, and health services to unaccompanied youth (Heidbrink 2014; Kennedy 2013). As it detains unaccompanied youth, ORR simultaneously and paradoxically provides funding to the nonprofit organizations that advocate for youths' release and that employ most of the cause lawyers I interviewed. Describing her contributions to what she hoped would be an influential policy report on Fujianese youth, one attorney concluded impatiently, "In the end, though, I just can't be affiliated with anything that challenges ORR practices. My hands are tied."

While state and federal public policy approaches differ, international human rights law presents an unequivocal approach to the rights of undocumented youth: "Everyone is entitled to all the rights and freedoms set forth in the Declaration [the Universal Declaration of Human Rights, or UDHR], without distinction of any kind such as . . . social origin, . . . birth or other status."[10] The Convention on the Rights of the Child [CRC] grants further specificity to the UDHR's general acknowledgement of children's rights as human rights. "If the UDHR laid the foundation for acceptance of Arendt's children's human rights vis-à-vis the state," writes Bhabha, "then the CRC, albeit cautiously, added the platform for these children to assert their human rights vis-à-vis their families, their teachers, and their communities" (2009, 420–21).

Yet while the CRC establishes children's rights as protection against the exercise of state power and promotes them in international migration and social-welfare policy, it cannot guarantee that these rights are effectively enforced. This has particular implications for unaccompanied minors in the United States. The only nation-state to not ratify the CRC, the US has only limited obligation to bring domestic law into conformity with the convention. Thus, despite the CRC's expectation that comprehensive guardianship and legal representation be provided to unaccompanied minors, undocumented youth in the US are not guaranteed the right to counsel. This illustrates a discrepancy not only between the rights guarantees of international law and the domestic realization of access to rights, but also between the substantive and procedural rights of documented versus undocumented youth in the US, as I detail in the following section. It also underscores the unique dilemma faced by legal advocates.

During a research interview with an immigration attorney in Nashville, I admitted, "I was surprised at the DC conference that the catch words seemed to be 'prosecutorial discretion' and 'best interests.' And 'best interests' was synonymous with 'avoiding deportation.' There's clearly a tension that exists here, particularly if a young person's expressed interest is to go back to her or his home country. Would you be willing to talk about that?"

"Welcome to the swamp!" said Anastasia. She leaned back in her lumpy office chair and laughed. It was a humid July afternoon, and we sat together in a disorganized cubicle on the main floor of a loud, dimly lit social-services office. The director of a small legal-services center, Anastasia wore a short-sleeved violet blouse and loose tan capris. Her blond hair was snarled, and a green scarf was tucked haphazardly around her neck. In dress and conversation, Anastasia quickly emerged as an outlier among the immigration cause lawyers I interviewed, the majority of whom wore dark, tailored professional clothing and responded abruptly, and somewhat distrustfully, when I inquired about issues like best interests.

"Now the best interests of the child is customary international law, according to *Beharry v. Reno*,"[11] Anastasia began. She explained further,

"Every country in the world except the United States and Somalia has signed the CRC.[12] The best interests of the child should be a no-brainer. . . . But is it actually applied, is it recognized as binding? Is it recognized as binding by ICE, who's making the decision for prosecutorial discretion? No . . . ICE is going to look at, okay, if we give [prosecutorial discretion] to this kid who has undocumented parents because it's in his best interests to be here, well then, all undocumented parents are going to be able to anchor their kids. So, we're not going to give prosecutorial discretion. That's what you're competing with. The reality is that the politics on the ground [matter more]. So, is international law useful? Not yet. Should we try to make it useful? Hell yes. Is it relevant legally? Yes, and we should be paying attention to the law and treating it as law and not just politics."

Anastasia's reflections thoughtfully summarize the inconsistency by which international law is applied in the US. In her experience, immigration judges' and trial attorneys' application of "best interests" for Arendt's children is entirely political, discretionary, and regionally specific. Of course, "best interests" as argued for by immigration cause lawyers are *also* political, discretionary, and regionally specific.

It's worth noting that the tension an attorney like Anastasia must hold in balance, namely between her knowledge of a modern, "universally-accepted" conception of children's "inalienable" rights and her experience of the arbitrary enforcement and provision of these rights, is weighted further by her own personal assumptions of unaccompanied minors' inherent "rights worthiness" as children. The aforementioned "natural rights" of individuals whose status is uniquely connected to *age* thus prove to be even more fragile, and more vulnerable, when tied up with state apparatuses that actively and capriciously act in spite of the pervasive construction of childhood as a protected, dependent, innocent space.

"On what grounds do you take a case?" I asked Anastasia.

"It's a matter of 'worst worses,'" she replied. "Sometimes it's if I have an attorney available. Basically, I try to take as many of the kids as I can. I have kind of a system, although it's informal, of preference. So I take children who I can do something for, who have a shot. Really, I take any and all children I can. And any and all persecution-based relief I can, and any and all domestic-based relief I can. And then after that I take court cases when they qualify for relief, like we'll take some tenure cancellation or LPR cancellation. I sometimes have taken kids just to help them with their voluntary departure, when you just know that nothing else is an option. Because, you know, *they're a kid . . .* "

A COMPARISON: THE RIGHTS OF
THE CHILD OF CHILD WELFARE

In the fields of child welfare and family law, considerable attention has been devoted to the complex and dynamic nature of representing children; to the idea of childhood as it had been interpreted, understood, and institutionalized for children by adults; and to the role of a young person's lawyer (see Appell 2004, 2006; Kell 1998; Koh Peters 1996, 2001; Guggenheim 1980, 1985). This work is important in creating a degree of additional legal protection (and a dialogue regarding the same) for many young people in the US. It also underscores the relative absence of these conversations in immigration law.[13]

In the 1960s and 1970s, attorneys for children were largely expected to play a guardian ad litem (GAL) role and to represent a client's best interests rather than the client her- or himself.[14] It was arguably Martin Guggenheim's "The Right to Be Represented But Not Heard" (1984) and the 1995 Fordham Conference on Representation of Children that signaled a fundamental shift in legal thought. The function of any attorney, these scholars argued, must be to pursue the legal objectives chosen by the client, so long as the client. is above a certain age. "To the greatest extent possible, legal representatives for children . . . should undertake a true lawyering role that is distinct from either a specialized guardian-like role or a hybrid lawyer-guardian role" (Guggenheim 1998, 312). Accordingly, writes Jean Koh Peters, "very few authors currently suggest that a teenage child, for instance, should be represented in the mode espoused by the early writers on the guardian *ad litem*" (2001, 48).

While this hard-won shift established clear principles regarding the proper roles and responsibilities of child welfare practitioners, strikingly little debate around the respective merits of the "traditional attorney model" (in which a lawyer advocates for a client's expressed wishes) and the "guardian ad litem model" (where she or he advocates for the client's best interests) has occurred among immigration advocates who work on behalf of unaccompanied youth. Indeed, many of the cause lawyers I spoke with vehemently espouse the GAL model, arguing that guardians ad litem should be assigned to every detained young migrant, no matter the youth's age. In many cases, immigration attorneys themselves serve as guardians ad litem, with very little or no communication with a client's parents or other family members.

At the heart of this issue is whether unaccompanied children are able to judge their own best interests (Byrne 2008, 37; Nugent and Schulman 2003)—and, likewise, what "representation" means when an attorney believes the answer is no. Here, recall one of the statements I heard during the "On Their Own" conference referenced in Chapter 1: "I was supposed to advocate for her expressed legal interest—it was a girl who wanted voluntary departure. But I didn't. I didn't think it was in her best interests to go back to her country." This contradictory "advocacy" is something I encountered frequently in my research and is likewise noted by other scholars (see, e.g., Thronson 2002; Carr 2009).

In the field of child welfare, the shift from the GAL model to "true law-yering" was undergirded by *In re Gault*, 387 U.S. 1 (1967), which holds that a juvenile accused of a crime in a delinquency proceeding must be afforded many of the same due process rights as an adult.[15] Not only did the precedent-setting case give (citizen) youth a constitutional right to counsel, but it also gave them certain substantive rights, including the right to remain silent.

As one legal scholar stated during an interview: "[This right] turns out to be deeply, deeply connected to autonomy. . . . Children have the substantive right not to coordinate. Now, I'm assigned to represent a child who has that right, and the question is, what would be best for that child? To plead guilty, or to deny the charges but maybe win where you are factually guilty but the proof isn't sufficient? A best interests lawyer would say, 'It's not best for my client to win merely because the evidence isn't sufficient, because my client's going to return to a life that's dangerous.' But that's a lawless choice. That is violating the Constitution, because the court already held that children have limited autonomy rights. . . . So my job as a lawyer is to enforce my client's rights. Now flash forward to immigration. What are my client's rights?"

I shook my head. "There's nothing," I replied. Youth with legal status in the US have different and more substantive and procedural rights than do undocumented youth.

"There is no *Gault* decision," he continued. "Therefore, the lawyers in the community . . . say, 'I'm going to advocate for what's best for my child ward.' They are not in any obvious way doing anything impermissible. . . . [Immigration attorneys] don't think of themselves as dangerous. They think of themselves as reasonable. So children do not get professionals who strive to achieve their objectives. They get professionals who try to change their life in some way, for what they believe is best."

THE CAUSE AS PROFESSION

As I demonstrate above, the restricted legal rights of unaccompanied and undocumented minors in the US establish a relatively clear "need" for immigration cause lawyers. This sense of responsibility is further compounded by a pervasive ideology of children's dependence. What results, then, are lawyers who do not dispassionately work for their clients, as in the "client service" model of conventional lawyering. Nor do they explicitly *partner with* clients to achieve moral and political ends or necessarily pursue objectives that transcend client service, the definitional "cause" of cause lawyering (Polikoff 1996; Sarat and Scheingold 1998). Instead, the cause lawyers in this study work *on behalf of* the legal and presumed "best interests" of young migrants, accepting unaccompanied Fujianese youth as legal clients because they believe no one else will and taking on a paternal or "guardian" role in the perceived absence of family ties and client autonomy.

This approach contrasts significantly with what many scholars argue are the essential features of cause lawyers: "They expressly seek clients with whom they agree and causes in which they believe," write Stuart Scheingold and Austin Sarat. "Cause lawyers often argue that the more closely they identify with their clients' values, the better advocates they will be." Significantly, however, the authors argue, "Cause lawyers tend to transform the nature of legal advocacy—becoming advocates not only, or primarily, for their clients but for causes and, one might say, for *their own beliefs*" (2004, 9, emphasis added; see also Simon 1984; Sterett 1998). This chapter has so far outlined a number of important tensions between the cause at hand and the broader cause-lawyering literature. In the realm of belief, however, the motivations my work documents firmly converge with the framework this scholarship offers.

While these beliefs certainly include the aforementioned "impulse" of legal and paternal responsibility, my data suggest that immigration lawyers' views are animated as well by bureaucratic and political structures and by personal disappointments and successes external to direct client service. This is, after all, *cause lawyering*, a form of human action in a field of institutional possibilities and, often, constraints (Sarat and Scheingold 2005, 4). In the remainder of this chapter, I explore the beliefs these attorneys maintain about the specific legal protections available to unaccompanied youth, the levels of bureaucracy in which they daily maneuver, the unique structure of immigration courts in the US, and the limited financial compensation afforded for their work. This provides a necessary introduction to a unique form of legal advocacy, but it also lends a more specific insight into the boundlessly intricate "uncontrollables" that cause lawyers navigate.

As I demonstrate here, these challenges both provoke and stimulate. Attorneys' encounters with what they describe as so many maddening scales of time, management, and funding often appear to delineate a specific course of action and to undergird professional identity and pride. These factors may not necessarily legitimate the strategies attorneys view as so constrained they become obligatory, but they do incite the reader to consider critically, and perhaps sympathetically, the complex and often very restrictive context in which immigration cause lawyers work.

MOTIVATING THE "CAUSE": LEGAL PROTECTIONS AND THE ADVERSARIAL, SUSPECT CAUSE LAWYER

Just as opposition to federal and state agencies appeared to unite the cause lawyers who attended the "On Their Own" conference, so also did it emerge in my research as an energizing force in lawyers' individual lives and practices. After talking with Russell, introduced earlier, I understood this opposition not simply as the likely outcome of lawyers' frustration with "the system," but as what many attorneys identified as a truly moral and political stance. "I'm a lawyer. I'm adversarial," said Russell as we sat together in his small Arkansas immigration law office eating pizza. The room's cinderblock walls were painted a dull yellow and lined with colorful tapestries and hanging plants.

"Is that something that's a personality trait," I asked, "or is that part of your training?"

"I think people are adaptable," he replied. "You fall into the world you're in. So yeah, it's us against the government. And I think it's partly self-selection, like, this is what we do. We fight the government all the time. We try to wheedle the government into giving us what we want. It's not adversarial like a criminal trial where you are really fighting. More often, it's more like persuading." He laughed. "Or attempting to persuade. And it's exasperating when it doesn't work."

Until this conversation, I was most familiar with "adversarial" as regards asylum procedures. Of course, that version of adversarial is not unrelated to Russell's characterization of himself and his profession. The attorneys in this study maintain "persuasive" or adversarial approaches to different legal protections like asylum, and also to the US immigration system more broadly. What many immigration cause lawyers believe to be the needless or counterproductive management of unaccompanied youth largely becomes a target of lawyering, contributing to the "us against the government" stance Russell described and that is often cited in the cause lawyering literature (Kelly 1994; Shamir and Chinski 1998).

Because their vision of a system is often procedurally centered, many lawyers accordingly construct and define a cause at the level of procedure (Hilbink 2004, 667), emphasizing the perceived unfairness of institutional treatment (Lev 1998, 447). Still, it is important to highlight that there is rarely so distinct a divide between substantive and procedural justice. In the cause at hand, lawyers oppose the US government's and/or immigration law's treatment of migrant *children* as substantively or morally wrong and also as procedurally unfair. The solution that cause lawyers present is largely procedural—namely the provision of lawyers (White 2001)—but with moral overtones, in that the lawyer may also assume the voice and power of a guardian ad litem. Throughout, as attorneys respond adversarially to "the system," more, and more abstract, barriers to *attorneys' own work* emerge. These include distrust, tenuous affiliations, and diminished success in securing now-suspect protections.

Consider asylum. If a USCIS asylum officer denies a petition for asylum, as the attorneys I interviewed claimed often happens with Fujianese youth, the unaccompanied minor then pursues the case in immigration court. This is extremely frustrating for attorneys who find themselves working against ICE trial attorneys in an adversarial setting they believe their clients don't deserve. "[You then have to] take down ICE," described one attorney. "They come to be the common enemy, I guess." Most of the lawyers I spoke with identified asylum as a particularly "bad" or nonexistent option for Fujianese clients. In his office's analysis of over five thousand case appeals in the Second Circuit, one attorney in New York reported that 4.96 percent of non-Chinese alien appeals and 2.33 percent of Chinese alien appeals were granted. "It is hard to avoid the conclusion that the Second Circuit does not carefully consider and evaluate the records, particularly in Chinese cases," he stated. Yet as other attorneys pointed out, this is perhaps not surprising given the relatively large numbers of fraudulent Chinese asylum cases filed by "snakehead lawyers" in New York (see Amon 2002). While this well-known racket certainly affects the experiences of *subsequent* Fujianese asylum applicants in the Second Circuit, it also hints at another related, and perhaps more relevant, issue—namely, the ease by which immigration lawyers, conventional or cause, come to be viewed with suspicion by immigration judges (IJs), trial attorneys, and other public and private actors involved in the management of unaccompanied youth.

While every cause lawyer I interviewed would be loath to be compared to snakehead attorneys in New York given the exorbitant fees, deceitful practices, and impossible guarantees they associate with this community of lawyers, they must likewise work "strategically" against a limited, adversarial, and often unreliable range of protections. They must also navigate the consequences of distrust associated with lawyers who work on behalf of young migrants.

"What about the segment of immigrants who are fleeing persecution?" an audience member asked during a panel at the "On Their Own" conference.

"The attention to this population is often very negative due to fraudulent asylum claims," replied the presenter. "*The New Yorker* had a very damaging article for us.[16] . . . When you bring up these issues, it's very tricky. You don't want it to seem like we're exploiting the system. With UACs, you have to increase attention to kids in the media, but you must present the many positive sides of the issue. . . . For instance, there's a growing interest in gang cases [as membership in a particular social group].[17] In the right hands, that's wonderful. But if someone focuses on one bad story, it could be bad."

When I returned to Chicago, I asked a local immigration attorney to clarify this. "Someone at the conference asked why no one was talking about asylum," I said. "The panelist said it's sort of a protection of last resort. There have been so many abuses of it that no one trusts asylum claims anymore. I was a little befuddled, because at a separate panel on Special Immigrant Juvenile status, it seemed like it was just another protection being used, manipulated, or potentially abused."

The attorney nodded vigorously. "Everybody's waiting for the jig to be up with SIJS. For now, you just want to get as much relief for as many kids as possible." From this statement, it is perhaps unsurprising that many of the cause lawyers I interviewed acknowledged the role and effect of suspicion in their work.

This suspicion is both regionally and remedy specific, as evidenced in Second Circuit Chinese asylum claims as well as SIJ status claims in Chicago. As I detail in Chapter 1, it is a three-part process to secure SIJ status: an attorney must get an SIJ predicate order from a state court, then petition for SIJ status (through USCIS, a federal agency), and finally file for lawful permanent residence with USCIS (if filing affirmatively) or federal immigration court (if filing defensively). What this ultimately means is that many immigration attorneys rely on well-established, trusted connections in local juvenile courts, which very rarely encounter immigration issues, to secure an SIJ predicate order.

For some, this is surprisingly easy. In my conversation with Anastasia, she mentioned, "We did have a case recently in Mississippi where we were able to get the order. The dependency and neglect order. We were able to get that in Mississippi from a judge, because we happened to know the judge well." An attorney in Texas described a similar situation: "I'm usually able to do an SIJ case in a few months, from start to finish. We had a nice arrangement with the state court, where we could file a declaratory judgment.[18] It's a remedy that exists in other states, but not all."

Yet when trusted connections do not exist, or when immigration attorneys are locally distrusted for the well-known and deliberate "waiting for the jig to be up" approach to SIJ, the legal protection is nearly impossible to secure. At the time of my research, this was the case in Chicago. "The courts are really resistant to SIJ [here]," stated one lawyer. "There are judges in Chicago and the state's attorney in Cook County who have been burned."

Jill, a local child welfare attorney, explained further, "We see very few unaccompanied kids [in juvenile court]. . . . We did have maybe three or four unaccompanied kids way back when, before the immigration world pissed off the child welfare world and the cases stopped coming in."

"Why did they stop coming in?" I asked. "I know with SIJ cases, you need a predicate order. So wouldn't those come through you?"

"Funny you should ask," she continued. "So what should happen is that immigration attorneys should be in the shelter interviewing kids, right? 'Okay. You, you, and you. It looks like you should qualify for SIJ; let's go in and get that predicate order.' And how do you get that predicate order? You've got to call DCFS [Department of Child and Family Services]. You've got to have somebody screen the case in the state's attorney's office. You call up DCFS, and DCFS says, 'I'm sorry, they're in a shelter. What do you mean they're abused? Someone's caring for them! The federal government's caring for them!' So, the state sees it as passing the buck, as the federal government wanting the state to pay for the care of these kids. And the state says, 'No! You have these kids in your care! We're not taking them.'"

She shook her head and sighed. "Of course, family court did take some cases . . . but then we had three cases in a row with really bad facts. One kid claimed to be the kid of a migrant farmworker from Honduras, spoke no English, and it turned out later she was a runaway from Washington state. But the immigration lawyers brought her case up anyway!" These lawyers, she added, were affiliated with a well-known immigrant rights advocacy organization in the area.

"And the judges found out about this." I responded.

"Yeah," Jill said. "And [cases like that] put a really bad taste in all the judges' mouths, and they said, 'Uh-uh.'" She knocked her fist on the table. "Like, 'No f-ing way.'"

"SO MANY UNCONTROLLABLES": SCALES OF TIME, CONFLICT, AND COMPASSION

In the above narrative, three scales of tension emerge. First, there is the local conflict between immigration attorneys and juvenile judges in Chicago—the willful presenting of "bad facts" that damaged the reputations of *all* immigration attorneys in the area, no matter their affiliation with the major nonprofit. Second, there is the broader "immigration world pissed off the child welfare world," a conflict that continues to limit advocacy efforts on behalf of undocumented youth. And finally, there is tension in the highest reaches of immigration policy, namely the state's perception of federal reliance on local juvenile courts as "buck passing." Rather than give up, the lawyers in this study often appeared motivated by these tensions, challenged by the belief that within this arbitrary legal system there remained space for knowledge, creativity, grit, and, thus, the possibility of success (Coutin 2001). At the same time, the challenge of balancing a concern for the individual client—or, as detailed below, a distressing glut of individual clients—*and* larger substantive goals also resulted in a sort of collective uneasiness. As attorneys explained, the demands of this balancing act fueled empathy with other stakeholders, but also intolerance. They legitimized a moral and professional identity as "altruistic" but also contributed to apprehension over longevity and personal commitment.

The attorneys I spoke with must operate within these multiple, divergent scales every day, and they must do so *quickly*. This was powerfully evidenced in a conversation I had with Roberta and Evelyn, two attorneys who oversee the Children's Project, a division of an immigration advocacy organization in Chicago. I arrived to our interview a bit early, and the waiting room was crowded. Around me sat a young man, two small boys who whispered to one another in Spanish, their mother, and another couple with a daughter. Signboards were lined up haphazardly along the smudged white wall behind us. On each was a close-up photo of a dark-eyed child, the agency's logo, and a statement about human rights. One of the signs had toppled over. The fluorescent lights above us were achingly bright.

A current of nervousness filled the room, all of us waiting to be called inside by the thus-far absent receptionist. "If one person leaned forward or motioned to stand up, I think we all would have," I scribbled in my notes. When the receptionist finally arrived, she slowly turned the scribbled "at lunch, I will be back at 2" sign over. "Who has appointments?" she asked in a flat voice. Simultaneously, two women stood and walked hurriedly toward the desk. Ignoring them, the secretary went through the list before her, calling our names in what seemed a random order. All told, it was nearly the same experience I had in 2011, when I waited to interview a separate attorney at the agency.

I quickly stood upon hearing my name, and the receptionist walked me to Roberta and Evelyn's office. With friendly welcomes, they ushered me in. Both in their late twenties or early thirties, Roberta was energetic with a quick, wide smile, and Evelyn, though more reticent, offered particularly introspective responses to my questions. Turning on my voice recorder, I asked, "How many youth does your program see?"

"Well, there are currently 448 beds [in shelter facilities] in the Chicago area," Roberta answered with a vigorous nod. I wondered if she, a relatively new hire, would experience the burnout her predecessors described. In less than three years of research, Roberta was the third staff attorney I had interviewed to hold the position. "So at any given point, there's a max of 448 kids."

Evelyn shook her head. "There are *always* 448 kids. And there have been since . . ." her voice trailed.

"Forever," concluded Roberta. "In a given month, we usually see approximately three hundred unique individuals. *Every month.*" Roberta estimated that over 80 percent of these youth would reunite with family, with the help of staff from the Family Reunification branch of the Children's Project.[19] This left people like Roberta and Evelyn to help with local legal cases or connect youth to pro bono attorneys across the country. But things have changed, Roberta stressed. "Right now, we've seen the release times [decrease] a lot," she stated.

Her colleague nodded. "About a year ago, we saw kids in facilities about four to eight weeks, generally, sometimes ten weeks. Now we're seeing them anywhere between one and three weeks, flipping over." In 2011, it should be noted, the number of unaccompanied minors brought to federal detention facilities began to increase dramatically, from fewer than four hundred in 2011 to nearly thirteen hundred in 2012. At the time of writing, there were seven child detention facilities in the Chicago area alone (Yousef 2013).

Evelyn leaned forward. "So that means a lot of them are released before they even have a court date. And in areas like Houston, New York, L.A., places where there's usually more of a pool from which to pull the pro bono attorney, because of the influx, they also don't have capacity. So where it might not necessarily be difficult to place them with the pro bonos, the length of time it takes to actually get an appointment or to start a case with them could also negatively affect their legal options. So now it's more difficult in certain areas, just because there aren't any attorneys familiar with these issues in certain states, and then where they are familiar, they're just totally inundated."

Coupled with growing numbers of detained youth, the limited nature of attorney networks that Evelyn described created a palpable sense of urgency among the cause lawyers I interviewed. This urgency was often exacerbated as attorneys moved beyond local scales of advocacy.

"There are so many unexpected things that can happen," said Roberta. "Things can change from one hour to the next, where a child might need something of you in a relatively quick amount of time. [And] we're constantly running up against deadlines. . . . There's *always* someone that's going to turn eighteen, and if you don't make a decision, that's going to impact them. And that is a challenge that others may not face in their practices. And then, of course, there are all the players that are involved with unaccompanied children. You know, you have to be very conscious of the fact that your role needs to play nice with the role of another individual in order to have a good end result. Having that really smooth communication between all the players is critical. And because there are so many players, the moment that one thing falters, it's just like a domino effect. That's a real challenge."

"And it's compounded by the time," added Evelyn.

"Right," answered Roberta. "It's compounded by the time. So I think if I could change anything, it would be developing [better] communication with the stakeholders in the area."

"When you say 'stakeholders,'" I asked, "who are you thinking of?"

Roberta paused, then began listing "stakeholders" as Evelyn looked on: ORR representatives in Chicago, individual staff at the shelter facilities, immigration judges, trial attorneys, juvenile officers of the enforcement and removal operations, officers who bring kids from the border to Chicago. "And even if we don't interact with the officers at the border," she concluded, "the decisions they're making at the border [affect us]."

"Yeah," agreed Evelyn, "I would echo those things." She paused, then introduced another scale of advocacy: "And not only is it the different actors, but the different steps that each kid has to go through. You know, we give the 'Know Your Rights' presentation and try to explain to a kid who might not have a government system and who might not have the social structures back home." Here she began to thump the table with her palm: "And so we have to explain DHS [thump] and the border patrol [thump] and ICE [thump] and the court and us and the advocates [thump, thump, *thump*]. And there are just *so many layers of the system*. From the best interests perspective, it could be good, you know, because there are different people looking out for them. But there are a lot, a lot of people involved, and a lot of that has to do with control. What can we control, and what can't we control? Or what can we— you know, as legal service providers, as attorneys, we like to control things, right? And there's so many uncontrollables. And when it's a kid's life, it just makes it that much more sympathetic or compassionate or whatever word you want to insert there."

ANOTHER LEVEL OF URGENCY: THE UNIQUE "LAYER" OF IMMIGRATION COURT

As perhaps the most obvious "contact zone" (Pratt 1992; Merry 2000) through which attorneys and unaccompanied minors move, the immigration courtroom is a space in which novel and taken-for-granted understandings of Chinese family, age, and rights intersect. Here, I focus on what immigration court means to attorneys, and how its unique structure constrains these individuals' work in some ways but permits surprising practices in others. I also highlight the role of IJs, including attorneys' impatience, and also empathy, toward these actors.[20]

As Roberta and Evelyn detailed, the growing number of apprehended unaccompanied minors in the US has resulted in a rapid turn-around time. Instead of being in a detention center for one or two months, youth can be released to a family member as early as one week after arrival. This puts a heavy strain on attorneys who must evaluate youths' cases and connect youth to appropriate pro bono services in their destinations. For IJs, including those who oversee juvenile dockets, this contributes to an already dramatic overload. A historic backlog is to blame, along with ICE agency goals of four hundred thousand deportations per year—about seventeen hundred cases per judge—at the time of this research.[21] Increased immigration enforcement means that IJs' workload is the highest it has ever been—three to four times larger than caseloads in other federal courts (Hsu and Becker 2010).

Of course, immigration courts are unlike federal courts in other significant ways. Unlike federal courts, immigration courts are run by an agency of the Justice Department,[22] the EOIR. And as many attorneys pointed out, particularly those with legal experience elsewhere, these courtrooms operate at a much faster pace than federal and state courts. "The last trial I had before I left civil rights practice was one month long," said Russell. "An entire month in front of a human rights commission judge about a woman's failure to get promoted because of her disability."

"And that was a long time?" I asked.

"It was a *really* long time," he replied. "I walked away from it thinking, that's way too much time to spend on an issue like that. And then I went to immigration court, where you get two hours over a person's claim that they're going to be murdered if they get sent back to their homeland. Two hours. Over a death penalty case, basically."

During an interview with an attorney in Wisconsin, I asked, "Do you think there are regional differences between immigration courts?"

"They're all pretty similar," Carl answered. "And they're all pretty isolated from real life, you know, what law practice is like outside of immigration court. There's just no comparison. People who work in immigration court forget that trials in the real world last longer than two hours. And you know, you have actual certified translators instead of—"

"—the phone," I interrupted.

"The phone, or whatever guy was hired who comes in and doesn't even speak the same dialect. And people go, 'Eh, close enough. It's fine.'"

These complaints were not exclusive to immigration attorneys. Lustig et al. (2008) report that IJs share similar sentiments about bureaucratic constraints and the subsequent moral questions about their work. Judges who face constant pressure to evaluate "which asylum claims are genuine: who has truly suffered horrors, and who has been coached by 'travel agents'" (Miner 2010, 1) suffer significantly from symptoms of secondary traumatic stress and job exhaustion. Many complain of an overwhelming volume of cases with insufficient time for careful review, a shortage of law clerks and language interpreters, and failing computers and equipment for recording hearings (Lustig et al. 2008; Preston 2009).

The attorneys who regularly work with these judges were often very sensitive to the exhaustion, and exhausting demands, they observe. Describing the anti-immigrant climate of her southern state, Abigail stated, "Our EOIR court has one of the highest if not the highest number of deportations per judge in the whole country. Because of the ICE glut, because of 287(g).[23] All of a sudden everybody pulled over for not stopping at a red light is now in immigration court. So there are two judges, and they have something like over five thousand cases on their docket. That means each judge is responsible for more than twenty-seven hundred immigration cases at once. I don't know how they keep it in their heads without their heads exploding. And they're both very good judges. We're really, really glad to have them here. They're very just and fair and smart, but they have twenty-seven hundred cases."

Erika, the director of a university immigration law clinic, explained further: "Because immigration court is an administrative court, IJs don't have the kind of freedoms they might have in a regular civil court. And they actually sit on the bench for something like thirty-five hours per week. And so that leaves very little time for admin work. And within that time, they have to not only prep for all the cases that are coming up, they also have to review all the cases that are going up on appeal. They're really constrained. I have a lot of sympathy towards the judges. I mean, they have huge time constraints put on them." She shook her head.

"So a lot of the work in immigration is all up front. . . . For instance, in an asylum case, you'll hand in something that's like, this big." She held her hands about eight inches apart. "It will have all the exhibits, and if you have witnesses, you submit something that indicates specifically what they'll testify to. You'll usually have an affidavit from the client that lays out specific details. So all the information that's going to come up in court will probably have been submitted before the actual hearing. And the theory behind it is that the judge would have reviewed all that information beforehand, so then they can ask more specific questions about what they have concerns over."

"In theory," I responded, "but in practice? I mean, if you're putting in thirty-five hours on the bench . . ."

"Yeah, it doesn't always work out that way. I do think judges are familiar with similar cases, like a domestic violence case we recently had from El Salvador. I think once they get used to that type of case, they know what issues to look for. But no, I don't think that they have a chance to look through everything. But there are ways—like when we submit a packet like this, we highlight all the articles, and in our table of contents we put a sentence or two of what is most important from there, so they sort of have a synopsis of everything. So yeah, it's a lot of prep work for us."

Like Abigail, Erika was considerate, and strategic, regarding IJs' work load, instructing her students to prepare, organize, and structure their arguments to best appeal to the insufficient time and consideration she knew judges could grant each case. Other lawyers took more explicit advantage of IJs' limits and the distinct structure of immigration court.

"Think about how evidence is considered in immigration court," said James, an attorney in Arkansas. "In state or federal court, civil or criminal, you've got really specific rules about admitting evidence. There are very strict rules about what can be considered. In immigration court? I don't know of any rules. There are guidelines, but . . ." His voice drifted off as he laughed and looked out the window.

"I mean, I've gotten reports off the Internet, from the State Department, human rights reports, articles, you know, whatever I can find. I try to keep it to a reputable source, but if I can't find one, I've got to do something! In a state court, there would be an issue with hearsay, because you can't cross-examine who wrote it. You can't challenge anything in it. So from a respondent's point of view, it's good to send all this stuff in. Like the last removal proceeding I had in Memphis—I didn't have a very good case. And so we were trying whatever. I was trying to compare the child's hometown in Mexico with our community, the great education, great economic opportunities she'd have here. I was taking things from chamber of commerce websites,

Forbes magazine, rankings of the region, saying, 'Judge, this is a top-ten place in America—virtually the world—versus, you know, what is probably a tiny, rural place in Mexico without potable water.' I was able to use those things, at least submit them. And I guess they could argue against them, but they don't have the opportunity to challenge the offer ever. . . . There's not discovery like in civil cases, no haggling over secret documents. And there's just no time."

Here, James highlights the sort of creative license attorneys have in immigration court, particularly in his presentation of a small town in Arkansas as "a top-ten place in America" alongside the seemingly *indisputable* association of Mexico with rural life and dirty water. That this practice is acceptable, or at least is unlikely to receive a thorough assessment, illuminates the significance of the attorney-authored practice advisories and policy reports I reference earlier. During my research, I was perpetually struck that lawyers could contribute to or even *create* the very documents they would later use and distribute as evidence and that the resources James laughingly described—chamber of commerce websites, rankings, magazine articles—might actually substantiate someone's claim for asylum. Of course, as we consider the broad parameters regarding hearsay and evidence that James detailed above,[24] along with the well-known and mounting burdens placed on IJs, perhaps I should not have been so surprised.

Yet not everyone lauded the permissibility of such savvy, creative techniques. After all, argued Russell, it's not an attorney's job to help IJs make their decisions, no matter how advantageous it may be for the client. "What's most important is to empower these kids," he stated, furrowing his thick eyebrows, "to have somebody who takes seriously what they want, who looks out for them, and who keeps their confidences, who counsels them, who stands up for their desires in court. It's an abdication by judges, I think, to say, 'I just want a lawyer to tell me how to do my job.'"

Lana, a young attorney in New York, was likewise flabbergasted: "And so I wonder, what is our role, really? Is our role to—I don't know. Often, I see myself up against the IJs. It's like they just don't want to listen to me. But if the IJs actually asked the *kids* more questions, not us . . ."

Similarly, and drawing back to the earlier discussion of youths' presumed "dependence," one attorney in Missouri commented, "And if you try to talk about children's legal rights versus their best interests versus their objectives, it can get quite tense. As adults, we don't trust children. That's why you have GALs and attorneys acting as GALs all over the place. Immigration judges *love* GALs, by the way. They love GALs because the judges have to make the decision of what's in the best interests of the child. And they want someone else to tell them what to do, and someone else to be giving them that information."

As Evelyn recounted in the previous section, IJs are but one element of a many-layered immigration system that also includes ICE trial attorneys, border patrol agents, ORR officials, and on and on. I focus here on IJs because to many cause lawyers, IJs not only evoke the broad problems inherent in the US immigration system, but they also symbolize opportunities to work creatively within it. Additionally, by exploring the "layered" strains placed on IJs, including a historic backlog, expanding federal quotas (euphemistically termed "agency goals") of hundreds of thousands of deportations per annum, and regional collaborations between ICE officials and local law enforcement, we can begin to recognize the knotty and intertwined context of US immigration as well as its influence on what cause lawyers believe are the necessary practices and possibilities of their work.

THE FUNDING GAME

In documenting the many "uncontrollables" of immigration cause lawyering, the financial side of advocacy—specifically, the overt *lack* of financial reward—was referenced as a notable constant. In addition to its predictability, the relatively low pay cause lawyers receive is significant, and in a sense celebrated, as a form of professional identity and legitimacy. Many of the attorneys I spoke with presented their work in the nonprofit sector as something of a public sacrifice—it was this, "on top of everything else," that conveyed the most recognizable and reconcilable form of compassion.

This sentiment helps lawyers position their work in relation to wealthier conventional lawyer colleagues, and it bolsters a more "altruistic" sense of satisfaction and pride, one that money may not necessarily provide. June, an attorney in Chicago, explained: "Oh *god*," she said theatrically. "I *wish* I was making the kind of money my friends at big firms make. I wish my office wasn't a dump. Nobody cleans. It's disgusting! And I wish I had a car allowance and a beautiful view. I mean, I work in an environment that my friends from law school would be horrified at. But," she shrugged her shoulders, "they all hate their jobs . . . so I feel at least happy that my eyes are open to these things, even if I can only fix or help the tiniest, tiniest bit in my little part of the world." She paused. "I do a book group. And it's all North Shore [a wealthy suburban area of Chicago] women. And they're *so* sheltered. They have no idea. I sit there, and I think, 'You are the dumbest bunch of people I have ever met in my whole life.' They have no idea what they're talking about. I want to say, like, spend a day in my office, and then you can talk."

As other attorneys pointed out, however, this satisfaction was neither easily won nor especially sustainable. Lana commented, "It's interesting being a public interest lawyer when you're twenty-six and you go into it being like, 'I want to be the most altruistic person in the world.' But now, you know, I'm living on a public interest salary. Literally, every day, I think, do I have to eat today? Do I have ten dollars? Fifteen dollars?"

Along with these personal constraints, most cause lawyers stressed the impact of limited public and private funds on their individual work and on broader national advocacy efforts on behalf of unaccompanied youth. Supporting what Sara De Jong calls "a crisis of legitimacy" (2011, 25; see also Pupavac 2006) in the nonprofit world, attorneys identified funding restrictions as a key aspect of the bureaucratic structures they must navigate in their daily work, often with considerable frustration. Even if these lawyers perceived their limited income as indicating personal and moral commitment, "sacrifice," and social awareness, they remained critically aware that tenuous funding also signaled broader fissures in the image and efficacy of nonprofit immigrant advocacy organizations.

As Erika noted, "In Chicago, we just don't have any resources to continue. It's a big challenge, and I think it's a challenge for most of the legal service providers that work with unaccompanied kids.

"So we're subcontractors with the VERA Institute of Justice, which is contracted by ORR to make sure children in their care receive legal orientation presentations and are screened for legal relief. We have some limited funding that allows us to do representation, but it's outside funding. And funding restrictions have changed in the last year, so we have to be really careful not to mislead the kids into thinking that we're actually their attorneys. For the most part, our funding isn't to represent these kids, it's just to determine if they're eligible for relief, to provide them with this information, to place them to a pro bono lawyer. It's confusing for them. It's confusing for us.

"The managers in each project are focused on direct service, but it's hard when you're government funded to be more creative. Budget cuts mean more intra-agency urgency and reaction. We have to be very reactive."

Taken together, the limited funding and time attorneys experienced contributed to a narrow and pre-delineated course of action. "The short-term option always wins out," said Lana. "I'm not blaming anyone for 'taking advantage' of the system, because it's so messed up and broken. People do what they have to do." She paused, then nonchalantly added, "Immigration lawyers—it's interesting, you know. If your only tool is a hammer, then the problem looks like a nail."

However glib or offhand, Lana's comment efficiently summarizes this chapter. Not only do the ideologies, legal rights, and bureaucratic constraints outlined here influence the "tools" available to cause lawyers, but they also shape the problem itself. As lawyers work to put Fujianese youth "in the right box," the problem—or perhaps, the *cause*—is at once a matter of age, of citizenship, of legal rights and protections. It is also very personal, involving more ambiguous questions of responsibility, identity, and proper (or necessary) action.

Moreover, and as the next chapter reveals, the intricate forces that constrain and delineate cause lawyers' work prove consequential and yet in some ways *insignificant* when held against the complex transnational histories and situated identities of young migrants themselves. In contextualizing and presenting these youths' reflections, I endeavor to expose readers—some of whom may be immigration cause lawyers—to the perspectives of clients, which are often missing from discussions of advocacy (Shdaimah 2009, 19), even among those who claim to speak on behalf of youths' best interests.

3 *A Poetic and Practical Bridge: Reflections on Youth Mobility*

W hen I admitted to the young people who participated in this project that most of my experience in China had been in Sichuan Province, and that Mandarin seemed nearly incomprehensible to me when spoken with a Fuzhou accent, I was often met with good-natured laughter and then an earnest and lengthy explanation. However uncomfortable it felt at the time, sharing my insecurities about language and place was typically, and rightly, interpreted by young research participants as an invitation for meaningful collaboration.

As youth began to self-identify as valued experts, the reflections they shared were increasingly vibrant, critical, nostalgic, challenging, and heartfelt. I remain compelled by and accountable to their accounts, and thus present extended vignettes in this chapter as opposed to shorter interview excerpts.[1] My reasons for this are distinct but interrelated. For one, these individual portraits illuminate local processes of change and likewise emphasize youths' own knowledge and influence in their families, communities, and this project (see Arnold and Blackburn 2005; Jeffrey and Dyson 2008; Sime and Fox 2015). As ethnographic "bridge builders," it is young research participants' voices that facilitate a "'crossing' into the sensibilities and sensitivities of others," writes Benson Saler. "[These] ethnographic bridges . . . allow the reading public to cross over to new understandings, new understandings of others and perhaps of themselves" (2003, 209).

Yet while valuable for their own sake, when held up against attorneys' interpretations of "Chinese culture and family," these new understandings take on additional power, intrinsically illuminating the insufficiency of so many largely decontextualized legal portrayals of Fujianese youth. In this chapter I accordingly move between—and likewise stress—multiple frames of reference. In hindsight, I realize this way of re-presenting my data largely reflects my fieldwork experience. Often, I would feel satisfied after a particularly informative interview with an attorney, only to have the material I collected almost immediately upended in a subsequent conversation with a young migrant. Neither perspective was incorrect, but situated, and divergent.

Accordingly, what may at times feel dissonant in this chapter is important, revealing how a young person's migration journey is shaped by her positionality within and against a range of geographic and temporal scales, from a rich regional history of migration to a local sentiment of "backwardness," from valued familial and community status to sustained and seemingly inevitable socioeconomic insecurity among peers here in the US and there in China. Juxtaposing the complex context of Fujianese migration with youths' nuanced reflections takes us further, implicitly calling into question what tends to be simplified as "unaccompanied Chinese migration" in immigration court. Whereas Chapter 2 details the complex legal demands and professional motivations that arguably necessitate these reductions, this chapter documents what is lost in the process.

"THERE'S ALWAYS THE MOUNTAIN": BRIDGING TIMELESSNESS AND CHANGE FROM ALABAMA

When we met, Bingwen was in his early twenties. He had lived in Alabama for nearly eight years and was more comfortable speaking English than Mandarin, he said. Short and broad-shouldered, Bingwen wore cargo shorts, a blue t-shirt, and flip-flops. He adjusted his glasses frequently. Accustomed to sharing his migration story but rarely ever the story of his life *before* migrating to the US, he appeared startled and pleased by many of my questions.

"Can you tell me about your life in Fujian?" I asked.

"Okay," he said. He closed his eyes. I waited. "Okay. You know when you are in a certain place, everything is just . . ." his voice trailed. "Every day is just Monday, Tuesday. There's nothing special about it. Now I think back to the place I grew up; it's really quite pretty. You know, China's had this economic boom, but it doesn't reach the little towns and cities until right about when I was coming to the US. So basically I grew up in a pretty pristine China, before the pollution kicks in. I used to remember the river was clean, but by the time I was thirteen, fourteen, it's black, you don't want to touch it. It's really sad. Now, my childhood? Okay, let me think. How do I put it? My village is very small."

"How small?"

"There are about two thousand people in the entire village. It's really a town. So the way the place I live at is structured, it's a whole bunch of villages, joined together. They become a town."

"What was the name of it?"

With a heavy accent, Bingwen said the name of a village in Changle, a county-level city over which Fuzhou has direct jurisdiction.

"So basically," he continued, "it's kind of backward relative to other parts of China. It's still an old-fashioned village setting. And there's pretty much no traffic when I was little. There's maybe two concrete streets in the entire area. Now, I understand, everything's concrete."

"I bet."

"Yeah. So, everything else was, you know, gravel or dirt road. I remember that between my village and the hill, there was a stretch that's maybe half a mile, just essentially clay and gravel. You just picture yourself walking from your house, all the way to where the mountains and the hill are. Everything to your left, everything to your right is rice paddies. It's kind of cool, actually. To me, the rice paddy has always been there, there's always the dirt road, there's always the mountain. That's just everyday life. But now when I think about it, you know, a lot of people in this country pay thousands of dollars to go to a place like that! But if that's all you know your whole life, there's nothing special about it."

"Were you living in a house?"

"It was a really small house, like a giant rectangle. Pretty basic amenities. Pretty much everything is on the bottom floor, and then you sleep on the second floor. You work and you cook here." He traced an outline on the couch cushion. "It's like I'm working here, and someone's cooking there. Some kids are running around outside. Dogs and chickens and cats everywhere. It's weird, it makes no sense, but everyone just runs around like nothing's going on. Nobody cares. And you know," he added, "I actually worked in the rice paddy."

"You did?" I asked. "What did you do?"

"So, when you see the Travel Channel . . ."

"Was that you I saw?"

He laughed. "Yeah, I did that! I actually did that."

"How old were you?"

"Eleven or twelve. It's completely normal, actually, because no one considers it underage working. It's just how life is."

"Did you mind doing it?"

"I don't mind. Well, when everyone else is doing it, you don't complain. It never even comes to you that [it's] something you should complain about.

It's not like the next-door neighbor has a kid who has a Mac computer or anything, you know? So there are frogs jumping around, some leeches try to suck your blood. . . . It's like that. And pretty much everybody in my extended family, my village, owns a piece of the land. You know," he said, "it's actually pretty cool. I think Western visitors would enjoy seeing something like that. It's seeing how life has always been, for thousands of years.

"My work on our farm was kind of a gradual thing. As you get older, you start to do more stuff. By the time I was twelve years old, we were outside, selling." He paused. "Man, now that I think about it, I pretty much did all kinds of third-world stuff." He laughed. "I'm just joking. Then for about three years during the summertime, my job was selling watermelon. I had a giant watermelon stand. It's fun. It's like a workout for me. I had *a lot* of watermelons. My dad would go to purchase a watermelon from a farm outside. He brought an entire truck of watermelons. So maybe once a week or once every other week I sleep where the watermelon is on the street. Just so no one would steal it! I have my mosquito net over me, sleeping."

"Were you going to school then, too?"

"I actually was. But in China, school is not free. You have to pay for it. And especially once it's high school, you're pretty much on your own. Even then, it's considered expensive."[2]

Later in our conversation, Bingwen mentioned he hopes to return to his home village to visit.

"How do you feel when you think about that?" I asked.

"I worry about whether I'm going to be able to find my way there!"

"Of course," I replied. "I'm imagining if there were rice paddies when you left, what is there now?"

"I heard there's no rice paddies anymore in the area. Everything's gone. It's like the city's growing out and it's growing into my village. So slowly it's becoming more and more like a city. It's almost *part* of the city now because of all that growth, all the concrete and buildings and expansions. The mountain is still there, though. You can't move the mountain."

A LEADING AND LAGGING PROVINCE, ITS LEADING AND LAGGING MIGRANTS

I was captivated by Bingwen's rich, straightforward descriptions of life in his home village and by the almost deceptive ease with which he "bridged" disparate worlds, expectations, and temporalities. However indirectly, Bingwen's words also lend clarity to what Julie Chu argues is a "nested set of inferiority complexes" (2010, 27) typical of Fujianese villages like Bingwen's. In his memory, Bingwen's village is a community with a unique landscape and history: "It's seeing how life has always been, for thousands of years." Yet Bingwen's words aren't unconsidered nostalgia. With characteristic directness, he describes how the village has been absorbed into a broader metropolitan area, in this case Changle City: "It's like the city's growing out and it's growing into my village." He also identifies the village, or the city, as "kind of backward relative to other parts of China." Though a transnational community, it is simultaneously a region that can't compete with the remarkable economic growth of nearby provinces.

Following Julie Chu, we locate in Bingwen's description a place that is both "a lagging or leading edge of China" (2010, 25). It's not just Bingwen's village, of course: The "edginess" and insecurity—and arguable inferiority—Chu describes also extend to Fujian Province more generally. On the national level, Fujian falls behind the more influential and cosmopolitan north, which includes Shanghai and Beijing (see fig. 1). At the provincial scale, Fujian is largely overshadowed by the expansion of Guangdong Province to its south. Within Fujian Province, Fuzhou, the administrative capital of Fujian and the region from which most contemporary out-migration occurs, is often viewed as a "mediocre disappointment" among national efforts to modernize China, falling behind special economic zones like Xiamen, also in Fujian Province (Chu 2010, 28). And finally, on the most local scale, villages like Bingwen's are at once geographically close but socially distanced from areas like Changle City. As Bingwen's reflections illustrate, his community "fall[s] between all boundaries as neither a proper, idyllic 'peasant village' nor a welcomed extension of urban life" (30).

As I demonstrate elsewhere in this book, attorneys and popular media often attribute the migration of Fujianese youth to deficient or dysfunctional parents, poverty, sophisticated smuggling networks, or political or religious persecution. And in certain individual cases, one or some of these explanations may be true. Yet to understand *why* youth like Bingwen left, we must first know *what* Bingwen left—that is, how he and other young migrants experienced and now imagine their communities of origin as profoundly connected to, yet somehow still on the "edge of," local and global processes of change.

It is likewise necessary to understand the physical and very personal reach of migration, or how the youth at the center of this study situate their personal migration stories within a broader regional history and a complex

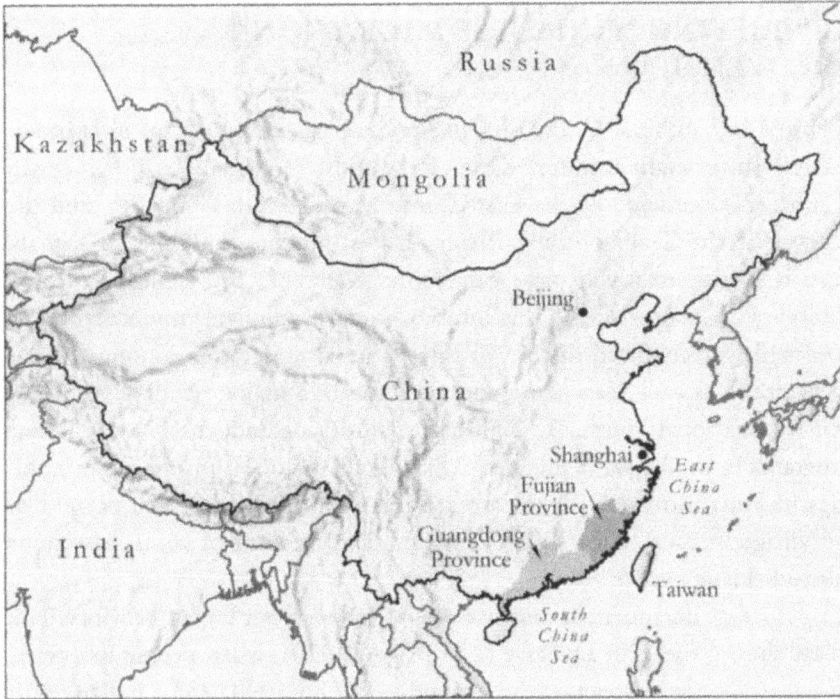

FIGURE 1: People's Republic of China
Micaella Penning, Geospatial Analysis Center at the University of Minnesota Duluth.
Data courtesy of Esri.

present in the US. Above, I employ the poetic view of these youth as "ethno-graphic bridges," yet I also recognize the very real bridges these individuals are as young migrants. Perceived of and self-identifying as valued conduits of money, status, and information, these individuals are in a sense like Fujian Province itself—lagging behind or leading, depending on one's position-ality and point of comparison. As my data demonstrate, unaccompanied Fujianese minors are keenly aware of the ways in which they "lag" behind other Chinese nationals in the People's Republic of China, behind Chinese-Americans and Chinatown peers, behind other unaccompanied youth, and behind distinctly Western or American presumptions of developmental stages and age-appropriate markers of success. Yet there is potential in this precari-ousness, for the young people with whom I spoke are simultaneously often the leaders of their "emplaced" families and of their relationships, employ-ment, and legal pursuits in the US.

CLARIFYING "FUJIANESE MIGRATION":
AN OVERVIEW

Located in southeast China, Fujian Province has a population of approximately thirty-eight million.[3] One of the most mountainous provinces in China, it is bordered by the East China Sea, the South China Sea, and the Taiwan Strait. Geographically, it is the closest province in China to Taiwan, and it is also relatively near Singapore, Malaysia, the Philippines, and Indonesia. Unsurprisingly, this location underlies Fujian Province's unique and widely recognized history of international emigration among China's provinces—as well as its contemporary status as a major "sending" province for transnational youth. By 2000 the majority of undocumented Chinese migrants in the US were Fujianese (Liang and Ye 2001). In some communities in Fujian, overseas remittances make up approximately 70 percent of all village income (Chu 2006), and almost 90 percent of youth have gone abroad (Liang and Ye 2001).

The first documented instance of emigration from Fujian Province took place during the Han Dynasty (226 BC–AD 220), when people journeyed to what is today known as the Philippines (Zhu 1990, 233). Fujian's port regions became increasingly important during the Tang Dynasty (618–907), and overseas trade flourished in the Ming Dynasty (1368–1644). At this time sea trade extended from Fujian Province to nearly every Southeast Asian country, with particularly strong ties to the Philippines.

The Treaty of Nanjing (1842), which marked China's loss to Great Britain in the first Opium War, stipulated that five Chinese port cities, including Fujian's Fuzhou and Xiamen (known at the time as *Amoy*, an approximation of the pronunciation of the city's name in its local vernacular), be opened for residence by British subjects and their families. Interestingly, and returning to the notion of Fuzhou as a "mediocre disappointment," the British were apparently so frustrated with Fuzhou's performance as a commercial port that there was discussion of swapping it for another city with better prospects (Fairbank 1969; Spence 1999). Fuzhou and Xiamen nonetheless became major sites from which individuals were transported to Southeast Asia as contract laborers, as well as to the US to work in mines and on the railroads.

External trade factors certainly influenced Fujianese emigration, but a powerful "push" came also from within China during the nineteenth century. Between 1779 and 1850, the Chinese population grew from 275 million to

430 million (Hsu 2000). This placed unprecedented pressure on Chinese production, particularly in Fujian Province, where 80 percent of the region was mountainous, and elite merchants and landlords operated the remaining arable tracts. Because of these conditions, growing numbers of Fujianese began emigrating overseas as contract laborers or debtor laborers: 16,683 people left Fujian in 1875 and 43,613 more in 1885 (Liang and Ye 2001,193). The majority of these emigrants settled in Southeast Asia. Approximately 80 percent of all Chinese in the Philippines and 55 percent of Chinese in Indonesia trace their origins to Fujian (Zhu 1990).

Though the contract labor system was later abolished in the early twentieth century, emigration from Fujian continued. Chinese labor was exported via a recruitment system by foreign governments, and a significant increase occurred during World War I, when contracted laborers were imported from Fujian to the US. Other major waves of emigration occurred with the start of the second Sino-Japanese War in 1937 and when China's civil war intensified in the mid-1940s.

With the establishment of the People's Republic of China (PRC) in 1949, strict controls were placed on emigration. For the next thirty years, Chinese citizens encountered chaotic realities that would ultimately shape and underlie later waves of migration. The agricultural collectivization and industrialization of the Great Leap Forward (1958–1961) brought about a catastrophic famine that resulted in as many as thirty-five million deaths, and the Cultural Revolution (1966–1976) produced further social, political, and economic upheaval. Very little out-migration occurred during this time.

As Deng Xiaoping consolidated leadership in the 1970s, China adopted a policy of "reform and opening up" (改革开放) regarding both its economy and international immigration. While comparatively restrictive, an exit visa system was established in 1980, and approximately fifty thousand individual applications were approved between 1979 and 1985 (Liu 2009, 316). In 1979, formal diplomatic relations were officially established between the US and the PRC, and the subsequent passage of the Law on the Control of Exit and Entry of Citizens (1985) importantly underscored emigration as the right of every citizen. The law remained restrictive, however, requiring work unit approval, household registration or *hukou* documents, official overseas invitations, and financial guarantees before a passport might be secured. Subsequent reforms made it relatively easier for a Chinese national to secure a passport, but important limitations remain, particularly for government officials, managers of state-owned enterprises, and, significantly, the residents of small cities and rural areas, including those in Fujian. Today, many provincial governments also establish their own separate regulations and reform measures, further complicating the national government's power to control exit and entry (Liu 2009, 320).

DIFFERENTIATING *FUZHOUNESE* YOUTH: COMPLICATING OR COMPROMISING THE CAUSE

As Peter Kwong explains: "The profound Fuzhounese feeling of marginalization—brought on by the combination of their geographic isolation, distinctive dialect, and seagoing vocation—all contributed to the equally profound Fuzhounese spirit of independence and political autonomy. . . . Yet for all their prowess and prestige in China as world travelers, very few Fuzhounese came to the United States before the late twentieth century" (1997, 26–27).

Characterizing these migration histories and patterns as "Fujianese" is in many ways insufficient, glossing over the unique geographic and sociolinguistic diversity within Fujian Province itself (see fig. 2). Largely isolated from the rest of China and from one another via the Min River and nearby mountain ranges, the distinct regional groups within Fujian boast the most heterogeneous dialects of any Chinese province.

Historically, most Fujianese emigrants were from south of the Min River, those who spoke the Minnan dialect. The first record of migrants from Fuzhou, which lies north of this region, involves a few hundred seamen who worked on US merchant marine vessels during World War II. After the war, many of these individuals gained residence in the US as reward for their service, and most settled in New York. Few ever obtained legal status, and those who did often did so through bogus marriages to American-born Chinese women. Regardless of status, as soon as many of these sailors became economically established, they began to bring members of their families from China to the US.

This was the beginning of the Fuzhounese smuggling network, writes Kwong: "a few primitive, simple schemes concocted by enterprising travel agencies to exploit this eager market of merchant mariners" (1997, 28). By the 1970s, Fuzhounese migrants began arriving in the US in more significant numbers. The modern era of Fuzhounese smuggling accelerated with the 1986 passage of the US Immigration Reform and Control Act (IRCA),

FIGURE 2: Fujian Province
Micaella Penning, Geospatial Analysis Center at the University of Minnesota Duluth.
Data courtesy of Esri.

which offered one-time amnesty to all previously undocumented migrants and enabled subsequent chain migration among the Fuzhounese (1997, 2001; see also K. Chin 1999, 2001; Chu 2006).

This migration was not, of course, motivated exclusively by economic opportunities in the US. Reiterating the unique position of Fujianese in China, and of Fuzhounese within Fujian, Chu writes: "As state classified peasants for four decades, the rural Fuzhounese were precisely not the kind of subjects authorized to charter moral careers as mobile cosmopolitans in China. . . . What they revealed through their persistent aspirations and dissonant strategies for going overseas was not only the normativity of mobility per se but also . . . the uneven and unequal positioning of different groups and persons in relation to various flows and movements" (2006, 403; see also Massey 1993). This interplay of positionality and mobility introduces an almost overwhelming array of potential motivations, suggesting that a young person's migration may be attributable to economic forces, state-building projects, family, community norms, religious hierarchies, transnational networks of obligation and support, local values, global fluctuations of power—and, of course, how the Fuzhounese youth herself experiences and imagines these phenomena from within and outside or, perhaps more accurately, on the "edge of" processes of change.

Though by no means exhaustive, youths' extended reflections here introduce a number of these distinct possibilities. They likewise reveal both the promise and troubling potential of ethnographic research, at once bridging the socio-spatial distance between the reader and the young person while simultaneously accentuating the relative gulf that exists between individual and legal accounts of migration. This is not to say that the "cause" as represented in the legal realm is inaccurate, but rather that it is rarely—and perhaps can never be—complete.

As evidenced here, youths' reflections neither explicitly support the characterization many attorneys suspect may be true but actively work against (namely that Fujianese youth are economic migrants), nor do they necessarily help validate cause lawyers' claims of trafficking, of severed kin ties and parental abandonment, or of fears of persecution for illicit immigration and unpaid smuggling fees. Moreover, youths' responses evidence a savvy and sometimes cynical understanding of Chinese and American policies, global economic realities, and cause lawyers' own strategies.

"I think the popular thing attorneys do is put everyone in a group," one young man told me later. "It's much more difficult to evaluate individual cases. Even cases that are very similar are *still individual cases*. There's always some reason back home that causes [youth] to be there to begin with. Many of them are similar, and many of them are different. Everybody experiences different stuff. It sucks for me that I was put in a group that's [seen as so] desperate."

To underscore the never-so-neat intersection and communication of information, expectations, and values in Fujianese migration, it is worth thinking more carefully about economic change and social status. Consider, for instance, the "reform and opening up" mentioned in the previous section. While the program presented new economic opportunities for the nation, it had complex and at times ambiguous effects on Fuzhou. The rapid development of new industries and Special Economic Zones in the early 1980s introduced significant foreign investment into Fujian Province. By 1992, the per capita income of Fujian's rural households had risen to eighth place among China's thirty-one provinces (Liang and Ye 2001, 195). At the same time, however, Fujianese farming and fishing communities, already limited by the aforementioned shortage of arable land, were largely displaced. As China's Special Economic Zones became destinations for millions of displaced inland Chinese—particularly those without permanent household registration status, or *hukou*, at their place of destination—job competition and unemployment rates rose steadily in Fujian's urban areas.

Fujian Province is not considered "poor" in relation to other Chinese provinces, but its GDP per capita is lowest among China's coastal administrative divisions. Additionally, 40 percent of Fujian's GDP is accounted for in just three municipalities, those of the "Minnan Golden Triangle": Xiamen, Quanzhou, and Zhangzhou. As a result, whatever "deprivation" Fuzhounese emigrants or sending families experience, it is largely understood in relation to Fujianese in the province's urban core, to individuals in other coastal areas, and to Chinese with wealth elsewhere in China and/or abroad. In other words, some Fujianese and other Chinese nationals are more in charge of certain kinds of mobility than others—intra-provincial mobility, national mobility, upward mobility. For Fuzhounese, it tends to be *international* mobility that is perceived of as easiest and most lucrative.

While grappling with local-level economic insecurity rooted in national reforms, some Fuzhounese individuals may also be motivated to migrate by state practices and purported human-rights violations. Claims of political and religious persecution were often a considered—and contentious—issue with earlier waves of Fujianese migrants, including those involved in tragic, highly publicized smuggling and rescue attempts like the 1993 Golden Venture boat drownings off Long Island and the 2000 Dover, England, truck suffocation deaths.[4] As I note in Chapter 2, however, immigration officers and judges tend to be skeptical of claims of forced sterilization, abortion, and persecution for religion or involvement in the pro-democracy movement, largely owing to fraudulent Chinese asylum cases and the diminished credibility of so many familiar stories.

Yet even if a young person does not or cannot claim overt political persecution, national-level policies often play a subtle and enduring role in youths' decision to migrate. Consider Ruolan, featured in the preface. Having emigrated at age sixteen, China's birth planning policy, more commonly referred to as the "one child policy," wasn't a personal concern for Ruolan when she lived in Fujian. Still, as Ruolan evidenced, the socioeconomic *outcomes* of the policy mattered to her, even if they couldn't lead to a cognizable claim for legal relief.

"I was at the crossing point," she told me. "The older generations still have the mentality where kids are supposed to work, to be obedient, to do everything your parents tell you. If I do something wrong, or if I didn't do something wrong, my parents beat me up. I'm not even supposed to complain, even if it was a mistake. It's because they beat you up for your own good, it's that idea. But there were also people in my village at that point, they disobey."

"There was some pushback?" I inquired.

She nodded. "[These kids] want pork instead of eating veggies. They don't want to eat their rice, they want some noodles instead. You know, it's like, I'm not that, but I was at that crossing point of a generation, or half a generation. It really depended on when the system was installed. [The birth planning policy was introduced in 1979.] By the time my parents were young, it was a really bad time. [Local officials] used to come in, break your house in, take your property if you're having more than one kid. But by the time I was little it wasn't as bad.

"Because the system has been in for some years, a lot of people only have one kid. So anytime you only have one kid, he's your treasure. If it's the first one, it gets spoiled and becomes disobedient. So I'm sure five years after me, every kid is like that. I was at that crossing point. You know, little kids in China, they call them 'little emperors' [小皇帝; see Fong 2004] because you give them what you want. You give them the best education. You hire tutors, even though not everyone goes to college in China. . . . It's very weird. It's like, you send your kids off to prepare for test, just to get into college, and you hire these educated people to live with them, do their chores, make their food, buy them clothes, buy them groceries, teach them. . . . And their parents, when they were growing up, they were completely obedient [to their parents]. But their own kids are treated completely different. It's because that's their only kid. That's how everyone else is doing it. . . . In just one generation, such a dramatic change. I think it's a combination of the one-child policy and the incredible economic boom."

Like Ruolan, most of the youth I interviewed never explicitly linked national- or provincial-level policies to their migration stories, yet their experience of mobility was clearly shaped by these forces in conjunction with broader economic, social, and generational shifts (see also K. Chin 1999).

"Okay, but here's a question," I said to Ruolan. She smiled expectantly and adjusted the front of her screen-printed t-shirt. "I understand how you were right at the cusp of this big change, and so it makes sense that if your parents came from a particular generation, they might push you to go to the US, and you would take part in this by being a very obedient child." She nodded. "But then what about these teenagers who are now sixteen, seventeen and still come to the US from Fujian? Do you think they're coming for a similar reason? Do you think it's because they're obeying their parents?"

She faltered, "I—I think it might be—I'm not sure, because I'm not in China right now." After pausing for a moment, Ruolan continued, "But I would say, from what I understand, the future is going nowhere if you are in a village in Fujian. All the growth you hear about. . . . Chinese are becoming billionaires, which was incredibly rare, but now it's a common phenomenon in all the big cities. All these people driving cars, people with bigger houses—These things would never go to the part of China I came from. All these buildings, all these middle-class people. And most of them live in big cities. Not just in big cities, but big coastal cities. And get government benefits. The majority of China is still, you know . . . I mean, the place I came from, you might have some growth, some towns growing. . . . But for the most part, the future doesn't come to me. So a lot of people from Fujian or, you know, most of China in general, they flock into the cities. Most of the people in Chinese cities are migrant workers, really. You can't even become registered in the city. . . . And if you are a migrant worker, you might always be a migrant worker. That's not a future you want, either. Some [recent young migrants] from China told me, it's actually even worse now. You used to have everything you want, everything you need, [like] everyone else in your village. But now, you know, you can't even buy a house because the growth of the big city, the growth of the economy, land becomes more expensive, property becomes more expensive. You can no longer afford these things."

As Ruolan demonstrates, even what is comfortably categorized as "contemporary Fujianese migration" is at once individual and relative, differentiated by political and economic policies, intersecting and often conflicting intergenerational expectations, and quickly changing modes of status and marginalization.

MOVING BEYOND THE "FAMILY FIRM": STATUS, SUCCESS, AND THE SEMI-AUTONOMY OF GLOBAL (FUZHOUNESE) YOUTH

When young Fuzhounese independently or with peers or family members begin to consider migration, they naturally evaluate their own experiences in their home communities. "I knew that in the US I would just work, work, work," said one young man. "I would not rest. I would be tired. But it would be much better than [where I grew up]. There, you have to work, but it's not really good. You can't afford anything."

Though youth often find these communities lacking in relation to wealthier areas of Fujian Province, China, or the US, it is also in these communities that they are exposed to a more global or cosmopolitan impetus to emigrate, what Julie Chu calls a unique "politics of destination" (2006, 398). Here, the identities of young "emplaced" Fuzhounese—those who will not or *have not yet* migrated—are actively remade in relationship with local accounts and ostentatious displays of transnational migration, including the construction of lavish and often empty mansions by overseas family members. The varied mobility of Fujianese youth is propelled in part by these established and affected ambitions, strategies, and connections overseas.

Alan, who identifies as a Fuzhounese software developer in the US, demonstrates this in a comment he posted on a blog about Fujian Province:

> I must say that my siblings [in Fujian] are very familiar with NYC even though they have never been there. They know exactly which street our relatives' restaurants are on. They even know that traveling from Queens to Chinatown in Manhattan, you have to pay a toll. They basically have no desire to stay in Fuzhou. All they want to do is to sneak into America and work in a Chinese restaurant. It's not just for money. It's also about status for a family.
>
> Suburbs in Fuzhou are known for overseas Chinese or expatriate Chinese households. They are the status symbol of success. Yes, almost all of the old illegal migrant workers plan to return to Fuzhou after working here for 15 to 20 years. But they do want their kids (those who come at a young age) to stay in America for a better life for their next generation. Sadly many of the young kids who came with their Fuzhou parents (in these cases, they are usually legal) suffer a great deal in America. They have no friends except for their own *Fuzhou ren*. Their parents don't speak English. Other more successful Chinese in school won't hang out with them. We all have heard stories of some overachieving second-generation Chinese Americans. But rarely do any of these second generation Chinese Americans belong to *Fuzhou ren* [people from Fuzhou] whose parents came here illegally.[5]

A 2010 interview I conducted with Len, an immigration law professor, revealed similar beliefs about the relative influence of economic and social status in Fuzhou. "Why do you think Fuzhounese youth emigrate to the US?" I asked.

"They're motivated by new opportunities—and definitely by money!" He laughed. "I think Fujianese are like the rest of the working folks in China, in the way that modernization and globalization has promoted this mass-migration of Chinese people within China. There's hundreds of millions of people moving from countryside to the city to find work, because the pay disparity is so, so great. And the Fujianese demonstrate that, not by migrating to a bigger city, but they actually go abroad. . . . So that's sort of their motivation, I feel, in coming. It's really to make money. And because there's so much cultural attachment to status and money, that you have made it as a person if you—and the kids say this themselves—that you've made it. You've been successful. You were not cowardly. You could proudly hold your head up with your relatives and their friends. There's definitely a lot of cultural attachment to that."

Like Len, other attorneys often portrayed Fuzhounese minors as the necessary tools of an otherwise economic unit, or what Susan Greenhalgh calls the "Chinese family firm," which exemplifies "traditional Confucian culture," China's supposed culture of familism, collectivism, and mutual benefit.[6] Arguably the dominant image of China in American eyes (Greenhalgh 1994, 769), it often featured in lawyers' reflections, particularly when individuals confidently expressed that Fuzhounese youth do not and must not act independently of their families. In a sense echoing Fei Xiaotong ([1947] 1992), family relationships emerged in these statements as ritualistic and institutionalized; young migrants were the unquestioned "subordinates" in normative ties of obligation to parents or other community elders.

During my pilot research, Margaret, another cause lawyer, noted: "You know, it's the same story, different kid. There are different circumstances that led to the child being smuggled, but the story has the same overtones, including financial pressure and filial piety. It's a cultural issue, for sure. Honor is so prevalent in Fujian; it's a tenet of daily life in ways we don't think of. Kids are doing something their parents ask of them without admitting it's unfair."

At the time of this interview, I was particularly interested in the role of the Chinese family firm in lawyers' cultural defense. Understandably,

Margaret's comments, as well as Len's—"There's so much cultural attach-ment to status and money"—felt especially meaningful. Yet when I return to these comments six years later, I find something different. Len may have fixed youths' "cultural attachment" to status and money in accordance with what he understood to be the traditional, dominant Chinese family firm, but his words simultaneously reveal an understanding of broader attach-ments and status that are not entirely limited to Fujianese migration. After all, Fujianese youth aren't exclusively like "the rest of the working folks in China," in that migration spurned by economic inequities and social disrup-tion is a historic and global phenomenon. Nor are Fujianese youth particu-larly unique among working poor or marginalized youth in the global south or north for choosing migration as a response to socioeconomic, political, and familial realities (Jeffrey and Dyson 2008; see also Gans 1995; Ignatiev 1995; Newman 1999).

Consider Len's and Alan's words, respectively, again:

> And the kids say this themselves—that you've made it. You've been successful. You were not cowardly. You could proudly hold your head up with your relatives and their friends. There's definitely a lot of cultural attachment to that.

> It's not just for money. It's also about status for a family. Suburbs in Fuzhou are known for overseas Chinese or expatriate Chinese households. They are the status symbol of success. . . . Sadly many of the young kids who came with their Fuzhou parents (in these cases, they are usually legal) suffer a great deal in America. They have no friends except for their own *Fuzhou ren*. Their parents don't speak English. Other more successful Chinese in school won't hang out with them. We all have heard stories of some overachieving second-generation Chinese Americans.

In hindsight, I realize these two comments powerfully evidence a broader tension that illuminates, and is illuminated by, the complex realities of global youth—one in which pride and suffering simultaneously exist and are in many ways implicated by success. Rather than contradict one another, these two perspectives succinctly detail what is already familiar to unaccompanied youth, regardless of their country of origin, *and* to their legal practitioners: namely, youths' complicated status as "terrain[s] of *semi*-autonomy" (Jeffrey and Dyson 2008, 6) and as intentional actors—even in passive or "dependent" states (see Coutin 2005; Das 1989; Statz 2016a).

Alan and Len's comments also introduce a more specific tension that exists between the identities Fujianese youth maintain as valued members, and even leaders, of their "emplaced" families and their simultaneous "lagging behind" other Chinese nationals, internal and international migrants, and second-generation Chinese-Americans.

THE MIGRANT, THE EMPLOYEE, THE CHILD, THE UNDOCUMENTED: ONE YOUTH'S ENCOUNTERS WITH FUJIANESE-NESS

I was first connected to Hua, a young woman in Arkansas, through Rita, an attorney who was applying for a T visa for Hua on the grounds that she had been trafficked by her parents and smugglers to the US. Rita had never met Hua. The turnover rate at the nonprofit where Rita worked was so high that she had simply "inherited" the case. Hua and I met in Jonesboro, where she lived first with her boss's family and then with her boyfriend, all Fuzhounese migrants. After being apprehended at the US-Mexico border in 2008, Hua had been placed in shelter care in Chicago. She was seventeen at the time. Hua was released for "family reunification" (though reunification with which family member was never clear) and soon after found work at a Chinese buffet in Arkansas.

When I first arrived in Jonesboro, Hua suggested we meet at a McDonald's near the buffet. She hugged me warmly when I introduced myself, and we laughed at our parallel dress: t-shirts, shorts, and sneakers, obvious choices for the hot day. Beyond the window, the dry grass and sky faded to sepia, shimmering in the afternoon sun. The air conditioning hummed on. Hua suggested we move our conversation to a nearby IHOP; it was quieter there.

Over the next few days, Hua and I spent most of our time together. She took me to the restaurant where she worked and to a local mall; we went to a movie; we purchased groceries and made cookies together at my hosts' home. Friends of my aunt, the older couple I stayed with were generous and exuberant, insisting that Hua and I accompany them on their Gator, a small utility vehicle, to visit the horses on their property. Hua was admittedly more enthusiastic about the idea than I, and she laughed heartily as the Gator bounced across the field, her ponytail whipping in the dry wind. However unexpected, this was one of my happiest fieldwork memories, a welcome contrast to what at the time felt like so many static and narrated portrayals.

Of course, our conversation at IHOP was hardly *still*. Tracing so many mobilities—transnational, social, legal—required a deep and at times very tiring concentration, a shared commitment to forging the most complete truth across different languages, socioeconomic positionalities, and ages. This was an energizing and vulnerable act for both of us. At times it felt sad.

"So you're from Fujian," I began.[7]

"Yeah, from Fuzhou. I'm from this little, little town."

"And you left when you were in high school? *Gaozhong?*"

"No, *jizhong*. Middle school."

"Were there a lot of people in your town who had come to the US?"

"Yes." She nodded. "Like, a lot of them are older, like thirty, or twenty-four. Some like me, younger. They have family here. They don't have green cards. So they have to . . ." She paused, searching for the English equivalent. "They have to *feifa yimin* [emigrate clandestinely, literally "illegal"]. You know?" she asked. I nodded. "They don't have parents here," she continued, "but they want to go out. They don't want to stay in China."

"Do most of the people in your hometown work in factories, or do they work in other businesses?" I asked.

"They always do something like seafood because our town is close to the sea. Just little businesses."

"How old were you when you came to the US?"

"Almost seventeen."

"Is this something you thought about doing for a long time? You wanted to do it?"

Setting down her coffee, Hua tilted her head to the side. "It was just . . ." she paused. "Just my parents asked me, 'Do you want to go to America?' And I'm like, 'Whatever.' I don't really understand what is different about here and China. I know it's different, but I'm young, so I don't really understand. They say, 'You don't want to go? We're not going to push you.'"

"Do you think they knew about America? Did your parents know people who came to the US?"

"A lot of people."

"What did they hear about the US?" I asked.

"Just work, work, work. And tired. Not rest, just work for everything. Tired, but it's much better than China. In China you have to work, but it's not really good."

"I understand," I replied. "You probably won't make as much money. And the working conditions might be worse."

"Right."

"So then you said, 'Okay,'" I continued. Hua nodded. "Can you tell me what happened after that?"

"The smugglers help us to do everything. Chinese New Year is coming, and they said, 'We are all ready.' And in the second day, there's some guy, he's Chinese. We take a train to Guangzhou."

"That's not too far, right?"

"Right." She added, "Guangzhou is really rich. Fujian is not as rich, but the people who have family members in the US are very wealthy. In Guangzhou we buy airplane ticket to Beijing. And to Frankfurt. And, and we go somewhere like Mexico. Honduras. . . . We get close to America somewhere. Mexico. Then we . . . just walked."

"Hua, is it okay if we back up a little?" I interrupted.

"Okay."

"Did your parents go with you to the bus station?"

"Yeah. My mom."

"Just your mom? Did your sister go?" Hua's sister was ten when Hua left Fuzhou.

"No. She was at school."

"Did she know that you were leaving?"

"Yeah, she know."

"How did she feel?"

"She is really young. She didn't really understand. She said, 'Oh great! My sister is going to America! I have a sister going to America!'" Hua laughed.

"How did your parents feel, do you think?"

"My dad was just a little bit worried and sad. My mom is sad, so worried. And when I left, we cried. For a long time. And when I ate my lunch, before I left, I just cried."

Hua looked down, quickly wiping her eyes with the back of her hand. She pushed the remains of her pancake back and forth on the plate with a fork.

I waited. When she again appeared comfortable, I asked, "When you were flying from Beijing to Frankfurt, what were you thinking about?"

Hua's eyes brightened. "This was my first time on an airplane. I was like, 'Wow! I'm on an airplane! . . . It's exciting, right? Wow! Different people! Different food! Everything was different."

I asked Hua about being smuggled into the US.

"After one week, [the smugglers] say, 'We can go to America right now.' And more Chinese came. One older. Three younger. The total is three women including me, and three guys."

"Did you talk with one another?

"Yeah. We can talk. They say to me, '*Ni zui shao de*' [You're the youngest]. They take care of me. We go at night. . . . We were with the smuggler and a lot of the Mexicans together. And there was this big, big mountain. A lot of trees and a lot of bugs. It was hot, really hot. . . . We have to walk again. Twelve hours. They told us twelve hours. . . . But at seven o'clock, the police."

"Was it the border patrol?" I asked.

Hua looked confused. "They were *strong* American guys." She laughed. "And really tall, and not really nice. They were like, 'You have to stay here.' And so we are just quiet. The lady and me. We are just quiet. And the police tell us, 'Don't cry! Don't cry!' And we still cried."

"I bet that was really scary. And then they handcuffed you?"

"Yeah."

"And you got into the truck?"

"Yeah, the truck. They just got five people. And one ran away. All Chinese. No Mexicans. The smuggler ran away first."

"Where did they take you?"

"Like immigration jail or something. They do everything. Take your picture, ask you some questions. They use the Chinese translator. On the phone," she added.

"Did you understand the translator?"

"Yeah. They asked me, like, 'Do you want to speak Mandarin? Or Fujianese?'" Suddenly, Hua changed her voice to a whiny whimper. "I said, 'Mandarin is fine.' I still *ku* [cry]."

"What did they say on the phone?"

"They ask you some questions, like, 'In China somebody hurt you?'"

"And what did you say?"

Here, Hua took on a pitiful and exaggerated tone. "Yes, somebody hurt me!" Recounting the phone call to me, she seemed bemused. I stared at her, startled. "I *have* to come to America!" She sniffed twice, still imitating her earlier self.

Recalling Hua's assumed eligibility for a T visa, I perhaps should not have been so surprised by the quick transition I witnessed—from quiet, discrete tears as Hua described saying goodbye to her mother to her shrewd description of abuse in China during the telephonic intake with a legal-aid provider. This preparation for, and arguable manipulation of, legal advocacy is discussed in more detail in the subsequent chapter. For now, I explore the ways in which Hua's migration journey, her work experience in the US, and her individual plans further evidence both the "leading and lagging" of Fuzhounese migrants. More broadly, Hua's account captures the "deeply ambivalent and uncertain" sociocultural fields revealed in youths' imaginaries and lived experiences of transnational mobility (Yarris 2014, 288).

Hua's migration story was not unlike others I collected. The details were different, of course: Some youth traveled through the UK, Cuba, Russia, or Thailand. Others flew directly to New York. Some described their journeys with relative nonchalance while others were evasive. Still other youth struggled to recall very many details, citing, "I didn't really understand what was happening at the time." In the latter two instances, I never inquired further.[8] While many of the attorneys I interviewed would vehemently argue this point,[9] most of the young people I spoke with took responsibility for the decision to migrate or, like Hua, explained it as a joint familial decision, one couched in feelings of uncertainty, grief, and excitement.

Yet Hua was also unique, and in ways she herself identified. When we talked later about her work situation, she said, "The staff isn't very big at the buffet. It's the boss and his wife, a hostess, six waitresses, and three *amigos*. [She always referred to the Mexican cooks as *amigos*.] The *amigos* can speak some Fuzhounese. Everyone here is older than me. The boss told me to tell customers that I'm twenty-one even though I'm nineteen so that no one will ask why I'm not in school.

"I'm the only one here who doesn't want to keep working in a buffet. I've been working really hard to learn English. You know," she said, rolling her eyes, "something besides, 'More water?' I talk to my customers a lot, and I watch a lot of American movies."

"What do you think you'll do after you pay off your debt?" I asked.

"You know about the debt?" she responded.

I told Hua more about my research with other youth. "Most of the people I speak with say that their debt is about eighty thousand dollars US," I said, carefully.[10]

"That's exactly it," she replied. "I have thirty thousand dollars paid and another year and half to cover the remainder and interest. After that, I want to leave Arkansas and maybe go back to Chicago and get my GED and go to college. I'm different from everyone else here."

"I think I understand how you're different from your coworkers, but what about other Fuzhounese kids, like the ones you were friends with in shelter care?" I asked.

"I think I'm different from them, too. Most of those kids want to go to New York and not leave. I'm happy to visit New York, and I mail things to my family from there because it's so much easier. But I don't want to live there. There are too many Chinese. It's too crowded; there are so many restaurants. But other kids like Chinatown. They have a lot of fun. A lot of Chinese, they can go to the bars because they don't have to show their IDs. And they can sing karaoke and eat a lot of Chinese food. And there are a lot of friends. And so they want to stay in New York. But I don't. When you stay in New York [you are only nominally tipped], not a lot."

"Oh?"

"And when you go out, you have to spend a lot of money. I don't want to stay in New York. I want to stay away. Make more money. Finish my debt, and then I can do everything I want to do. My friend asks me, 'Do you want to come to New York?' I say, 'No, I have to work.' She's like, 'Relax, take vacation. Come on with us.' And I'm, 'No. I need money. I don't want to go. You want to pay my [restaurant] tip?'" Hua laughed. "They say, 'Okay, you win! You just stay there.'" She gave me a wide smile, then looked down at her plate. "No, I just want to work."

Later, I asked Hua about her plans for the future. "What do you want?" I asked. "What are your goals?"

"So I really want to get my documents. I really want that."

"And then once you get them, what happens?"

"I will have to pay the tax. I won't have to worry that. . . . Now," she lowered her voice, "somebody will check me, I say I don't have a job. . . . I want to show the manager I got the document right now. I don't want to worry about that. And I want to try to get a license. A driver's license. And . . ." She fidgeted with her napkin and smiled at me with excitement. "And a green card. And I want a debit card. And . . ." She paused. "I just want. . . . It should be more easy. I don't want my boss to be afraid, like when they talk to me, they are afraid. 'You know,' they say, 'we don't want to be afraid, but you make us afraid [because you're undocumented].'"

Sensing her discomfort, I changed the subject. "Hua," I asked, "do you think that most other Fuzhounese youth want to stay in the US? Or do some want to go back to China?"

"I think a lot of people want to stay in America. And they got a green card, so go back to China and . . ."

"Just visit," I finished. She nodded. "What do *you* want to do?"

She paused. "I want to stay in America."

"Yeah? Why?"

"Because it's different. Here it's more people, more friendly. Before I stay in China, I didn't have anything. I couldn't do anything. No restaurant, nothing."

"What about school, or college?"

"Yeah. Well, if you are old like me—if I go to school, it's not easy right now because in China, I'm old. But here, you can go anywhere. If you want to go to school, you can go to school. Like GED."

"If you had never come to the US, if you had stayed in China, what would have happened?"

"Maybe I would've gone to the middle school. Or high school. But probably no more. No college, because it's expensive. Even if I went to college, and I graduate, and I look for a job? Nothing. Because a lot of children with college [degrees in China] might not even find a job."

I asked Hua about her parents. "Do you think they're proud of you?"

"Oh, yeah," she replied. She nodded quickly.

"Think about when your parents are talking to their friends. What do you think they say about you?"

"They say, 'Oh, your daughter in America? Amazing! You don't have to worry about your life right now. Much better right now.' My mom say, 'I hope so.' Hua slowed her speech. Imitating her mother, she shrugged weakly. "'But she's tired. My daughter's tired.' And somebody say [to my mother], 'You no good. Your daughter is so young, and you send her—'"

"People say that?" I asked, surprised.

"But not to my mother's face. Just—"

"Really? I guess I thought that . . ." I hesitated, keenly aware of my own assumptions about Fujianese migration.

"*A lot* of people say that," she answered, "and to me, too. 'Why go to America?' A lot of Fujianese ask me, 'Your dad and mom sent you to here? And you're so young! Sixteen, seventeen? Why do you have to come?' I say, 'I want to come! I want to come! I like it here!'"

I looked at her carefully. "Is that true?"

"That's true," she replied, her voice steady. "They say, 'Really?' I say, 'Yeah! I like here!' That's true."

"But not always," I noted, thinking about the long hours and working conditions Hua had earlier described.

"Yeah," she agreed. "Sometimes somebody's not very friendly, and I'll be alone, and I'll feel so bad. I don't like here. I want to be home then. Sometimes. Sometimes."

"Do you think your mom knows that people talk behind her back?"

Hua nodded. "She knows. Before I come to here, she said to me, 'If somebody ask you, Why you come to America? Your dad and mom so bad. What do you think about that?' 'That's fine,' I tell her. 'I want to go. You don't have to worry.' My mom say, 'Really? Are you sure?'"

To clarify, I asked, "*You* say, 'It's fine?'"

"Yeah. I just don't want them to worry."

"You know, Hua," I responded, "I'm listening to you, and you want your boss and your manager to be safe and not worry about your documents. And you want your mom and dad to not worry and not feel bad. What about you? Are you okay?"

She smiled wanly. "Just fine. I don't want—Sometimes I just think a lot. I don't want to think a lot. Just give me two more years and everything's good. I'm not afraid. I can do everything I want."

Hua was tired, I could tell. "I think we should stop talking." We had planned earlier to see a movie, Hua's choice. She smiled and nodded. "Before we do, Hua, is there anything else you think I should know?"

She squinted and looked out the window. "Yeah," she said abruptly, and with startling energy. "I think lots of people, like from China, or maybe from Fujian, they're *yimin*. *Yimin*."

"Mm-hmm," I agreed. "They're immigrants."

"Yeah. *Feifa yimin* [undocumented immigrants]. They know about the system. No good. One time I talked with my [Chinese] friend, he's not from Fujian. He said, 'Do you know Fujianese always *feifa yimin* to America?'"

"He said that?"

"Yeah," and with some hesitation, Hua admitted that she had lied to him. "I just told him I go to school, I don't work. I don't have to pay the debt. And he said, 'A lot of Fujianese, a lot of people know Fujianese come to America and always [emigrate clandestinely].' I said, 'Really? How do you know that?' He said, 'Everybody know that, okay?'" She laughed. "I say, 'Oh, really?' And then I think about it. A lot of Fujianese come here with family. Father, mother, and they just *yimin* [migrate] here. It's good. They go to school. I have a lot of friends like that."

"Friends who came here legally."

"Right. Like, they had a passport."

"So do you think," I stopped. "So you're telling me that you think it's important for people to know that some Fujianese are not *feifa yimin. Youde Fujianren hefa yimin* [Some Fujianese migrate legally]. Is that right?"

"Yeah." Hua furrowed her thin eyebrows and said gruffly, "Fujianese in America so bad." She shook her head. "I think that a lot of American think that. Like, they know. Fujianese come, no good."

"But you're good!" I felt desperate.

"I try to be. I try to be nice."

"Do you feel like that puts pressure on you?"

"Yeah. A little bit. Like when I go out and meet somebody from Beijing or something, they ask, 'Where you from?' 'I'm from Fujian.' 'Oh, Fujian?'" She wrinkled her nose. "So I want to finish the debt. Be something different. I don't want to be, oh, Fujianese, restaurant, restaurant, restaurant."

LEGAL—AND PERSONAL—INTERPRETATIONS OF AGE, CHOICE, AND SUCCESS

This book centers on the representation of culture, age, and young migrants' individual experiences in and beyond the legal realm. Accordingly, I believe it is all the more important to let youths' reflections largely stand for themselves, without unnecessary layers of explanation or analysis. Their experiences and perspectives consistently unsettled what I thought I knew or was learning or what had just been described to me by an attorney informant. In the same way, young people's accounts powerfully complicate and counter the broader legal representations, and often misrepresentations, this book examines. Even so, the reader will recognize that my most "distanced" or "objective" anthropological intentions are fraught. Hua was responding to the questions *I* asked on a Tuesday afternoon in July. I selected the interview excerpt above; below, I reiterate what I find important in it today. The political and poetic aspects of this ethnographic "moment" are perpetually, and very self-consciously, in flux (see Behar 1992).

Similarly, my ongoing friendship with Hua continues to reveal my own assumptions about individual success and normative pathways to adulthood. A year after I spoke with Hua in Arkansas, she called me to share that she was making significant progress in paying off her debt. "Hua, what's next?" I asked. "This is so exciting! You can do so many different things once your debt is paid off. Will you start going to school?" I must admit I had actually forgotten that getting her GED was one of Hua's original goals. Asking about school was simply my own assumption about what she *should*, rather than could, do next.

Hua didn't hesitate: "No," she replied. "I want to keep working. All this time I have been saving up money to pay off the debt and interest and to send money to my family. *Now*," she said energetically, "I want to make money for myself! And I want to learn how to drive and have a car." A few months later, when Hua received word from her attorney that she had been granted a T visa, she sent me a text: "I got my visa!! I can have a drive lisence [*sic*]! ☺☺ so lucky!!" *Everyone's allowed to change their minds*, I wrote in my notes later—a reminder.

It would be unfair to claim an explicit connection between the change in Hua's goals and the vague pressures and desires of economic independence, her transition to adulthood, peer pressure, or the derogatory "Fujianese, restaurant, restaurant, restaurant" reputation she wanted so badly to counter. Instead, I include the incident here because it evidences a tension Hua continues to embody, namely the simultaneous "leading" and "lagging" of young Fuzhounese migrants. It also reflects what Shao-hua Liu identifies as the "two layers of individualism" present in migrant youths' pursuit of modernity (2011, 20–21). As Liu argues, young Chinese migrants demonstrate a "consumption-oriented individualism" that is shaped by China's market reform and the corresponding growth of youths' desire for autonomy and purchasing power (see also E. Chin 2001; Yan 2003). Yet as the young people in this and Liu's research come of age through migration, they also experience "institutionalized individualism," a precarious, constrained freedom in the context of late modernity (Beck and Beck-Gernsheim 2002).

The individual and perhaps "consumption-oriented" accomplishments Hua identified include paying off a debt of $80,000 US plus interest, obtaining a visa and, eventually, LPR status, and getting a driver's license. Related, though less unambiguous, achievements include Hua's courage and equanimity as a young migrant; her savvy navigation of the legal process;

her industrious work at Comet Buffet—and indeed, her deliberate choice to remain in Arkansas; and her determination to master English.

To Hua, these successes are incredibly meaningful. They are a source of personal, as well as collective, pride and status. In the particular context of US law, however, they signify a precarious reality of economy and age. Consider, for instance, how the "reason" and autonomy that Hua demonstrates—which notably includes the simple but somehow still disconcerting act of *changing her mind*—clash with popular and institutionalized assumptions about maturity, innocence, and dependence, and with the corresponding legal provisions of "protection" and "best interests" by cause lawyers. As Hua's attorney successfully argued in her T visa claim, it was an extraordinary and sad thing for Hua to have *had to* do the things detailed above, alone, before she was twenty.

Lana likewise viewed independence, let alone success, as antithetical to the migration experiences of the youth for whom she advocated. "We're talking about, like, sixteen, seventeen, eighteen, nineteen, twenty year olds, right? And that's what drives me. People are always like, 'Well, the kids, they chose to come here.'" She leaned toward me and raised an eyebrow. "You were *sixteen years old*, and you just got up to go to another country where you don't speak the language, you don't know anyone, you're not going to be able to go to school, you're working twelve hours a day?" Lana shook her head. "Something had to be going on to make you choose that, right? That's the premise we [lawyers] come from. Something's *wrong* if a sixteen year old feels they need to pack up and move across the world. Usually, in our cases, it's because they were forced to, basically. They just don't call it forced."

Like Hua, Bingwen at once reiterates, complicates, and subtly challenges this interpretation of success and choice: "As a migrant, you might be thirteen, fourteen years old. Well, twenty years ago, people had kids when they're fourteen years old! So in a way, you're almost an adult now. And if you try to go somewhere, make yourself a better future, then [he raised his forearms in a gesture of defeat, imitating a Fuzhounese parent], 'My hands are off, you're on your own. If you cannot make it, come back, bring me some money. Otherwise, I've raised you to a certain point, and now you can be on your own.' So I think it's done with parenting [i.e., a cessation of parenting]. Now that I think about it, from a Westerner's standpoint, what my parents or any parents from the area did might be almost evil, like sending your little kids out abroad to work. But I think, you know, part of that, it's the local culture playing to the mentality of the parents. It's like, if you stay in this place, you're just going to be stuck here, your worth is like everybody else. And there's more stuff out there. And, you know, you're on your own out there. You're on your own to explore. You make it out alive, maybe you can come back a 'wealthier person.' Because in the US, even a very poor person makes far more money than a very wealthy person where I came from."

As Hua and Bingwen's reflections suggest, Fuzhounese youth must continuously evaluate and move between conflicting expectations of age and status at each step of their migration journeys, which notably coincide with youths' transition to adulthood (see Gonzales 2015; Rumbaut and Komaie 2010).

Consider the balancing act Hua detailed. Returning to her statements, we see that she steadily situates her and/or her family's decisions against or within broader regional, national, and global phenomena: "[Fuzhounese migrants] just work, work, work. . . . Not rest, just work for everything. Tired, but it's much better than China. In China you have to work, but it's not really good. . . . Guangzhou is really rich. Fujian is not as rich, but the people who have family members in the US are very wealthy."

There are also local interpretations of success that Hua must confront, in a sense returning us to Ruolan's description of being "at the crossing point," or the intersection of regional and generational beliefs that either children should support their parents, or parents affected by the one-child policy should sacrifice everything for their "little emperor" children. When asked, "Do you think your mom knows that people talk behind her back?" Hua answered, "She knows. . . . [My parents' neighbors say,] 'Oh, your daughter in America? Amazing! You don't have to worry about your life right now. Much better right now.' [Other neighbors say,] 'You no good. Your daughter is so young, and you send her . . .'"

Consider the role of age in these statements. Like Hua's lawyer, neighbors tell Hua's parents, "Your daughter is so young." So too do the migrants Hua meets during her journey, who say, "*Ni zui shao de*" [You are the youngest]. As Hua describes her workplace in Arkansas, she herself admits, "Everyone . . . is older than me. The boss told me to tell customers that I'm twenty-one, even though I'm nineteen."

Though clearly sensitive to the ways in which her age was used by others to disparage her parents' intentions or downplay her independent labor, Hua also drew on her age to reiterate the unique freedoms and opportunities she had as a young migrant. As the youngest employee at her workplace, she maintained, "I'm the only one who doesn't want to keep working in a buffet. I've been working really hard to learn English. . . . I'm different from everyone else here." Later, she stated, "I can do something different. I'm young. I'm just—really, I'm not afraid of anything. I want to try something different. But I don't know what's different yet. I only know right now!" To Hua, then, her young age was at once a liability, particularly with regard to her parents' and boss's reputations, and a boon, a clear symbol of skill, individuality, and a long future rife with possibility.

"BE SOMETHING DIFFERENT": IDENTITY AND RESPONSIBILITY IN COMMUNITIES OF RECEPTION

There is another level of significance in Hua's reflections, namely the responsibilities and identities she independently managed as a not-entirely-independent Fuzhounese migrant:

> I want to show the manager I got the document right now. I don't want to worry about that. And I want to try to get a license. A driver's license. And . . . a green card. . . .When I go out and meet somebody from Beijing or something, they ask, "Where you from?" "I'm from Fujian." "Oh, Fujian?" So I want to finish the debt. Be something different. I don't want to be, oh, Fujianese, restaurant, restaurant, restaurant.

In these comments, we see Hua as undocumented but striving to act lawfully—securing her visa, a driver's license, a green card—so as not to threaten her boss's credibility or her own position at Comet Buffet. This resolve was not unique. Many of the youth I spoke with described the ambitious efforts they took to accurately record earnings and remittances, file taxes, and seek out educational opportunities and medical services that did not request proof of legal status or employer information. Yet in the above statements we also find another sort of obligation, one connected to an identity of being *different*, of countering the image Hua believes Chinese nationals, Chinese-Americans, and even American restaurant-goers hold of Fujianese migrants. Think again of Alan's comments: "[Fuzhou youth] have no friends except for their own Fuzhou *ren* [people]. . . . Other more successful Chinese in school won't hang out with them."

The reputation Hua and Alan described is pervasive. It is an identity of isolation, of being itinerant and marginalized (see Guest 2004), and something I encountered often in my visits to Chinese service organizations in Chinatowns across New York City and Chicago. Having volunteered with a Chinese mutual-aid association in college, I was at once familiar with and baffled by these spaces. Each was a study in contrasts: the relative disrepair of a structure against the liveliness of the (typically elderly) people inside; the sweet smell of incense in an entryway against the abrasive bleach used to clean the stairwell; the perpetually evasive responses to my questions against the genuinely warm welcome I received throughout. While I was offered many cups of tea and even more business cards, insight into the status of and response to Fuzhounese youth in these service organizations was rarely forthcoming.

Some of the organizations I visited were private, founded and funded by donations from Hong Kong, China, and/or Taiwan. Some were consolidated Chinese benevolent associations, originally organized around regional loyalties as *huiguan* (see Lai 2004). Others were broader social-service organizations, receiving local funds to aid immigrant groups including, but not exclusive to, Chinese. Many provided after-school help to first- and second-generation students, as well as ESL classes and citizenship assistance with naturalization and green card renewal. It was usually quite easy for me to learn about the structure of these organizations, but information about their work on behalf of Fuzhounese youth was often vague at best and uncomfortable at worst.

At one mutual-aid association, I asked a staff member, "Can you tell me about your youth programs?"

Enthusiastically, she listed off the music and dance classes the center offered, along with math and language tutoring and a Saturday SAT preparation course.

"Do you primarily help youth who have legal status?" I asked.

"Oh, yes," she nodded.

I told her more about my research. "Right now," I said, "I'm trying to understand what sorts of services might be available to Fuzhounese teens here in Chinatown, like health care, education, legal assistance."

As I said "legal assistance," she looked at me quizzically, then shrugged. "They work in restaurants," she responded. "They don't really need legal status."

I received a more nuanced picture from individuals who worked with these organizations but who self-identified as "outsiders" to Chinatown communities based on their own immigration histories and experiences: Ernesto, a youth-program director at a Chinese settlement house, Ming-Yue, a social worker, and Sal, a labor-rights advocate.

"One of the major reasons we can't help the Fuzhounese kids," said Ernesto, "is funding. We get a lot of grants, including state and federal grants, and so we can only help in-school [enrolled] youth. Other programs are evaluated and tracked through a person's documents. Or with our work-readiness program, we help kids who have a social-security card, a residency card, an alien card—you know, whatever they need to be considered for a job.

"But there are social aspects to it, too," he added. "I mean, things were a lot different back in 2000, like the fact that the Fujianese *are* an established community now. They're more established than they were before in Manhattan. They're being heard more as a collective group. So, you know, they support us, we support them. . . . Of course," he paused, "there are still people [who say], 'Oh, you're Fujianese? Uhhhh.'" Ernesto groaned, imitating the skepticism and hostility he observed.

"But now it's like, 'Oh, you're Fujianese. You look pretty decent, whatever.' Still, even [at this organization], Fujianese are not looked upon in the most graceful light. Even when we saw a spike in the number of Fujianese people seeking services from us. The Chinese here have a very stereotypical view of them, as thugs, gangsters, you know, nasty people."

Like Ernesto, Sal also identified bureaucracy, legality, prejudice, and insularity as powerful inhibitors of community support for young Fuzhounese migrants. "I think the Chinese service organizations are not very successful in connecting with undocumented people. Undocumented migrants think [these organizations] are connected to the government. It's hard for people from mainland China to understand the difference between a government-funded and a government-directed agency. A lot of these places are sympathetic to undocumented individuals, but services just aren't accessible. An agency might be Hong Kong-centric, or the Mandarin competence of staff is below average. But there's also a kind of 'legal' attitude among clients and staff," he added.

"China is so large, and the Chinese people here tend to be very provincial. Like, to the Cantonese people I work with, anyone who is not Cantonese is suspect. Anyone north or west of Canton is a northerner. And there are also a lot of negative stereotypes of Fujianese. They're aggressive, abrasive, ruthless. They would do whatever it takes to get what they want. I mean, of course there are also positive stereotypes; they're seafaring, adventurous."

While Ming-Yue identified a tension between Fujianese and more established Chinatown residents, she extended the disconnect further, namely between Chinese immigrants in Chinatown and those elsewhere, or what Peter Kwong (1996) distinguishes as "Uptown" Chinese and "Downtown" Chinese. The "Uptown" Chinese, Kwong writes, can be American-born or new immigrants. Typically, they have legal status and more education and higher incomes than the national US average. They do not live in concentrated ethnic communities, unlike the "Downtown" Chinese, who tend to be new immigrants, speak little English, and work in unstable industries or an underground economy not protected by American labor law. Ming-Yue referred to "Uptown" Chinese as "mainstream":

"I think the people in Chinatown, they are not only separate from American mainstream, but also from the Chinese immigrants mainstream," she said. "They're so different from that mainstream."

"You mean immigrants who came here with documentation?"

"Yeah," she responded. "For example, the kids [Fuzhounese youth] might go to a church in Chinatown, and then everybody asks, 'How can you come? How did you come?' You know what I mean? They have to hide it. They feel uncomfortable being asked, 'Oh, your family's here?' No. 'You come here to study?' No. 'How did you get in, then?' They don't want to talk about it. It's difficult. [Before emigrating] they cannot imagine how difficult it might be to get a connection with fellow countrymen. They don't understand your reason for coming, and you don't want to expose what the facts are of how you came" (see also Guest 2004).

"So, it's like you made your family proud, but you still feel ashamed," I responded. "You're always *different*," I added, thinking of Hua.

"Exactly. You know, it's great when you go back to Fuzhou, but then here, there is no support in the mainstream Chinese community. . . . Most of my friends, they ask, 'Why do you help this group of kids? They're illegal. They just make up stories.' I mean, you can imagine, there are a lot of rumors, and it might be true, too. I can imagine this. The kids are told to get a story. But if you are not in [my] field, it's so difficult to explain your feeling of attachment to this group of kids because they are caught. They are caught by the environment. The whole environment."

In identifying Fuzhounese youth as "caught," Ming-Yue's words are compelling and not inaccurate. Yet they are also incomplete and, as this chapter demonstrates, not necessarily reflective of Fuzhounese youths' own interpretation of their migration experiences. After all, while the motivations and ongoing migration journeys of Bingwen, Hua, and Ruolan share certain characteristics with those of other Fuzhounese migrants and with global youth more generally, the mobility of these individuals is differentiated by time, region, economy, and politics. It is also uniquely affected by age, social and familial values, multiple and shifting identities, and regionally specific experiences of semi-autonomy and independence.

Just as this chapter begins with Bingwen's reflections, I also wish to close it in his voice. Below, Bingwen is again a thoughtful "ethnographic bridge," this time linking a view of Fuzhounese youth as vulnerable, dependent, "caught," or lagging to another, equally real version of himself as transformed, successful, and leading:

"I feel bad, but I think through my entire life, I'm always very obedient. People used to think I'm a big nerd. Now I'm an educated nerd. But essentially, everybody [in my village] thought I'm almost like a dumb-headed person. I don't do anything. That's because I'm not a sneaky person. . . . I'm actually well known in my village, because I'm the fruit guy. I'm the watermelon guy. I'm the guy you see cutting rice in the paddy. Other kids weren't doing it. Only a small group of me—a small group of Bingwens are doing all these things. Everybody else is—you know, they already pass through the transition. I'm still in the middle process. No one would ever think of me as being a person to think of other options, but—I think I came to the US, I realized I'm alone, I realized how desperate I am, and I changed. . . . I'm no longer so obedient to my parents, because they're not there. I'm on my own, and I start to do things differently. And I think back now, I made some pretty damn smart decisions."

4   *Selecting Identity, Rejecting Context: "The Child in Her Context" and Collapsing the Cause*

> *[In the law] there is always conflict and always loss: the stories of the two parties conflict or compete. . . . Neither story, neither language, is the sole source of authority; at some points choices will have to be made that favor one or the other. And both must yield, in much if not in all, to a third force, the language of the law that governs the process as a whole. (James Boyd White 1990, 262)*

Young migrants experience real, and increasingly well-documented, vulnerabilities. These include the disruption of family relationships, developmental trajectories, and educational attainment (Gao et al. 2010; Perez 2015); heightened exposure to harsh labor, living conditions, and violence (Hashim 2010; Suarez-Orozco and Suarez-Orozco 2001); and inadequate institutional interventions (Honwana 2011; Panter Brick 2002). At the same time, research on transnational migration has begun to also recognize the more nuanced and *power-filled* dimensions of youth mobility, including the role of age, relatedness, and belonging in family migration decision-making (Caneva 2015; Moskal and Tyrrell 2015; White et al. 2011); the fluidity of households over time (Chung 2013; Pribilsky 2001); and young migrants' agency as social and political actors who powerfully redefine transnational families, communities, and institutions (Dreby 2007; Heidbrink and Statz 2017).

Amid—or perhaps despite—these nascent efforts to contextualize the diverse experiences and meanings assigned to youth migration, this chapter is ultimately about the strategic *rejection* of context. As I demonstrate, this rejection is a dialogic process, one negotiated by immigration cause lawyers and their young clients across complex imbalances of power (Lopez 1992). Through this process, a young person, her relationships, and the unique circumstances around her migration are largely reduced to abstract dichotomies. "Family" is selected as an explanatory tool instead of inequality or socioeconomic change. "Wrongs and needs" are emphasized instead of—or in contrast to—rights and rights protections (see Chanock 2000).

There are multiple reasons for the decontextualization of young migrants' experiences. Most simply, it helps situate a client within one of the narrow legal frameworks available to unaccompanied youth. To many attorneys, these frameworks demand even more specific and impossible either/or calculations: parents as either bad or not bad, youth as agents or victims, the client alone or in context (Green and Dorhn 1996, 1310).

The strategic dismissal of context can also be read as a professional response, however intuitive, to the broader reality that young migrants lack the right to have rights, as discussed in Chapter 2. Here, the failed ideals of supranational, "inalienable" rights are accompanied by a global shift toward "humanitarianism"—a moral and political project promoted largely through the widespread development of the sort of nongovernmental organizations that many of the cause lawyers in this study work for or direct (Ticktin 2014). In their efforts to protect the "bare life" (Agamben 1998) of displaced and undocumented people, these organizations implicitly recognize—and in a sense reify—a trend in which complex political questions of immigrant rights are reconfigured into a focus on *charity* (Merry 2007). This is what Liisa Malkki (1996) calls the process of bureaucratized humanitarian intervention: through it, the specificities of individuals—in this case, a young migrant's circumstances and particular historical experiences—are reconstituted as "pure victims in general."

As a final level of consideration, this reduction or rejection of context also enables attorneys to reconcile their own professional and moral goals. Here, the aforementioned imbalance of power—one maintained by attorneys' understandings of professional expertise, age, and even mobility (see Jones 2016)—emerges discursively through the questions cause lawyers craft, the responses youth offer, and the subsequent "scripting" of a legal narrative (Heimer and Staffen 1998, 5). An international children's rights expert described this process more simply and with audible bitterness: "It's attorneys' conforming of kids' stories. That's what it is." While the process generally abstracts the young person from her or his broader context, I argue that it simultaneously distorts this context, normalizing an image of Chinese parents as dysfunctional and Chinese children as uniquely needy (Timmer 2010). It also upholds the US as an implicit standard, one in which childhood is maintained as a developmental stage dependent on parents, or, in their presumed absence, *professionals and guardians* (see Appell 2009). The identity that is produced is institutionalized, forming a collective representation of "Fujianese UACs" and an unequivocal moral narrative, the consequences of which I discuss in Chapter 5.

This is a chapter about choices. It identifies the choices lawyers make as they interpret and disaggregate the shifting challenges, accomplishments, and identities of young Fujianese migrants and the ways in which "the language of the law" demands and reinforces these decisions. It also recognizes the choices Fujianese youth themselves make. Unlike Roger Zetter, who emphasizes the "extreme vulnerability" and "non-participatory nature and powerlessness" of immigrants in processes of bureaucratic legal labeling (1991, 39), I recognize most unaccompanied Fujianese youth as active and informed, and sometimes misinformed, participants in the selective scripting of legal narratives and identities (see Calavita 1998; Menjívar 2011).

In a sense, this participation is akin to mirroring: Fujianese youths' accounts lend detail and depth to what is often put forth as a sure image, "The Fujianese Child" or "The Chinese Family," in legal representation. Depending on place and proximity, the metaphorical mirror takes on a variety of curvatures. At times, youth directly and deliberately reproduce attorneys' expectations, lending the account a sharper and more tragic focus. At other times, these narratives are refracted through divergent expectations and interpretations: in their ambitions, negotiations, and spatial strategies, youth complicate and powerfully distort the image, or "the cause," of their own selves. Characterized in the introductory lines above, their stories are in part magnified, disguised, and even lost in the conflicts and competition inherent in law.

PRIVILEGING THE CHILD VICTIM: AN EXAMINATION AND SIMPLIFICATION OF TRAFFICKING

> *But who's scamming, right? The whole question of scamming doesn't focus as much on the child as on the child's family. . . . So there's sort of a division: there's the good child, and then there's the scheming parent. –Michael, legal scholar*

The legal protections immigration cause lawyers evaluate for unaccompanied young clients are limited. The most likely claims are asylum and SIJ status, as well as T nonimmigrant status, which this chapter largely examines. Amid increased political and public awareness of trafficking,[1] initiatives to specifically identify and support *youth* who may have been trafficked are often criticized as inadequate or ad hoc (Goździak and MacDonnell 2007; see also Maloney 2002; Nugent 2006). When young people are expressly considered in these efforts—and sometimes, in critiques of these efforts[2]—they are typically depicted through the "universal child" imagery, i.e., as having disappearing, lost, stolen, or invaded childhoods (Stephens 1995; see also Statz 2018). Youth are further folded into the category of "women and children" and, in this way, almost always portrayed as victims of sexual exploitation (Goździak and Bump 2008; see also Merry 2003).[3]

What largely results, then, is the construction of a typical or "ideal" victim of trafficking (O'Brien 2013; see also Bernstein 2010; Hill 2014) and what Erin O'Brien characterizes as a "hierarchy of victims": "Firstly, the victims are primarily trafficked for the purposes of sexual exploitation; secondly, trafficking victims are primarily women and girls; thirdly, trafficking victims are compulsorily vulnerable and innocent" (2013, 316). Considering this "hierarchy of victims" in light of the previous chapter, and particularly in light of the nuanced motivations, interpretations, and relationships I documented, it's worth asking: Where, or how, does a Fujianese youth fit in here?

This is not a book about trafficking. Still, the topic is significant, for just as cause lawyers and anti-trafficking advocates utilize popular, "universal" constructions of childhood as an apolitical stage of dependence, development, and inherent (or compulsory) vulnerability, so too do they rely on what Jyoti Sanghera (2005, 6) describes as the "dominant anti-trafficking discourse"[4] to position youth as eligible for a T visa. This discourse is based on a set of assumptions largely rooted in anecdotal evidence and strong moralistic positions.[5] These include:

- Most trafficking happens for the purpose of prostitution;
- Poverty is the sole or principal cause of trafficking;
- Trafficking within the Asian subcontinent and the region is controlled and perpetrated by organized crime gangs;
- Strategies which club women and children together will be equally beneficial to both in extending protection against trafficking and redress after being trafficked;

- All persons under eighteen years of age constitute a homogenous category—children, devoid equally of sexual identity and sexual activity, bereft equally of the ability to exercise agency, and hence in need of identical protective measures. (Sanghera 2005, 4–5)

The federal definition of "severe form of trafficking in persons" includes "the recruitment, harboring, transportation, provision, or obtaining of a person for labor or services, through the use of force, fraud, or coercion for the purpose of subjection to involuntary servitude, peonage, debt bondage, or slavery."[6] As my data evidence, in the case of Fujianese youth, immigration cause lawyers—and often, their clients—largely appeal to this definition through a heavy reliance on the assumptions Sanghera details.[7]

Attorneys' moves may be interpreted in two not inconsistent ways, namely as reflecting the narrow parameters and arbitrary conditions of US immigration law (see Barsky 2006, 2016)[8] *and* as reiterating the inherent ambivalence of the dialogic process by which Fujianese youth are positioned within these legal frameworks. In the following attorney-authored excerpts, this process is presented as a strategic, ambitious, and ultimately *exclusive* professional effort. As I demonstrate, however, young people steadily inform and guide the development of a legal framing, at once resisting, misunderstanding, informing, and expertly mirroring their attorneys. This "mutuality of differences" (Holquist [1990] 2002, 41) matters: it is the meaningful and uncomfortable core of the steady exchange through which clients are "fit" into the trafficking framework or, as discussed elsewhere, the SIJ framework. If we are to understand it and its consequences, we must recognize this negotiation as carried on by different means and informed by different situated knowledges and practices (Haraway 1988; Mayer 2004; Shdaimah 2009).

In a legal practice advisory, "It Was(n't) My Choice: Identifying Human Trafficking in the Unaccompanied Chinese Youth Population," Lauren Burke describes how attorneys might or must "fit Chinese clients into a trafficking framework." Doing so requires a certain maneuvering between the federal definition of trafficking (relevant clauses from which are highlighted below) and assumptions about both trafficking and the client's family more specifically:

Utilizing [the federal definition of trafficking] can be difficult. . . . A filially pious mindset is deeply ingrained in many Chinese youth and convincing a youth to open up about the pressures that had been placed

upon her by an adult to come to the US is often a lengthy process. . . .
In my experience, however, there is an entire world that lies beneath the
surface of these youth and often, their experiences fit into the trafficking
framework. (2011, 9)

The author, who at the time of this research was a prominent immigration cause lawyer in New York, details the step-by-step process by
which attorneys might delineate and satisfy the statutory language of this
framework:

The Chinese youth I have worked with are *recruited, harbored and
transported,* by their parents and/or the snakeheads in charge of bringing
them from their homes in Fujian province to the United States. Some
Chinese youth are packaged by their parents as a way to make easy
money, others are targeted in their communities as being easy victims
to the snakeheads' exploits. All these children are brought between
border lines, often locked in rooms, kept at gunpoint and under
constant physical threats to their safety. The youth are *obtained* by the
snakeheads, or *provided* by their parents or other adult caregivers, for
the express purpose of earning capital—first for their captors in the
form of debt exchanged for their passage, then for their parents in
future earnings from working in the US. The element of *force, fraud,
and coercion,* can be found by exploring the false pretenses, idealistic
promises, physical violence and outright psychological force, placed
upon the children by adult caregivers, snakeheads, and "middle men"
in order to get them to "agree" to come to the US. Finally, nearly every
Chinese youth encountered is forced to pay off unthinkable debt, now
often ranging close to one hundred thousand dollars, in exploitative
working conditions for most of their young lives. (Burke 2011, 8–9;
emphases in original)

In this advisory, Burke selectively codes, interprets, and highlights her
clients' experiences in accordance with the US federal law (see Goodwin 1994;
Mann 1999). While underscoring the challenge of tracing and defining this
shadowy phenomenon—how to obtain and expose the family realities of
reticent, "filially pious" children, for instance, or how to recognize the "false
pretenses and idealistic promises" of adults—the report provides a number of
instructive and presumably sufficient solutions. Detailed below, these solutions

hinge on very specific ideological and legal understandings or productions of age, childhood, culture, and family and on the pervasive mythologies of the dominant anti-trafficking discourse.[9] Consider the following excerpts:

> With the Chinese child population, there are a number of aspects which make them unique from their adult counterparts. Most notably, of course, is the fact that they are children. Often under the age of eighteen at the time of their recruitment and smuggling, such children are thus legally incapable of consenting to assume any sort of debt obligation and, arguably, intrinsically unaware of the consequences of utilizing the snakehead network. Thus, even in the instances where the child claims it was his/her choice and he/she *did* agree to the conditions imposed upon him/her . . . the scenario of straightforward smuggling as applied in the adult context does not work due to the simple fact that we are discussing a *child* who is protected under the law. (8; emphasis in original)

> If the child is under the age of 18 at the time of trafficking, then given current standards of contract, labor, and sexual consent laws, as well as international standards on child capacity, they cannot legally consent to the migration, contract of transportation, and lifetime of exploitation. (30)

> Many unaccompanied Chinese youth are also eligible for T-nonimmigrant visas for victims of human trafficking as provided by federal law, as they have been victimized by either their parents . . . or snakehead smugglers to prospect off of the children's coerced labor. . . . Children who are coerced or forced to come to the US with snakeheads for the purpose of making money to send home once the debt has been paid off, are arguably victims of human trafficking at the hands of their parents. (29)

> Many Chinese children report fearing their families will be killed or report instances of actual violence and harm used against the relatives of those who come to the US and fail to pay their fees. This pressure tactic is even more effective on Chinese youth as, in Chinese culture, the family clan is the most important unit in society. An individual's identity is closely linked to her family. This Confucian tradition of taking care of one's parents is reflected not only in Chinese moral life but also in the practice of Chinese laws. Thus, children who have had not only their

lives but those of their family members threatened and the children reasonably believe such threats will be materialized should they not continue to work, it can be found that the children are coerced into their involuntary servitude and debt bondage. (34)

In Chapter 3, I discuss the shifting, often unexpected roles and identities of young Fujianese migrants. As youth independently make respected improvements to the economic and social status of "emplaced" family members, they come to self-identify as leaders in their communities of origin. Youth similarly take pride in their increasing autonomy and purchasing power, as well as in their own skilled management of employment, taxes, health care, language acquisition, friendships, and romantic relationships in the US. These are valued markers of success and of successful transitions to adulthood. Of course, Fujianese youth concurrently experience other and often negative understandings of self and responsibility. In certain contexts and communities, "Fujianese" emerges as a pejorative label, one associated with regional inferiority and illegality. Youth are often isolated or "caught." They are semi-autonomous and in legal limbo.

Yet as Burke's report suggests, in the legal realm these complex negotiations, endeavors, and constraints are extraneous at best. They are dismissed or rejected as cause lawyers "fit" Fujianese clients within the "right box" of the trafficking framework, and more specifically within the "homogenous category" of individuals under age eighteen that Sanghera details. They are *children*, writes Burke, protected under law and unable to consent to migration. They may have been *coerced* by snakeheads. They are "victims . . . at the hands of their parents" (2011, 29) who remain financially and culturally obligated to their ultimate identity, that of the Chinese family firm. It's worth noting, of course, that if we uphold these same understandings of age and vulnerability, the process by which such details are elicited and decontextualized might likewise be seen as coercive (McKinley 1997; see also Dawes 1999).

CHILD VICTIM, DEVIANT PARENT: FROM THE TRAFFICKING FRAMEWORK TO THE GRAND NARRATIVE

That immigrants' complex negotiations are flattened or standardized to satisfy legal categories is relatively well documented in law and society scholarship. Relevant to this study is Sarah Morando Lakhani's (2013) examination of the dual narratives immigration attorneys craft on behalf of petitioners for U visa status,[10] namely "clean" victimhood and migrants' civic engagement as contributing members of society. Consider also Susan Coutin's (2000) study of Salvadoran immigrants' struggles over the legitimacy of lawyers' asylum claims and Susan Berger's (2009) examination of the "cultural restructuring" of battered women as worthy of immigration relief through Violence Against Women Act (VAWA) provisions.[11] Michelle McKinley's (1997) exploration of life-story narratives that have been recast as necessarily tragic and brutal in attorneys' "zealous pursuit" of refugee women's rights is likewise significant.

Other scholars have examined moral legitimacy and the multiple "legal registers" through which citizen and rights-worthy subjectivities are discursively formed (Comaroff 1995; Osanloo 2006; Ticktin 2011) and the processes of citizen subject-making as necessitated by the modern nation-state (Fitzpatrick 1992). As Aiwha Ong argues, citizenship is itself "subject-ification," the dual process of self-making and being-made via power relations of surveillance, discipline, control, and administration (1996, 737–38; see also Foucault 1991). This process is made clear as we consider a necessary qualification for T nonimmigrant status, namely that the applicant complies with law enforcement for assistance in the investigation or prosecution of the crime experienced. Here, establishing an individual as a protection-worthy subject simultaneously— and most importantly—contributes to ensuring the security and prosperity of the nation-state, the political justification for this "subject-ification" (Ong 1996, 738).

The phenomenon of legal scripting is not *new* to law scholars or to legal practitioners. Yet as my data demonstrate, however standard (and ostensibly obligatory[12]) the selective creation of a legal fiction,[13] the practice is neither straightforward nor consistent. In this section, I attend to lawyers' oppositional understandings and uneasy utilization of youths' families as they attempt to "fit" their Fujianese clients into the trafficking framework.

First, it is important to highlight cause lawyers' fluctuating, sometimes apprehensive interpretations of trafficking. Most of the attorneys I spoke with were not as firmly convinced as Burke of the nearly indisputable applicability of T nonimmigrant status for Fujianese youth. Often, lawyers' understanding of trafficking had less to do with statutory definitions than with bureaucratic constraints and associations. Kim, a lawyer in San Francisco, stated, "When I first started [taking on Fujianese clients], we weren't seeing the cases as trafficking . . . but over time we looked at them and were like, this is really an issue of trafficking."

"How did this shift occur?" I asked, recalling the often slow, tentative process by which cause lawyers try out and network new strategies with others.

Surprisingly, Kim listed an actual year. "It was 2004," she stated. "That's when the Office of Refugee Resettlement came," she added, referencing the dissolution of the US Immigration and Naturalization Service (INS) through the Homeland Security Act. With it, responsibility for the custody of unaccompanied minors was transferred to the ORR.[14]

"The Office of Refugee Resettlement does the initial approval of benefits for trafficking victims," continued Kim. "And so when it was them instead of the Justice Department . . ." she paused. "Well, now it's related to trafficking. We have to frame it that way. That's when things started to change."

While a number of other cause lawyers situated their choice to pursue T nonimmigrant status in broader administrative shifts, the majority of those I spoke with also moved beyond the language of federal regulation to the explanatory paradigm of the Chinese family.

"The definition of trafficking is codified in law," said Damien, another attorney in California. "However, every helper, every attorney, every social worker, every advocate has a different personal view on what trafficking is. And the biggest snag is whether they feel that the youth coming from Fujian are being trafficked. . . . If the child is honest enough, they'll say, 'I came here because I wanted to make money.' This is hard, because if the person looks at the law, there has to be an element of coercion, or being forced to come here to work, for trafficking to be defined as trafficking . . . so people think [these youth] are just immigrants like anyone that will cross the borders. But my view is that would be missing a lot of cultural and family dynamics."

Many of these cultural and family dynamics were viewed, or at least presented, by cause lawyers as unequivocally *bad*. This powerfully reflects and extends what Matthew Fraidin calls "the Grand Narrative of Child Welfare" to the immigration context. "The narrative is one of brutal, deviant, monstrous parents and children who are fruit that doesn't fall far from the tree" (2012, 98–99). The narrative, Fraidin writes elsewhere, has little to do with parental authority and instead emphasizes parental culpability; the implicit corollary is that youth are "child-victims" (2010, 14; see also Best 1993).

The "deviant parent, child-victim" narrative featured prominently in my attorney interviews. One individual stated, "Children should not be made to take primary responsibility to provide and support their parents. Instead, it is parents who have the primary responsibility to secure, within their abilities and financial capacities, the conditions of living necessary for a child's development." Later, he added, "It is the snakeheads who are abusing the immigration system, not the children *who are only acting at the adult's direction.*" Similarly, other cause lawyers commented:

Childhood is an immutable status at the time that you migrate. Eventually you'll outgrow this, but at the time that you're a child, you can't change that. And that vulnerability is certainly part and parcel to why you're the target. And the fact that a child's been sold to snakeheads? They don't make that decision. It's the parents that make the decision for them.

And this is the difference: If a parent chooses to come—if you are an adult and you want to sacrifice everything to come to America and work to the bone and send money back to your kids, fine. You chose to have those children. If you're an adult and you say, "My child's obligation is to do that for me," well, I think that's the fundamental difference. . . . The idea that you belong to and for your parents is very strong; that's a big cultural thing.

A lot of the kids, when we talk about trafficking, it's like they're [unable] to think that their parents would put them through something like this. So I say to them, you know, "People are people. Your mom might be a good person, but once parents choose to have children, that's a job they're choosing to fulfill. And so we're not saying anyone's a bad person, we're saying that maybe they just weren't as good at this specific job in their life."

I do think the snakeheads are very predatory. But I think that coercion happens less often than the parents being the ones who take advantage of their kids.

In these reflections, we trace the development of a "grand narrative," one that unhesitatingly assigns blame to parents and suggests they are the *real* danger to a young person (see Bernstein 2000). This is, again, a sort of selective process, one in which attorneys appeal to, make, and ultimately maintain a series of inflexible legal and moral choices as they elicit necessary and ostensibly predicted details about their clients' families.

"As an attorney, what do you need?" I asked Marsha, a cause lawyer in Chicago. "What do you think would help provide better legal services to youth?"

Marsha was still for a moment; then she thoughtfully adjusted the heavy beaded necklace that hung over her green blouse. "I think it would be helpful to show coercion," she said. "You know, to prove coercion, to be able to have a better understanding of 'family tells child to do this, child does that, if child argues with parents, then this is what happens so the child would never argue.' So to be able to prove duress or coercion . . ." She tilted her head, waiting for a response. Suspecting that Marsha hoped I would eventually *supply* this required evidence through expert testimony, I remained silent. Finally, she continued: "I think it's different in Chinese culture. In our culture, if a parent wants a kid to do something they don't want to do, they're probably going to say, 'I hate you. I don't want to do that.' But it seems like that doesn't happen in these cases." Looking toward her window, she asked distractedly, "Does it not happen in Chinese culture?"

Unlike Marsha, Lana was certain—and explicit—in her moral interpretation and legal "selection" of Chinese family dynamics: "I have kids [clients] whose legal argument I've written, that their parents trafficked them. But their parents don't see it that way. And that can be hard, where legally this is what happened, but perceptually, that's not what took place in the kid's mind. I still have clients who I think are in complete denial about their parents' involvement. I think there are parents who are over-exaggerating [*sic*] the snakehead threat and are over-exaggerating how much money needs to be sent back every month. So basically the kids have been put into this really horrible situation by their parents who only talk about the snakeheads . . . and the kids are in total denial about it. Or it's just not their reality yet. They're just not ready . . .

"So I do my intakes with Chinese kids the opposite of how I was trained—where it's all open-ended questions, and you're supposed to never want to make the kid feel like they're agreeing with you. There have been times when I've asked a kid a question, and they've agreed with me, and I've tried to get more detail, and it turns out they were just agreeing with me.

"So now it's, 'Who did you come to America with?'

'My *ayi*—my auntie, my uncle.'[15]

'Oh, is your auntie's name *Snakehead?*'

"And they'll laugh, but they're not going to tell me it's a snakehead. . . . So you have to really dig into it. You can't just ask a kid, 'Was it your choice?' Instead, it's, 'Who was the first person who ever brought up

America? How did you learn about what America was? What were your perceptions of what America was like? How did you have those perceptions?' You know, it's about building it that way . . . [because] they're kids, and that's what people forget."

As in scripting T visa claims, a narrative of parental blame and child vulnerability occurs when attorneys evaluate and pursue SIJ status on behalf of a Fujianese client. Recall that to be eligible for SIJ, a state juvenile court must find that reunification with one or both of the youth's parents is not viable because of abuse, abandonment, neglect, or similar basis found under state law.[16]

A number of attorneys described the process by which they "fit" clients within the SIJ framework, namely by satisfying the language of "neglect" and "abandonment": "I told this kid, 'I don't see any relief for you. I really think you might have to go back; how do you feel about that?' And he said, 'Bad, because my mom needs back surgery, and she sent me here to work so she could get the surgery.' And I was like, THAT'S abandonment! I'm sorry, but you don't send your kid who is school age to work! For your back surgery! That kid was neglected, abused, or abandoned by his mom."

Another attorney stated, "An approach I've started to take is saying that parents who send young people with snakehead smugglers to come to the United States just in and of itself is a form of neglect." She shrugged. "So even if there isn't any past history of abuse, or even if the kids are still talking to the parents, the fact that the parents would put them in such a precarious situation and expose them to such dangers, that . . . should be enough to win a Special Immigrant Juvenile status case in family courts."

"DOES INTENT HAVE TO BE MALICIOUS?": UNEASY INTERPRETATIONS OF PARENTAL INVOLVEMENT

Of course, other attorneys were less convinced of, though no less reliant on, the image of Chinese parents as neglectful or coercive. As a potentially significant aside, all these lawyers were themselves first- or second-generation immigrants to the US and perhaps viewed mobility as more normative than did many of their colleagues (Jones 2016; see also Cresswell 2006; Deleuze and Guattari 1987).

Lisette, a cause lawyer who had immigrated to Missouri from Western Europe, openly admitted her doubts about the families of her clients. "It's hard for me to understand why anyone would pay to smuggle their child across so many countries," she said as we sat together in a loud, humid coffee shop. She fanned her face with her hand and shook her head. "On the other hand, I haven't lived a day in the shoes of those parents. We're easy to judge, and we're easy to not actually look at the picture. . . . I mean, you're the parent, you're the boss, and you know what's best for your child, and you make that decision. But sometimes [lawyers] are very patronizing of families."

While rare, the notion that smuggling a child to the US could actually reflect foresight or a parent's devotion was introduced by other attorneys, as well. "Does intent always have to be malicious?" asked Ife, an attorney who had herself been an unaccompanied young migrant. "I don't know. Think about parents who may be smuggling their kids in their kids' best interests." She raised an eyebrow emphatically and shook her head. "But it's still substantive law, and we have kids that are circles in square pegs. They don't fit, and so we have to create these elaborate cultural accounts."

Len was similarly uneasy with the "Grand Narrative" I traced above: "If we take seriously the idea that each family can only have one child, what's going on with them sending that one child off? It could either be that they're doing it for the family's interest, but that seems a little odd because now you're sending your one child far away. Or you might really think the child being sent away is going to have a better life, in which case it fights this idea of neglect. They're doing it as a way to have a better vision for their child's future. . . . I have a hard time, you know, condemning parents, saying that they're doing it purely for their own fiscal interest. I think older models of Chinese culture would say, yeah, of course. You use your children; the family unit is number one; the children's interests are not as important, right? But I think it might be different nowadays."

Nelson, a lawyer who had emigrated from Hong Kong to New York City, offered perhaps the most unambiguous interpretation of Fujianese families. "Fujian is different," he said. "You seldom see a person from Sichuan send a child halfway around the world. The Fujianese have a different kind of culture. It's not like the parents don't care about the welfare of the kids. They care too much—enough to smuggle a kid to the US alone."

It was August, and Nelson and I sat together in his stifling fifth-floor office. The space was brightly lit and dingy. When I first arrived, Leslie, Nelson's secretary, had walked me along a low-ceilinged hallway, passing rooms with desks piled high with papers at which older Chinese women sat steadily working and chatting. Metal fans whirred loudly. "Here, Mr. Wei's office," Leslie said unceremoniously as she abruptly left me at his door. I stood before Nelson and said hello. He did not smile.

I remain unsure about the nature of Nelson's work, though many of the cause lawyers I interviewed readily identified private, Chinatown-based attorneys like Nelson as allied with snakehead smuggling organizations. At the same time, a noted scholar of Chinese migration referred me to Nelson, and in our conversation he exhibited a deep understanding of and concern for Fujianese youth. While his motives may be disparaged in certain circles, I appreciated Nelson for his knowledge and, in hindsight, for unintentionally serving as something of a wrench in the professional dichotomy many nonprofit cause lawyers extol—namely themselves as needed moral and political activists in contrast with conventional lawyers (or, worse, sinister snakehead attorneys) as value-neutral "hired guns" (Sarat and Scheingold 2008, 2).

"Do you think parents know how dangerous the smuggling journey is?" I asked.

"Yes," Nelson replied flatly.

"What about working conditions?" I asked. "Are parents aware of that?"

"Yes." His face softened. "But when kids arrive in the US and they find out how hard they have to work, that's hard. Most are good kids. They work hard. Some even go to school. A lot are doing well. But some—I just saw on a Chinese newspaper, some become criminals. Some have legal status; some don't."

I described my observations, noting in particular the long hours that so many youth worked in Chinese restaurants and nail salons. Nelson nodded sympathetically. "The goal for most is to make money and pay off fees. My sense is that most don't have a long-term plan. The parents just want to send the kid here and pay off the smuggling fees. Their thinking is that the US will be better for their kids." By destabilizing assumptions about parental coercion, Nelson's interpretation struck me as markedly compassionate—even if his professional identity was suspect to many other cause lawyers.

SELECTING—AND PLAYING—THE VICTIM

Above, I examine one way in which many immigration cause lawyers reduce the "context" of Fujianese youth, namely through the introduction and selection of oppositional moral claims about a client's parents. Here, Fujianese parents are brutal, deviant, and entirely responsible for their child's migration to the US. It is the "Grand Narrative" of Fujianese families, as a sampling of attorneys' comments exemplifies: "The parents [are] the ones who take advantage of their kids," "The kids have been put into this really horrible situation by their parents," and "The parents . . . put them in such a precarious situation and expose them to such dangers."

Yet at the same time, sending a young person to the US can be interpreted as an act of compassion and sagacity, a decision parents make in their child's best interests: "You're the parent, you're the boss . . . you know what's best for your child and you make that decision," "[Parents'] thinking is that the US will be better for their kids," and "[Parents are] doing it as a way to have a better vision for their child's future."

These interpretations reveal much about the language of immigration law—and perhaps most obviously about the limited nature of the trafficking and SIJ frameworks. Yet if we look carefully at these statements, we see something else. Both views selectively dismantle or dismiss *youths'* participation in their migration journeys and often reveal a deliberate disregard for youth themselves. Squarely situating unaccompanied Fujianese migration as the parents' choice, whether malicious or altruistic, abstracts young people from the narrative and likewise elides the complex circumstances, responsibilities, and relationships underlying their individual migration journeys. It is a subjectification that recasts the young person as a (however compulsory) victim and fractures her or his broader context. Significantly, this is both an intimate and a formal fracturing. Reframing parents as traffickers or abusive will most likely exclude them from obtaining derivative nonimmigrant status. A person who becomes a LPR through SIJ status is no longer considered the child of his or her parents for immigration purposes, even if parental rights were not terminated.

Even for attorneys like Lisette, who were cautious in their evaluation of parents and uniquely aware of the "patronizing" tendencies of legal advocates, the young person is largely unconsidered as the lawyer expertly scripts the responsibility and motives for her or his migration journey. This absence evidences what many cause lawyers may unconsciously categorize as a second opposition, an "either/or" choice that is in their strategic interest not to make. Though youth (or, more specifically, youths' volition) are omitted from the family narratives that attorneys craft, every cause lawyer I interviewed grappled with the role their clients played in their migration journeys, journeys that extended prominently into the legal realm.

Not only were attorneys unsettled about youths' insistence on their participation and management of migration—and, naturally, by the fact that these assertions could inhibit or undermine a lawyer's work *on a youth's behalf*—but some lawyers were also frustrated and perhaps threatened by the legal knowledge and skilled maneuvering their young clients demonstrated. "Half of the kids I work with never thought they'd be apprehended [at the US-Mexico border]," said one lawyer. "But half of the kids tell me they were ready to be caught because, like they say, they wanted to get an asylum case." Whether her expression conveyed disbelief or defeat, I couldn't decide. "I guess some of them know the system really well."

During a follow-up interview with Len, I asked, "What is your sense of the role of youth in making the decision to migrate?"

"I don't know," he replied. "That's a good question. It's always difficult because the children themselves are always going to say it wasn't their idea."

"Yes?"

"Because it helps their case." He shrugged, indifferent. "I mean, you know, if you say, 'It's my idea,' it's not, 'Oh, you were afraid to come.' I mean, obviously the argument can be made: It doesn't matter if they wanted to come; they're not adults. They don't have that agency to make that decision. But I, you know, I've said before, I am always confronted with this notion that it is a strange, paternalistic view of a people to say that they would deliberately put their children in harm's way, without at least some sense that it's for the children's good." He knocked on the table as he said it—that they would *deliberately* put their *children* in *harm's way*. He was quiet for a moment. "I think most [youth] say it's not their idea. And do I think most of the time they're sincere? Probably. But I am not ignorant of the fact that it helps their immigration case for them to not take agency or ownership over that decision."

"Which is interesting," I noted, "because the very fact of a young person deliberately not taking agency is a pretty savvy move."

"Yeah." He nodded. "And that's the thing, too. As lawyers, we tend to sometimes not give our clients enough credit. You know. I think our clients, for the most part, despite how difficult and how confusing immigration law is— and it certainly is—our clients know in general what's going to get a judge on their side. And they know that if they say, 'It's my idea,' it makes it very difficult to make the argument about fear and abandonment. It makes it very difficult to make this argument about being a victim, as traumatic as [migration] is.

I'm certainly not placing any kind of blame or any kind of judgment on it. . . . They sort of know a little bit [about law]. Now, it doesn't matter to me, right? I think they're not old enough to make that decision. They're not old enough to take ownership over that decision, so it shouldn't matter to me whether or not they want to do it, or they have agency to do it."

While Len rather swiftly solved this tension by relying on social and legal standards regarding youths' capacity to consent, other attorneys were less convinced by this argument, noting the relatively older age of unaccompanied Fujianese minors. As two attorneys whom I interviewed together stated:

If the child has never disclosed any sort of red flag for trafficking, we could talk [again] to the child and say, 'Look, are you sure there's nothing going on, do you want to tell us more?' in the hopes that they will kind of put their guard down. . . . But if the child very solidly maintains that everything is fine . . . our hands are tied, and we can't move forward with anything at that point.

When working with minors, there are certain ethical provisions that do allow us to kind of dig a little bit more and kind of collaborate with other actors and with other stakeholders [such as ORR shelter staff]. But because the Chinese minors are sixteen—you know, fifteen to seventeen, they have the sufficient capacity, and they have the competency to make their own decisions and to speak for themselves. Because of the age of these minors and the capacity and competency levels, we have to work with what they give us.

Rather than be dismissive or wary of the "capacity" or "competency" their Fujianese clients demonstrated, a few of the attorneys I interviewed appreciated these qualities, and even admired them. "Framing kids [as victims] has been going on for a long time," said Angela, an attorney in Alabama. "For the lawyers representing kids, a T visa is great! It's excellent that we can use it. And [the youth you're studying] play the victims, right?"

"Right!" I said, startled by so forthright a question. "And to me, doing so is the opposite of victimhood."

"Yes," Angela replied. "In this case, children are the interpreters of the law, and the ones with power."

"THE ONES WITH POWER": COLLABORATING, MIRRORING, AND REJECTING LEGAL ADVOCACY

Recall here the abuse Hua described during a telephonic intake with a legal-aid provider, detailed in Chapter 3—"Yes, somebody hurt me!" she imitated herself and laughed. Later in our conversation, I asked, "Can you tell me a little bit about what you shared with your attorney?" We were discussing Hua's smuggling debt and how her mother turned all the money Hua wired home over to the snakeheads.

Hua nodded. "Yeah. My mom never keeps the money. But when I talk to my lawyer—" She altered her tone once more; this time it was strained, distraught. "'She used *all* the money! She doesn't pay the smuggler, and I have to work a *long* time.'"

"You change your voice like that?"

"Huh?" She squinted at me.

"Whenever you tell me about how you talk to your lawyer, you say, 'Ohhhh, ohhhh, ohhhh,'" I mimicked Hua's mournful cadence.

"Oh. Yeah. A little bit." She sat back thoughtfully, then tried again: "My mom . . . *Many* years they got to give the money to smugglers. I have to work a *long* time. I'm *tired*."

"Do you think your lawyer believes you?"

"I'm not sure," Hua answered. "But it's good for me."

In this instance Hua is a mirror, cleverly putting forth the account she knows her attorney needs, one in which her mother can be reframed as a trafficker and which emphasizes the crushing smuggling (now trafficking) fees she is obliged to pay. Still, it's important to stress that Hua clearly never expected to deceive her lawyer, nor is her experience universal. During another conversation, I mentioned, "When I talk to attorneys, many of them say the same thing: 'Chinese kids come here because they're Christian. Or because they have bad parents.'"

"No," she quickly replied. "No. They know more. I think they know more. Because, you know, they know that's not true, but they're doing their job."

I waited.

"They do a lot of different cases," she added. "A lot different. So I think they know why you come to America. It's because you're poor. You don't have a lot of money. And you don't have choices in China. Coming to America is a good choice. It's much better than China. I think they know."

In Hua's reflections, we find what Foucault calls "the modern attitude" (1984, 37), a mode of self-production within shifting fields of powers. Significantly, this is both a form of belonging *and* a task. Recognizing "what we are" (50), argues Foucault, demands acknowledging the structural limits imposed on us and necessarily experimenting with the possibility of going beyond them. As utilized here, "the modern attitude" is uniquely connected to agency, or what Carisa Showden identifies as a product of both autonomy—i.e., an individual's capacity to act—and freedom, the conditions that facilitate action. Taken together, these concepts accentuate the ongoing process and deeply intimate reality that what we are, and what we can do, is "a capacity that is shaped by subjects' temporal and relational circumstances" (2011, ix). Accordingly, how a young person like Hua interprets the conditions or constraints of this capacity shifts over time and also in relation to her attorney, peers, family members, smugglers, and other sources of expert knowledge. In the process Hua described, becoming a citizen is not a top-down process; it depends on how Hua is constituted by attorneys and how she reconstitutes herself and her family *to* attorneys (see Ong 1996).

Lixue, another young migrant, similarly identified the scripting of a migration and family narrative as a shrewd, collaborative process between herself and her lawyer, a specific "self-making" that engaged with the T visa framework as both a task and, following Foucault, a potential source of belonging.

"The first time I met with my attorney," Lixue told me, "we didn't talk. We just went to court. Bonnie [Lixue's attorney] said, 'I'm your lawyer.' That's it. Later we talked."

"What did you talk about?" I asked.

"She said to me, 'You don't have to be a Christian' [i.e., how Lixue earlier self-identified]. You don't have to lie. We can help you with your case."

"What did she mean?"

"She said, 'We can try to get a visa for you.' It's the—" Lixue looked toward the ceiling, trying to recall the name of the legal protection.

"SIJ?" I volunteered. "T visa?"

"Yeah! T visa."

"Is that what you're trying for now? The T visa?" Lixue's removal proceedings had not yet concluded.

"Yeah."

"What do you know about the T visa?" I asked. She tilted her head at me quizzically.

"I mean . . ." I paused, trying to explain. "So, pretend you are Bonnie, and I'm Lixue."

Lixue laughed.

"Bonnie, can you tell me what a T visa is?"

"Okay!" She leaned forward. "The T visa is something for children."

"Yes?"

"Not adults. And it's because in China, your parents—or somebody—has hurt you. You can't stay in China anymore. So you have to go to America. It's something like, your parents don't like you. They hurt you. They try to kill you. Or it's like, nobody wants you. You don't have anywhere you can stay. You have to go to America."

"Okay," I said, "But what if my parents were nice to me? Then what?"

Lixue nodded knowingly. "Bonnie didn't ask me, 'Are your parents good or not?' She just asked, 'Why did you come to America?' And I said, 'I need money.' Or 'My parents are bad.' You can say, 'If you don't send money, the smuggler will hurt your parents and your brother. And the smuggler is bad. If you do not give them money, then they will hurt you.'"

Significantly, many youth garnered these strategies *from* smugglers. Aware of the legal options available to youth traveling alone, some snakeheads instruct young migrants to lie about their age if apprehended and to prepare a specific narrative of abuse or exploitation for the telephonic intake evaluation they will receive from an attorney, as Hua did. A number of youth recounted how smugglers diminished or even celebrated the threat of apprehension, describing to their charges the free legal aid they would purportedly receive if designated as UAC, as well as the provision of food and shelter to youth in ORR custody.

Uniquely positioned between and able to access a variety of perspectives, youth continuously evaluate lawyers' and smugglers' advice against the transnational connections and communication they maintain with other Fujianese through social media. Not only does the information youth obtain from other migrants include discursive strategies for "collaboration" with attorneys, but it also contains a variety of perspectives on legal advocacy more broadly. While the majority of the youth I interviewed did utilize an immigration cause lawyer, some declined these advocates' offers of free assistance. Explaining the decision to me, one individual recalled the advice of peers who had already migrated to the US and with whom she communicated on social media. It's better to hire a private attorney, warned her friends. Private attorneys might cost more, but they work faster, and they're more successful than pro bono advocates.

Chaoxiang, a young man I first met in Chicago, decided with his father (in Fujian) to hire a private attorney when he aged out of an ORR detention center and moved to New York. "It's such a bad decision!" Joan, Chaoxiang's legal advocate, told me when she heard the news. "He's going to go with Davis, I know it." Marty Davis, a private Chinatown attorney, was infamous among immigration cause lawyers for dispensing misleading advice and ignoring the particular forms of relief for which unaccompanied Fujianese clients could be eligible.

Chaoxiang *did* go with Marty, and things proceeded as Joan predicted. The attorney was evasive with Chaoxiang, rarely returning the young man's calls. He never asked Chaoxiang for information and only gave vague assurances when they did finally speak, usually in a waiting area outside an EOIR courtroom in New York City. Sitting beside Chaoxiang on one of his court dates, I listened as Marty leaned toward the young man and said confidently in English, "You have a 75 percent chance of winning your case." Chaoxiang nodded, not understanding. He sat stiffly in his new navy suit below the buzzing fluorescent lights, his gelled hair swept carefully across his forehead. It was an impossible and unethical claim, but Chaoxiang seemed too tired to care when I translated it to him in Mandarin.

It was clear that whatever impatience Chaoxiang felt in New York was matched by his frustration and regret about the time he had spent in Chicago. To Joan's chagrin, Chaoxiang was never particularly concerned about the quality, cost, and overall altruism of an attorney—he simply wanted to work and obtain legal status. "The person I was smuggled here with was twenty-one," he told me. "She didn't have to go into [an ORR shelter facility in Chicago] like me. And she's been working for years. She got asylum right away because of a Falun Gong claim."[17] He wrinkled his forehead, "She's already legal. I had to wait in Chicago, and now I have to wait here. I'm losing a lot of time."

BETWEEN STATUS AND CARE: THE FRAUGHT CAUSE AND PROFESSIONAL PURPOSE

While Joan was aggrieved and frustrated by Chaoxiang's decision to partner with Marty, she was also not particularly surprised. Like other immigration cause lawyers who work almost exclusively with Fujianese youth, Joan often felt "used" by this population of unaccompanied minors. She had frequently encountered youths' singular urgency to work and their individual or shared family resolve to pursue certain legal outcomes. This was a doggedness that might lead to creative youth–attorney collaborations, as with Hua, or in the case of Chaoxiang, an outright rejection of what Joan identified as the better prepared, more sympathetic, and *free* advocacy that she and other immigration cause lawyers could offer.

In a chapter about choices, this tension introduces a final and arguably impossible binary, one pertaining to the broader purpose of cause lawyering on behalf of unaccompanied youth. Is advocacy ultimately for the provision of legal relief, or is for young people's welfare and safety? In many cause lawyers' minds, a choice can and must be made between the two. At the "On Their Own" conference, an attorney presenter stated, "Immigration judges aren't bad people, but there's confusion among them about whether SIJ is just for immigration benefits or for *the right thing*—the protection and care of the child." Audience members nodded in agreement.

In a later panel on the benefits of U visas and T nonimmigrant status, a lawyer described to her colleagues her experiences with local law enforcement:

> I don't know about you, but law enforcement is very hesitant to sign certification of the victim.[18] They're worried it's all about giving benefits, but it's not! And it's the same thing with DCFS. In Chicago, they won't sign for anyone who's not in their care and custody, and it's rare that they do for the children who are! And DCFS has authority to do this because they have investigative powers. The people at DCFS are afraid that they're granting them immigration [status].

In these and other instances, attorneys publicly diminished a relatively concrete outcome of legal advocacy, namely LPR status, in favor of a more ambiguous objective, the professional and ethical provision of *care*.[19] While some attorneys continued to emphasize best interests over LPR when discussing Fujianese youth, it was clear that the appreciation and deservedness they expected from their clients was neither straightforward nor wholly satisfying.

As I trace in this chapter, unaccompanied Fujianese youth present a series of uneasy oppositional choices many attorneys feel they must make, both as they "fit" their clients into the appropriate legal framework and as they ostensibly identify and address youths' best interests. Are these youth, *or should these youth be re-presented as*, alone (unaccompanied) or in context? As children or as young adults? As child victims or as agents of their own migration journeys? As dependent on legal advocacy or as "collaborative" or even *independent* clients? Are Fujianese parents neglectful and coercive, or are they acting in their daughters' or sons' best interests?

To many cause lawyers, Fujianese youths' compulsory vulnerability (O'Brien 2013) and anticipated "worthiness" of legal relief is unsettled by their relatively older age, language(s), economic goals, and transnational relationships. Moreover, they do not always appear to merit—or want—lawyers' best-interests advocacy. Why, then, do these attorneys continue to advocate so diligently on behalf of Fujianese youth? In the next chapter, I suggest that this advocacy is rooted in a vision of professional success that privileges the figure of the tragic Fujianese child rather than the law as its most marketable political and moral purpose.

5 *The Spectacular Case*

FROM CASE TO CAUSE: AN INTRODUCTION TO THE TRAGIC ACCOUNT

On a July afternoon, I rode with an attorney from her office in Chicago to an ORR detention center. It was a long drive, nearly an hour, and we were quiet as she steered her minivan onto the highway. The heavy whir of cicadas echoed into the open windows. While Maria[1] haphazardly grabbed for her sunglasses at a stoplight, I watched as teenagers walked together along the paths of a nearby park. Beyond them, young children shouted to one another, careening after soccer balls on a worn grass field. A garbage truck screeched to a stop behind us. Ahead was Lake Michigan, a streak of indigo against the bright sky. It was a beautiful and quintessential Chicago summer day on all sides—yet how surreal, I thought, to be traveling to an unassuming, sealed-off *detention center*. Trying to conceal what had become a familiar sense of apprehension, I began asking questions:

> How many Chinese youth are usually in this particular detention center?
> Why do you think they're here?
> How did you first learn about them?
> What were you doing before you started your organization?
> Did you always want to practice immigration law?

Signaled by the ease with which Maria answered them, these were easy questions, the natural outcome of so many conversations with reporters and policy makers and potential funders over the years. Still, she responded respectfully, and with characteristic steadiness and conviction began to tell me about Young Zheng, a young Fujianese migrant on whose behalf she had advocated years before. Young's was a gripping legal, familial, and migration narrative, a story that both inspired and helped explain Maria's ongoing work.

I begin this chapter by re-presenting to the reader the account of Young Zheng as I heard it that day and throughout the early stages of my fieldwork. To many, Young's journey had a hard-won and happy conclusion. To others, myself included, it is less straightforward. It is an intricate story, rife with angst and elation, technical details, and moments that surge to the fore of retellings and remembering. It is a very personal story. It is also partisan, a composite construction in which the abiding concerns and constraints of lawyers emerge as forcefully as those of Young, if not more so (see Rosenwald and Ochberg 1992). For this reason, I rely almost exclusively on attorneys' retellings of this case and very little on Young himself; however, many of the reflections Young shared with me are incorporated elsewhere in this book under a pseudonym.

Ever cognizant that this chapter represents but one more version of an individual's experience, I believe that as an ethnographer I am as accountable to my own fragmentary and disorienting *exposure* to the narrative as I am to the interpretations I collected and the facts of the case. To be absent from this text would be a betrayal (Toor 2017, quoting Ruth Behar), for I ultimately put forth the story as I encountered it—urgent, uneasy, and fraught with contradiction. Indeed, I argue that to understand the significance of this "spectacular case" is in a sense to recognize it as markedly uncertain—or, put differently, as hardly as simple and representative as it was often made out to be by many of those I interviewed.

There was this boy named Young Zheng, Maria began.[2] *He was from a small province in China. He was smuggled by ruthless traffickers at the age of fourteen, and expected to work off a debt of sixty thousand dollars. Zheng was the second child born to his family—he was an involuntary lawbreaker subject to government punishment. His mother was dead, and his father had decided it was time to get him out of the home he shared with his new wife. He made a deal with the snakeheads, promising that Zheng would work to pay the debt.*

Out my window, cyclists in colorful jerseys sped along the lakefront path. Our car fell under the heavy shadow of Soldier Field then eased into the bright light, now filtered by low trees and the sailboats bobbing in the harbor.

But instead he was nabbed at Newark Liberty International Airport and spent a year at a Berks County, Pennsylvania, detention center, where conditions were so bad that the place was later shut down. Then Zheng was transferred to the Chicago shelter, where staff members summoned me. He was terrified and traumatized. He didn't understand why he was in the US. He thought he was here to go to school.

When he was transferred to Chicago, we started serving as his child advocate and advocating on his behalf so he could be reunified with his uncle.

We were also advocating with the lawyer who was representing him at this time. This lawyer wouldn't return any of his calls. He would send letters to the lawyer, and the lawyer wouldn't call him back. Sometimes the lawyers are associated with the smugglers and the traffickers—they'll hire the lawyers to get kids out of custody.

We were able to get Young released and reunified with his uncle in Ohio. There, he attended school and received straight A's. He also had to go and meet with immigration officials once a month. He did this dutifully. He would ride two buses and a train to get there. And one month they told him, "You can wait three months before you come back." But then the next month they called and said, "Where are you? You're supposed to be here." Young went to their offices, and he was handcuffed and shackled and the very same day flown to Chicago, which was where we were able to meet with him again. And we put him on the phone with the lawyer who had been representing him, and the lawyer basically said, "There's nothing I can do, there's nothing I can do, but you need to pay me more money, but there's nothing I can do."

Before us was the upward expansion of 300 E. Randolph, where heavy steel beams jutted from the office building's roof and loomed over the edge of Millennium Park. In time I would hear Maria tell this story again, only then from the fiftieth floor of the completed building to a crowd of colleagues, friends, and benefactors seated along a wall of windows in Baker and McKenzie's new law offices, joined together for a fundraiser on behalf of the organization Maria directed.

In Chicago, they took him to the airport to deport him to China, and he was so upset. He kept throwing up on the way there. And once they arrived there, he was still shackled, and he was so panicked about returning to China that he hit his head against a concrete pillar at the airport. He hit his head so hard that he passed out.

As so many media and anecdotal accounts would prove, this was a particularly gripping, if not essential, moment in Young's story:

"He was so scared to return. He bashed himself against a wall to avoid being sent back to China" (Chinese Boy Asks for Stay of Deportation, Citing Fear." *New York Times*, Ralph Blumenthal, June 8, 2005).

"In a desperate attempt to stay in the US, [he] beat his head into a wall to avoid deportation back to China, where his unpaid smugglers awaited his arrival" ("Fulbright Attorneys Successful in Getting Green Card For Young Zheng," *Business Wire*, September 27, 2006).

"And then there was that Chinese kid who beat his head against a pillar" (Immigration attorney in Memphis, research interview, May 14, 2012).

"He was so terrified of being deported back to China that he . . . smashed his head into a wall, knocking himself unconscious and requiring a brief hospitalization. 'I will be killed if I return to China,' Zheng told the Associated Press in a phone interview from a federal juvenile detention facility" ("China Teen Fears He Will Face Death if Deported to China," Associated Press, Kristie Rieken, June 6, 2005).

"Young's fear [was] so great that during a deportation attempt in April, he repeatedly hit his head against a wall in an effort to stop authorities from putting him on a plane to Hong Kong" ("Smuggled Chinese Boy Pleads to Stay in US," *Reuters*, Jon Hurdle, July 11, 2005).

"Handcuffed and escorted by US immigration officers to a plane bound for China, the teen momentarily escaped and slammed his head into an airport wall so hard that he blacked out and had to be hospitalized. So intense was his fear of returning to face his smugglers in China that Zheng said he was willing to do anything to stay here" ("Teen from China Sees Asylum as Only Hope," *Houston Chronicle*, Edward Hegstrom, June 8, 2005).

He'd been told he was better off dying in the United States than coming back to China and putting everyone at risk, Maria continued. *Men had shown up at his father's house to ask for the money because he hadn't been paying off his smuggling fees. The concussion didn't kill him, but it did prevent the government from putting him on a plane to China. He was sent to a secure facility in Houston, where we found him pro bono attorneys. He remained under constant threat of immediate deportation. During his first two weeks in lockup, he was closed, quiet, blank.*

It was a tragic case, and also one of redemption. As I would come to know Maria better, along with Young and the team of attorneys who took on his case in Houston, my admiration for the tenacity and commitment these individuals demonstrated would only grow. Incredibly complex, the case revealed the exhausting intricacies and contradictions of the US immigration system, as well as the almost incomprehensible dedication and legal skill needed for success. Yet the *story* of Young, or, more specifically, the broad and steady retelling of this story, continued to unsettle and perplex me. As I encountered it at fundraisers, in media reports, or in interviews with immigration cause lawyers who were themselves only anecdotally aware of it, my unease with the narrative grew in proportion to my familiarity with it.

THE STORY OF YOUNG, THE STORY OF HIS LAWYERS

When I first learned about Young, I was volunteering with the UCA and meeting regularly with Li, a young man from Fuzhou, in a nearby ORR detention center. We talked about his family and about how we each liked to run and swim. Li described his running route in his hometown, tracing it with his finger on a piece of paper. I told him about seeing a fawn on my run that morning, drawing a deer when my efforts to recall its Mandarin equivalent failed. He laughed easily as we sat in sunlight filtered by mirrored, one-way glass.

When Li had a court date, I took the train downtown and sat beside him and other young men from the detention center, most of whom were from Guatemala. In the gray light of the waiting room, I sneaked pieces of gum to everyone, and Li translated my questions to his friends from Mandarin to Spanish, which he was learning in the shelter facility. He was relaxed as we waited. Older and considerably taller than those lined up beside him on the heavy wooden bench, he cracked jokes quietly, a clear endeavor to interrupt the anxiety around him, the nervousness betrayed by wrinkled foreheads and wan half-smiles.

"Every child has their own story," Maria said, "although I will say the situation of all of the kids coming from China actually is nearly identical to Young Zheng's story. They're all coming from one very small province in China . . . from very similar situations of having debt, not really choosing to come here but being sent here by their families and coming from cultures where they can't say no to their parents."[3] Yet as I got to know Li, and so many other young Fujianese migrants, I grew uncomfortable with this claim. Was his story really the same as Young's?

As discussed in Chapter 4, the explanatory paradigm of youth "being sent" to the US by deviant and abusive parents and being financially and culturally obligated to the Chinese family firm is prevalent and arguably necessitated as lawyers attempt to fit Fujianese clients into limited legal frameworks, or what Russell called "the right boxes." Yet how to explain the circulation of strategic narrative elements *beyond* the legal realm? How to make sense of the very public pervasiveness of so many brutal details, collapsed personal histories, and insufficient political geographies? How, I wondered as I came to know Li better, could his experience be compared to Young's—and even be characterized as "nearly identical?"

In Young's case, the ubiquity of these practices is compellingly evidenced in so many media accounts of Young's visceral, frantic moment at the airport. As this chapter demonstrates, however, accentuating a heartrending act of desperation is not simply a tactic of—or at least not limited to—sensational journalism. It is also a compelling practice among many of the cause lawyers I interviewed, one in which the figure of the child, rather than the law, surfaces as holding the potential for social change.

Arguably elicited in such a way to present Young in "the most tragic and convincing light" in the courtroom (McKinley 1997, 71), Young's legal narrative represents an ongoing exchange. Young's Houston lawyers were new to immigration law and the challenges of representing an unaccompanied Chinese minor. Viewed in this context, they are neither explicitly rebellious nor regnant: "traditional" or preeminent-problem solvers in fits and starts, these lawyers have a nascent knowledge of immigration law such that Young never *defers* to the particular drafting of a legal narrative (Lopez 1992). Instead, the dialogic construction of his story is situated, ongoing, and productive, in a variety of senses.

At the same time, writes Michelle McKinley, "once the narrative is in circulation, its 'owner' has no meaningful control over its interpretation, repetition, and use" (1997, 76). Accordingly, in many ways the continued refinement of Young's story is "un-dialogic" (see Barsky 1994) insofar as the utilization of one particular version and discrete period of Young's experience depends on but largely occurs outside of Young, even as he *is living his life*. Indeed, and as this chapter evidences, the story is continuously negotiated by cause lawyers in tension and in tandem with the work of other colleagues, the media, funders and institutional supports, immigration experts, activists, and the broader public. Amid the unpredictability of immigration law and the instability of nonprofit work, Young's story provides cause lawyers a fixed motif intended to reveal tragedy and need and, as I discuss later, a very specific remedy. It is intrinsic to defining the cause and, however unintentionally, the cause lawyer.

In 2013, a Chicago public radio program featured Maria in a discussion about the expected influx of unaccompanied youth to the US.[4] Young, now a graduate student, was also asked to participate in the conversation; his story, noted Maria and the program host, would give listeners a picture of UACs.[5] After sharing some introductory statistics on unaccompanied youth, Maria began to narrate Young's migration journey and experience in the US. As the dramatic tension grew—"he was handcuffed and shackled and that very same day flown to Chicago"—she paused. "And, Young, I'll let you tell the next part of the story, which is when they took you to the airport." It was a telling moment.

On the one hand, Maria's conspicuous turn to Young to provide these details may have been in deference to his story, the recognition of a traumatic juncture that only he could or should appropriately voice. Yet her careful reminder—"which is when they took you to the airport"—could also reveal a watchful resolve that the story follow a specific, tragic path. Read as *directing* the narrative, this moment invites us to consider Amy Shuman's work on storytelling: "In listening to or even retelling other people's stories, narrators become witness to others' experiences, and storytelling provides some hope for understanding across differences" (2005, 5). In many ways inspiring empathy, urgency, and support, advocates like Maria often feature the personal accounts of young migrants on public platforms to draw attention to their respective causes. Yet Shuman also warns that the appropriation of such stories may ultimately use one person's tragedy to serve exclusively for another's inspiration: "It rarely changes the circumstances of those who suffer. If it provides inspiration, it is more often for those in the privileged position of empathizer rather than empathized" (2005, 5).

The dramatic storyline sells, both as compelling legal testimony and in the popular press. How it sells a *cause*, and why, is the more uneasy and meaningful question considered in the following pages. To do so, I first introduce the "Young Team," the group of private attorneys who agreed to take on Young's case pro bono when he was moved to a secure facility in Houston. While interesting in their own right, these lawyers' candid recollections also underscore the relevance of practice site;[6] the meaningfulness of sustained, relatively autonomous advocacy; and the unique "entitlement" they and Young have of this legal and deeply personal account.

I then move to a more empirical overview of the case. Drawing extensively on court documents, I trace the discursive development of many of the oppositional categories I examine above—the vulnerable child and the suspect parent, for instance—while also highlighting other moral judgments and perceived cultural values that emerge as the case progresses. While this scripting is important in qualifying Young for SIJ status, the Young Team's primary struggle ultimately proves less about appealing to the limited *language* of legal relief than about *access* to pursuing legal relief. Indeed, these attorneys' eventual success reveals much about the bounds and possibilities of professional practice, the opaque nature of the US immigration system, and the rewarding potential of legal advocacy.

Yet however critical these hard-won insights, particularly when gaining access to a forum for legal relief is the primary challenge, they are for the most part absent when the story is taken up and disseminated by cause lawyers. In this chapter's final section, I explore the ramifications of the spectacular, and almost exclusively tragic, version of this account in more detail, when I return to the "Chinese kid who beat his head against a pillar."

THE YOUNG TEAM

I met Young in the spring of 2012. Later that summer, I visited him and the attorneys who took on his case in Houston. At a sandwich shop near the looming glass building where they worked, I met with three of the attorneys who composed "the Young Team," including Hannah and John. While they had been quite formal when we first met, the three grew disarmingly animated as they began to describe Young's case. They shook their heads with frustration, sighed, waved their arms across the table, and interrupted one another. I asked very few questions, furiously taking notes and the occasional bite of a sandwich.

"We had three days to file an application for a stay of deportation," Hannah recalled. Contacted by Maria, the team took up Young's case when, after one night in Chicago, he was flown to Houston and placed in a Southwest Key secure immigrant- youth center.

"We filed under emergency basis, and when we received the letter that had the stay, I'll *never* forget that moment." She unclenched her clasped hands and stretched open her fingers. "I wasn't breathing. It was our first victory, and at a really difficult time." Suddenly, she laughed loudly. "Both John and I had car wrecks that summer! We were driving everywhere, and often with other attorneys in the car." John, the lead attorney on the case, a tall, staid man I would come to know as particularly warm and generous, rolled his eyes.

"We drove everywhere," Hannah continued, "and every person in the car would be on the phone, trying to get information and file papers. The second step," she added, "was a publicity campaign. There was a story about him on NPR, and we got Young listed on the first page of the *New York Times*.[7]

"So we stayed deportation," Hannah continued. "But what we were trying to do with the third circuit and the BIA [Board of Immigration Appeals] was never going to work. It was so hard. I remember being on the floor in my kitchen, crying. I called John. 'You'll think of something,' he told me." She shook her head and smiled. "He was always so calm. He and Young were always so calm and full of faith."

John, who was indeed the most composed of any at the table, smiled slowly. "I don't know how calm *I* was," he said, "but Young always surprised us." His colleagues laughed, nodding. "We would always have to find the perfect time to talk to Young [who was in a Houston detention center] about his case," he said. "And I would explain it to him very carefully and tell him everything we were planning, and then I would ask, 'Is there anything you need? Anything I can get for you?' It was such a complicated case, and I knew I was giving him a lot of information. And Young would simply reply . . .'" Here everyone leaned in, smiling with anticipation. "'Yes, can you get me some lotion? My skin is really dry.'" The laughter was raucous.

Quickly, however, John's face grew dark. "At the time, John Pogash was the National Juvenile Coordinator at DHS and ICE and the only person who could grant consent for Young to enter state juvenile court." By then, Young's counsel had learned more about and chosen to pursue SIJ status, knowing it would require a Texas family court to determine that Young was eligible for long-term foster care because of abuse, neglect, or abandonment and because it was not in his best interests to return to China. Since Young was initially detained by DHS, only DHS—or more specifically, John Pogash—could consent to this dependency hearing.[8]

Without offering any evidence to refute Young's claims of abandonment or neglect or to support his own denial, Pogash nonetheless refused to consent.[9] As Young neared his eighteenth birthday, his attorneys explained, legal options and time grew increasingly limited: Young would soon be ineligible for SIJ status because Texas family court would no longer have jurisdiction over him. Young's lawyers requested consent to proceed in state court four times. Pogash denied every request.

"He was the 'czar,'" John continued. "I did everything I could with this guy. At a conference we both attended, I took him out for drinks, and at the end of the meeting, I said, 'Please. This case is legitimate. This is serious.' And Pogash, who was clearly all about power, loved it. You could see that. We would have very cordial, informative email exchanges, but then at crunch time, he would pretty much say, 'Mmm . . . No.'

"A key factor to our ultimate success was that I got someone to ask Pogash about the criteria he followed in making a decision to grant permission for a child to go to state court, and on the record he said something like, 'Well, I don't really have any guidelines I follow, I just decide on an individual basis if someone seems believable to me.' This lack of standards allowed us to later appeal under the Administrative Procedures Act, arguing that Pogash was acting in an arbitrary and capricious manner in his determinations of allowing applicants to go to state court. Young should have had permission to go to state court [to get a dependency order for SIJ], and he wouldn't grant it."

Here, John looked at me directly. With uncharacteristic emotion, he added, "Until you get into something like this, you think the government operates fairly. But this seemed like a third-world dictatorship—drugging asylees or refugees and putting them on a plane." He scowled. "The government became *vindictive* that we would try to use the law and procedure to prevent deportation. We were granted permission by the federal judge to go to state court, but an ICE lawyer followed us there and filed an opposition! I mean, he didn't even have standing in family court! But still, the state court judge allowed it." John shook his head.

In January, 2006, the Young Team appealed Pogash's conclusion and sought a preliminary injunction to apply for SIJ status to the federal district court in Houston.[10] DHS sought dismissal of the action, arguing that the court lacked subject matter jurisdiction to consider Zheng's injunction and that Pogash's denial of consent was not an abuse of discretion.[11] Yet at a preliminary injunction hearing on February 13, 2006, District Judge Hittner determined that DHS had indeed abused its discretion in denying Young's requests for specific consent to pursue SIJ status. Young's appeal of the denial of specific consent and his request for a preliminary injunction were granted.

John's disgust with ICE, and his frustration with the US government more generally, were familiar. I traveled to Houston near the end of my field-work. By then, I had already encountered many cause lawyers who expressed and appeared motivated by impatience at what they identified as an inconsistent, ineffective, and ultimately unjust immigration system. Still, it is important to point out that John and the others at our table that day would most likely *not* self-identify as cause lawyers, a detail most prominently indicated by their practice site (see Sarat and Scheingold 2005). At the time of our interview, they worked together at a private Houston firm known for its success in oil and gas litigation. John's primary practice was commercial disputes, and he also specialized in energy projects and transactions. Hannah's focus was business litigation and appeals.

When Maria contacted John and he agreed to accept Young's case pro bono, "it was without any experience working on behalf of unaccompanied youth," he told me. "We were so naïve. We didn't know what we were getting into." Hannah nodded vigorously. According to one case-time summary, John logged over five hundred hours working on it, and Hannah nearly four hundred. Combined with other attorney and timekeeping personnel, the firm granted over fifteen hundred hours to Young's case.

"It was financially and emotionally grueling," said John. "And we've since done other [related] pro bono work—'Know Your Rights' presentations with unaccompanied youth, screenings, you know. And there are compelling, sympathetic stories, but they're not all perfect cases. There was an Indian kid, he was like a Young from India, but he wasn't truthful. He was convinced of his story. It's like it *became* true to him." John was sympathetic. "But we were disappointed. He convinced us, too, and we had to withdraw the application even though the DHS was prepared to give us permission to go to state court. Pro bono work of this magnitude is challenging because you have to be careful and dedicated in order to be successful, but you also have to manage your paying cases and clients because most firms are not going to give too much financial credit to lawyers for pro bono work."

"And pro bono work changes all the time," added Hannah. "At Fulbright,[12] they wanted us to do pro bono, because it was good publicity and would be attractive to potential new hires. But at the smaller firm we're at now, they can't really support it. The attitude is just, 'Do it if you can.'"

For John and Hannah, then, cause lawyering was not so much an identity as it was an opportunity, a choice weighed against other commitments, strategies, firm demands, and professional relationships and reputations. "Pro bono programs in *corporate firms* entail the greatest constraints," write Sarat and Scheingold. "In return for a more than comfortable income, the time open for cause lawyering is very confined, as is the choice of causes and the means to pursue them" (2005, 12; emphasis in original).

Still, John's advocacy on behalf of Young extended far beyond the general expectations of a pro bono program in a corporate firm. As I spent more time with him and his family, it was clear that Young's case had become a uniquely meaningful endeavor, one that represented and profoundly integrated his personal life, religious beliefs, and legal practice. Once Young turned eighteen, he was offered temporary housing through Catholic Charities. He was also invited by John and his spouse, Kriste, to move in with them and their four daughters. He accepted. In 2011, he changed his surname to Sullivan.

"My parents [John and Kriste] really have a great heart," Young told me. "They are—and I'm not, you know, dramatic—they are two of the best people I've ever known—in my entire life. Two people with great heart and genuine desire to help out a person. There's no way I could say no. So I came and lived with them. After a little bit, I start mixing right in, sort of became one of the kids."

Still, however intimate and sustained his relationship with Young, never did John's legal advocacy appear to incite a deliberate reorientation of his career for the singular promotion of "a cause" (see Sarat and Scheingold 2005). He is now a partner at a different Houston firm specializing in oil and gas, and still committed to pro bono service.

WHOSE STORY? EMPATHY AND ENTITLEMENT

Of course, the question this chapter explores is not whether someone is or isn't a cause lawyer. Instead, I am more concerned with the production of a cause, and what I believe to be both its impetus and its outcome—the considered *production of a cause lawyer*. Consequently, the Young Team, while composed of conventional lawyers, is important to consider. As private attorneys, the professional identities and successes of John and Hannah were not entangled with or dependent on a cause in the same way as they were for Maria, the director of a legal advocacy nonprofit, or most of the other lawyers I interviewed for this research. Still, they play a critical role in shaping an account that took on a larger meaning, what Amy Shuman calls "the process of transvaluing the personal to the more than personal" (2005, 4).

The Young Team's shared experience with Young permits a sort of entitlement claim to his story, an intimate understanding evidenced in the assured and profoundly heartfelt retelling I encountered at the sandwich shop in Houston and in later conversations with Young, John, and the rest of the Sullivan family. Yet in the course of my fieldwork—and indeed, even in my first conversation with Maria—many cause lawyers also exhibited or claimed a sense of "ownership" of Young's story, including those who had only anecdotal knowledge of his case. In an ironic and troubling twist, I believe this reappropriation reveals fissures in—and perhaps even thwarts—the relationship and moral commitment presumed intrinsic to cause lawyering (Sarat and Scheingold 1998; see also Menkel-Meadow 1998). "The use of entitlement claims [to others' personal stories] . . . sometimes undermines empathy and the possibility of understanding across differences in experience," writes Amy Shuman. "Often, entitlement claims are alibis for a failure of empathy" (2005, 4).

THE SPECTACULAR CASE: THE THREAT
OF SMUGGLERS, THE THREAT OF FAMILY

> *Cause lawyers, in short, are not simply carriers of a cause but are at the same time its producers: those who shape it, name it, and voice it. (Shamir and Chinski 1998, 231)*

As we find in in the strategic recounting of Young's story, the case was gripping, infuriating, truly spectacular.[13] While the complex motivations underlying Young's migration journey were likely not so different from those of Li or other Fujianese youth—and certainly exceeded the Chinese family firm paradigm Maria offered—it was what he encountered in the US that so vividly initiated and intensified the dramatic storyline. There was a conniving attorney in Chinatown, a youth detention center in Pennsylvania that was eventually closed,[14] shackles at the airport, and John Pogash arbitrarily preventing progress on a viable legal claim.

Yet as the Young Team began considering different legal strategies, and as so many elements of Young's story were correspondingly asserted or defused in the legal realm and later deployed beyond it, I believe the case came to represent all that *could* be wrong with Chinese families, the Chinese state, and "Chinese values"—and more certainly, all that *was* wrong with the US immigration system. In its enduring and broader circulation, it also signified all that was right about cause lawyers. To demonstrate this, I here trace the development of Young's legal case from its inception as a matter of suffering from and resistance to the Chinese government to its eventual conclusion as a narrative of parental neglect and American in/justice.[15]

Young's father was born in Fujian in 1961, his mother in 1963. When Young, their second child, was born in 1988, his mother was forced to pay a five thousand yuan fine and undergo a forced sterilization procedure. She was killed in a car accident in 1996. Young's father remarried the same year. According to Young, sometimes his stepmother beat him.[16]

Young left China in 2003. On January 24, he arrived in the US, where immigration officials quickly identified the counterfeit passport and green card the smugglers had given him. He was detained at the Berks County Youth Center for a year, during which time a private Manhattan Chinatown-based attorney, Henry Zhang, applied for asylum, withholding of removal and protection under Article 3 of the Convention Against Torture (CAT)[17] on Young's behalf. Zhang's argument centered on the "persecution and discrimination" Young and his family encountered from the government's one-child policy (namely the fine and forced sterilization of Young's mother), as well as the "even more prevalent" persecution incurred when Young started school. "His parents had to pay at least double the tuition that other students had to pay."[18] Young would also be persecuted if he returned to China, added Zhang. Because he left unauthorized, Young would be forced to pay heavy fines and jailed.

The IJ was not convinced. Acknowledging *In re C-Y-Z-*,[19] which extended the scope of refugee protection to include the spouses of one-child policy victims, he stated, "I see the Board's decision in *C.Y.Z.* as being based upon the special relationship, or kinship if you will, of one spouse to the other. Essentially they're the nucleus of the family and share that special relationship, thus persecution to one . . . would be accorded deference to the non-persecuted spouse as persecution. I don't believe a child, even a juvenile in this matter, would fit within these parameters." The judge further noted that the forced sterilization took place when Young was a baby and that he had grown up and "seemingly prospered" in China. After all, while Zheng's parents were required to pay increased school tuition, never did Young assert that he was not able to attend school at all.[20]

The IJ denied the application for asylum and withholding of removal that September, and Zhang filed an appeal of the decision with the Board of Immigration Appeals (BIA) days later. The BIA dismissed the appeal in December 2003. The attorney then filed a petition for a review of the BIA's decision.[21] It included the following:

Arguments 5

The IJ agrees that one spouse's persecutory act of forced sterilization can flow to the other spouse, but only because they have a special relationship or kinship of one spouse to the other. The IJ does not find that a relationship between a mother and child fits within these parameters of a special relationship. The IJ did not find that *the persecutory act suffered by the Petitioner's mother flowed to Petitioner*. However, parents and children also have a special relationship or kinship with each other. China's coercive family planning policy does not only affect the mother in a household, but also, the rest of her family. . . . If it were not for *Petitioner's mother's resistance toward China's coercive family planning policy*, Petitioner would not have been persecuted and discriminated against at all.

B.3. Petitioner has a well-founded fear of future persecution if he is returned to China. . . . If he returns to China, *he will continue to be persecuted solely on account of his mother's resistance to the coercive family planning policy*. (emphasis added)

While Zhang's argument is not particularly convincing, the above sections are still significant. As the first instance or "draft" of a legal and family narrative, we find here the tentative creation and delineation—however contradictory—of Young's mother's role. There is a special relationship or kinship between a mother and child, writes Zhang, enough so that "the persecutory act" suffered by Young's mother intimately affected Young. Yet almost immediately, Young's mother is no longer presented as a victim of persecution. Instead, she is portrayed as culpable, someone who *resisted* China's family planning policy and left a son vulnerable to ongoing discrimination. The blame shifts.

In June 2004, the US Third Circuit Court of Appeals upheld the BIA and IJ's ruling. In the government's response, Young's asylum claim was reexamined. It is significant that in the case's early stages, the decision to migrate was presented as one Young and his father made together: "Zheng did not learn that his mother had been forcibly sterilized until approximately 2000 or 2001, after asking his father why he had to pay higher tuition rates at school. Zheng thus told his father that he did not want to stay in China because of the discrimination to which he was subjected, and his father found a way to help him get to the US in 2003."

Ultimately, the Third Circuit confirmed that the IJ and BIA properly denied Young's requests for asylum and withholding of removal to China. "Zheng was merely a young man who sought to leave China because he did not like paying higher tuition fees for his education and felt he was discriminated against as an extra birth child," the document states. "To rule otherwise would, as at least one Circuit has recognized, 'effectively open our borders to unlimited immigration.'"[22]

After the Pennsylvania facility was closed down, Young was moved to an ORR-managed detention center in Chicago. He remained there until July 22, 2004, or about a month and a half after the US Third Circuit Court of Appeals affirmed the denial of his original asylum claim. In July, Young was released for family reunification with his uncle in Ohio, with monthly reporting requirements to the DHS office in Cleveland, Ohio. He began attending school and earned a four-point grade point average.

According to an affidavit Young made in May 2005, as soon as he was reunited with his uncle in Akron, snakehead smugglers began calling the uncle and demanding immediate payment of Young's smuggling debt. Young also learned that smugglers had begun visiting his father and stepmother in Fuzhou:

> My father told me that my parents are very afraid the smugglers will torture and/or kill them. My father also explained to me that the police visited him and demanded that he pay the smugglers. Smugglers have little impact in the United States, and my father explained to me that as long as I remain in the United States, I would be safe. My understanding is that my uncle and my father are being threatened because they are my sponsors in the smuggling agreement.[23]

In February 2005, DHS officials told Young he needed to report to them only every three months. When he did not arrive to the office in March, an officer called Young and requested that he come to the Cleveland office. An appointment was set for April 5, 2005. When he arrived in Cleveland, Young was informed he would be deported to China. He was shackled and taken to the shelter where he had previously stayed in Chicago, where he met with Maria and was able to speak with his attorney and family members in China.

The next day, Young was transported in a van to the airport. Upon arriving, he hit his head against a wall and blacked out. He spent that night in Chicago and the next day was flown to Houston, Texas, where he was placed in a Southwest Key secure immigrant-youth shelter. His affidavit continues:

> My father has explained to me that if I returned to China my life will be in danger. If I return, the smugglers will try to kill my family and torture me. The thought of returning to China and placing my family and me in danger terrifies me. I fear for my own life and the lives of my family. . . . My father and stepmother have told me that they are terrified of the smugglers. They also told me on May 19th, 2005 not to come home. If I am deported to China, the smugglers will find me, torture me and could eventually kill me. The smugglers have also threatened my family and I fear for their lives and safety.

With its considerable emphasis on the threats posed by snakehead smugglers, this affidavit, filed by the Young Team on May 26, 2005, was included in a motion to stay enforcement of the Third Circuit decision that had rejected the appeal filed by Young's original attorney, Henry Zhang. At this point, Young had been in the Southwest Key facility for over a month and a half. He had fired Henry Zhang, and John Sullivan, initially contacted by Maria, had agreed to take on the case pro bono.

The first thing John did was submit a Brief in Support of Respondent's Motion to Re-open and Remand and Motion to Stay Removal (dated May 25, 2005).[24] It begins:

> Every once in a while, a case comes along that truly cries out for justice in a crowded judicial system and tugs at the heart strings of us all. In such a case, the bar waits with bated breath in the hope that justice will indeed be served. In such a case, those raised in America expect that our system of justice will indeed do honor to the unalienable rights that we all believe to be self-evident. This is such a case.
>
> Young Zheng is an exemplary seventeen-year-old boy who, if deported, will not be greeted by the warm embrace of his parents who have now abandoned him, but rather by the wrath of unpaid

"snakeheads" (human smugglers) who brought him to the United States and who have repeatedly threatened his torture and death.

The primary argument in this brief was that new facts, namely the smugglers' threats, had been raised since the BIA's original decision, which could form the basis for a new CAT claim. The brief continues:

It is reasonably likely that Young will prove to the IJ that it is more likely than not that he will be tortured and murdered by the smugglers if he returns to China.

Young Zheng lived in Fujian Province in China. In an effort to provide Young with better opportunities and to free him from continued discrimination, Young's father and uncle arranged for him to be smuggled out of China. Young's family agreed to pay the snakeheads approximately $60,000 to help Young escape.

Young is truly terrified of the smugglers. His father told him on May 19, 2005 not to come home, that Young is not his son anymore. If Young is deported to China, the smugglers have said that they will find him, torture him, and eventually kill Young and his family. Young has nowhere to turn for help other than this Board, through this motion to re-open and remand and motion to stay removal.

It is well-established that torture and murder by smugglers in China occurs and occurs with the acquiescence and support of the Chinese government. . . . Within Fujian, family pride and community pressure have led to a general complacency by local officials and the community toward snakehead activities. . . . Sadly, in a recent telephone call with Young and his father in China, Young's father stated that he cannot return home and that Young is no longer his son. Young's father told Young never to call him again. Young's counsel therefore is proceeding to confirm Young's father's intent to abandon his child and is working to secure SIJS for Young. Young has no one to return "home" to in China if he is deported. Young will be homeless. Further, Young will be confined by the government and tortured by the smugglers with no one to even attempt to protect him or to help him try to escape.

Our own constitution protects children from death, even as punishment for their own heinous crimes. Young has committed no crime. His father and uncle arranged to have him smuggled to the US. Even if

Young played a role in the decision to come to the US via smugglers, which he did not, Young was only fourteen years old at the time. In the US, we do not allow fourteen-year-olds to be sentenced to death for their crimes. . . . The US should protect all children within its borders from the evils of torture and murder. Young is an unaccompanied child in need of and eligible for protection under US' asylum law and the CAT, as well as the US constitution.

He is a child with a dream—the American dream—and he has shown this Board and every person he has interacted with, from his teachers to his detention officers to his attorneys, that he has the perseverance, dedication, resilience, and heart to achieve it.

As a rousing, melodramatic incitation—"a case comes along that truly cries out for justice . . . the bar waits with bated breath . . . he is a child with a dream"—as well as a frenetic portrayal of Young and his family, this document is particularly significant in the development of the "spectacular case." Of course, it is also important to consider the context in which the brief was produced. Recall John's description of the early days of the Young Team: "We were so naïve; we didn't know what we were getting into." In just over a month, and in addition to other professional obligations, the attorneys familiarized themselves with Young's story and compiled and filed the motion. As John explained, the initial strategy to emphasize the smugglers' death threats was largely based on the advice of an immigration professor at the University of Texas.

This tactic is overwhelmingly apparent in subsequent motions, in which a compelling, urgent argument is made: "It is reasonably likely that Young will prove to the IJ that it is more likely than not that he will be tortured and murdered by the smugglers if he returns to China." This is further underscored in excerpts from a letter of support submitted by Maria on May 11, 2005: "I am writing to express my extreme concern about Zheng, Young's situation. . . . Young is a good, well behaved teenaged boy. . . . I am very concerned that it is not safe for Zheng, Young to return to China. . . . Young's family [told him] 'you must not come back to China; because the smugglers will know about your case and they will kill you and will kill us.'"

Yet alongside the largely anecdotal and insistent, almost tedious emphasis on snakehead threats, we also find in these documents the development of a parallel and progressively more dominant family narrative.

Similar to the "Grand Narrative" detailed in Chapter 4, the account outlines two corresponding tropes: the deviant parent and the vulnerable, dependent child. Here, these characters are still underdeveloped. Their existence is peripheral, malleable.

At one point, Young's family members appear to act in Young's best interests: "In an effort to provide Young with better opportunities and to free him from continued discrimination, Young's father and uncle arranged for him to be smuggled out of China." As the smugglers' threats escalate, both his father and uncle stress that Young must stay in the US, presumably for his own safety: "His father told him on May 19, 2005 not to come home, that Young is not his son anymore. If Young is deported to China, the smugglers have said that they will find him, torture him, and eventually kill Young and his family."

Yet as the case develops—and, significantly, as the Young Team becomes more familiar with SIJ status—Young's father emerges as himself responsible for Young's smuggling. "His father told him . . . that Young is not his son anymore. . . . If deported, [he] will not be greeted by the warm embrace of his parents who have now abandoned him." Together with the increasingly deviant parent, we also find the development of a dependent child. "Young has nowhere to turn for help other than this Board. . . . Even if Young played a role in the decision to come to the US via smugglers, which he did not, Young was only fourteen years old at the time. . . . Young is a good, well behaved teenaged boy."

Of course, Young is not just a child "who is only acting at the adult's direction," as many Fujianese youth tend to be characterized in the legal strategies I discuss elsewhere. Though ostensibly featured to underscore smugglers' threats, Young is nonetheless celebrated in these early documents for acting independently, and for *not* doing what was expected of him. "Young is not like most smugglees who are returned to China because he was released from detention and *could have* gone underground, worked illegally, and paid the snakeheads but *did not*, instead going to school" (emphasis in original).[25]

Notably, while Young's counsel was working to demonstrate to the government the young man's "perseverance, dedication, resilience, and heart" despite the tremendous fears he had about the smugglers, Young himself was strategically emphasizing his fear of the US immigration system to his family to justify attending school. As he explained to me, "Fortunately enough, my record was with immigration. I actually *had* to go to school. It's not an option. It worked out in my favor. Because otherwise I would not have an excuse to tell all the people in my family why I go to school, because I was supposed to be working, pay back the money. So I never told them that. I kept it secret. I'm really happy that [I was apprehended]. So I get up at six, go to school, take the bus to Akron, come back, take the bus, you know—snowy day, same thing."

EXPECTATIONS AND EXCEPTIONALISM

Used by the Young Team to incite sympathy and admiration, and by Young to deflect family expectations and economic obligations, Young's American education is a significant component in his case's development. This is not surprising: school is a recognizable space in which to chart developmental markers. And as we find in the supplemental letters of support provided by Young's teachers in Ohio and Southwest Key, it is a way to distinguish an individual's propensity for hard work, cooperation, responsibility, rationality, and other qualities associated with good citizenship: "Young Zheng is a very ambitious young man who has great educational plans for his future."[26]

Consider also the connection between "deservingness" and *self-management* in the context of education. Not only are schools nexuses of internal discipline, surveillance, and order (Foucault 1991, 165) but, writes Michael Peters, they are also sites in which contemporary "entrepreneurial selves" are cultivated. To Peters, the entrepreneurial self represents a necessary cultural—or in the case at hand, moral or civic—shift from dependency to self-reliance, a "responsibilising [*sic*] of the self": "It is the relationship, promoted by neo-liberalism, that *one establishes to oneself* through forms of personal investment . . . that becomes the central ethical component of a new individualised and privatised consumer welfare economy. . . . [Here] education and training are key sectors in promoting national economic competitive advantage and future national prosperity" (2001, 60; emphasis in original).

Peters' argument is relevant, for in tracing Young's case documents we can distinguish between what is clearly a "proper" kind of "responsibilising," namely the fostering of a self-controlled, globally competitive, highly skilled citizen (or citizen aspirant) via education—"Young is a good, well behaved teenaged boy"[27] and "Young [wishes to] finish school and chase his dream of becoming a biologist"[28]—and "improper" responsibility, the illicit underground employment Young would otherwise pursue, a commitment that would benefit neither the state nor, presumably, the individual. One advocate described him as follows: "Young Zheng is a bright young man who spends most of his time reading and doing extra homework. He is very well behaved. . . . If given an opportunity to stay in the United States he will be very successful in life."[29] Another vouched: "Young Zheng is a well behaved, cooperative young man. . . . [He] has voiced his significant desire to reside in the United States . . . this is part of his life-long goal (to obtain a better education)."[30]

The emphasis on education also extends to and permits an inherent moral claim about Young's family. Recall from Chapter 4 the comment made by one cause lawyer: "I say to [Fujianese clients], 'Your mom might be a good person, but once parents choose to have children, that's a job they're choosing to fulfill. And so we're not saying anyone's a bad person, we're saying that maybe they just weren't as good at this specific job in their life.'" By expecting Young to work rather than pursue an American education, Young's parents do not fulfill their proper role as parents. They are *different* from Young; their personal goals are not as commendable as his. It is a singular interpretation, and one that effectively rejects other conceivable claims about Young's family, including the notion that if Young performs well in school, a symbolically "American" endeavor,[31] his parents could be presumed to have helped cultivate their child's character and aspirations (Morando Lakhani 2013). It also puts forth and perpetuates an arguably Western and sacrilized childhood ideal, one that negates the socially specific value accorded youths' labor and may even render youth more vulnerable to underground employment and exploitation (Nieuwenhuys 1996; Zelizer 1985; see also Qvortrup 1999). Consider here a recorded statement made by Young's father, Yu Ping, during a call with John Sullivan:

I do not want to talk to this son anymore, and I don't want to have anything to do with this one because he put my family in a jam, not just financially. . . . I need to tell you the mistake he make [*sic*], because, you know, we are living in the village. You need members of the family to support the family. He only wants to go to school. In reality, in our village, if you cannot support yourself, you are not going to school. And we have a lot of difference of opinion, you know, so he did not want to accept the fact and reality to help and work instead of going to school.[32]

Without dismissing the very intimate consequences of lawyers' efforts to elicit statements such as this, I want here to consider the unique context from which Yu Ping's words may have emerged. Recall again the complex negotiations of Fujianese youth as "lagging" and "leading": as unaccompanied migrants, these young people are often identified as leaders in their families and communities of origin via their own skilled management of their migration, legality, and labor. Yet in both Fuzhou and the US, youth like Young may simultaneously and somewhat despairingly self-identify as lagging behind other Chinese nationals and their American peers, as well as behind distinctly Western markers of adulthood and success.[33]

In Young's father's statement, we find frustration over Young's rejection of what is likely a locally valued identity, the opportunity to "lead" by providing his family with a particular kind of social and economic capital. Yet at this point, Young had been in the US—and for the most part, in US detention centers—for two years. To the reader, it is perhaps unsurprising that his solution to financial, social, and perhaps even legal success was in the resolute pursuit of education: "Fortunately enough, my record was with immigration. I actually had to go to school . . . otherwise I would not have an excuse to tell all the people in my family why I go." In the shifting spaces of expectation and opportunity that Young and his father occupy, Young has, in a sense, "abandoned" his father. And in the realm of law—and to Young's sorrow—his father's own abandonment of him is amplified. Here Yu Ping is inscrutable and aberrant, a criminal.[34]

There is another corollary to the depiction of Young as deserving and wanting of an American education, a future, a dream: "a child with a dream—the American dream," as John wrote. What Young has "found" in the US is indisputably lacking in Fujian. Recall the universal child model put forth by advocacy organizations, the popular imagery of disappearing, lost, or stolen childhoods (Chapter 2). Though Young is only *sometimes* an "unusually vulnerable child," most obviously in relation to dangerous snakehead smugglers, the possibility of a "normal" childhood in China remains perpetually unimaginable. "The bar waits with bated breath" to ensure it is not stolen now.

As Young is celebrated in these documents as capable, resilient, and worthy of American education and justice (i.e., citizenship), his family, his community, and his culture of origin are inferred as negligent, dangerous, and corrupt. Consider this parallel:

It is well-established that torture and murder by smugglers in China occurs and occurs with the acquiescence and support of the Chinese government. . . . Within Fujian, family pride and community pressure have led to a general complacency by local officials and the community toward snakehead activities. . . . In the US, we do not allow fourteen-year-olds to be sentenced to death for their crimes. . . . The US should protect all children within its borders from the evils of torture and murder.[35]

While not always so pronounced, this comparison is also not new. Much of the data I collected exhibits an inherent strain of American exceptionalism[36]—a (mostly) unspoken confidence in an ideology of individuality and individual freedoms; opportunities for social and economic mobility; American education; and the "American Dream"—alongside a more disparaging portrayal of Chinese families and/or society. Consider this depiction of "Mei," a pseudonymous youth described to me by an international children's rights expert: "In so many ways, Mei is an American success story. She is a success because of her courage, her resilience, and her hard work. And a success because in her case, the systems set up to protect children in the United States eventually worked. Mei was born into the family of two unemployed parents in Fujian province, China. My mom is illiterate [Mei said]. She doesn't even speak Mandarin Chinese."[37]

Although Mei is significantly *not* presented as a child victim in this vignette, it is equally notable that she, like Young, is celebrated for her "American" qualities of courage, resilience, and hard work, while her parents are simultaneously castigated as poor and illiterate Fujianese. The narrative is familiar. In my research, an image of Chinese parents as allegedly "un-American" (not valuing education, unemployed, and/or financially dependent on their children) was as pervasive as—and certainly connected to—the arguably necessitated legal framing of parents as deviant, coercive, and neglectful. An amicus brief[38] supporting Young's eligibility for SIJ status correspondingly states: "It is in Young's best interest to terminate Young's father's rights because . . . Young [should] be cared for by individuals who, unlike his father, desire to have Young be a part of their family. . . . Young has plans to eventually become a biologist and those who seek his custody [in the US] are likely to help him pursue those goals."[39]

While likely loath to consider it, lawyers' assertions of American exceptionalism are powerfully rooted in a history and ideology of American gatekeeping—one that is, of course, intimately connected with early Chinese migration to the US. The first instance of immigration restriction in the US was the Chinese Exclusion Act of 1882, which depended on and perpetuated stereotypes of Chinese as racially inferior, crafty, dishonest, and unwilling and incapable of assimilation (Lee 2003, 24–29; see also Leong 2000; Statz 2016b). Just as these stereotypes reinforced white supremacy in the early twentieth century, so also do the claims cause lawyers make about Chinese parents reinforce implicit assumptions of the superiority of US law, education, and family systems today. "Chinese families don't trust pro bono help," one attorney told me. "They don't understand that shelter care is good, that even if it delays kids working it gives them the opportunity to learn English. I don't think families quite get that. Or they may not value education, which is a big issue, too."

In a sense underscoring the significance of the "entrepreneurial self," Annette Appell writes, "The [American] legal regulation of children assigns responsibility for their development to families, schools, and professionals, with regulations primarily operating through . . . educational standards and assessments, safety requirements, and a general presumption against paid child labor. . . . All of these regulations aim to shepherd children into a self-sufficient, democratic, productive, and autonomous adulthood" (2009, 709). Accordingly, when individuals cannot meet their responsibilities as parents—"We're not saying anyone's a bad person, we're saying that maybe they just weren't as good at this specific job"—it is presumably up to someone else, here the cause lawyer, to shape and script the youth as having the capacity for education, good citizenship, and the "responsibilising" that produces an independent adult with national value.

When I described my frustration with attorneys' claims to a law professor who specializes in children's rights, he nodded knowingly. "What you're finding meets a narrative that's an important part of American culture. It's all about an American savior, particularly [when it comes to] immigrant kids. We use children for broader purposes, and demonizing parents is a well-worn idea. Atomizing children and seeing them as unconnected to family is part of what we do. . . . That's why repatriation is not an option, right? Children are better off in the United States."

Whether unambiguously or subconsciously rooted in American exceptionalism, attorneys' condescending language about clients' parents may also be somewhat strategic. If parents are uneducated, devious, and coercive, then they don't have to be—and indeed *shouldn't* be—included in the legal process.

"I don't talk to the parents," one attorney told me and laughed. "What holds these kids back from being able to succeed are their parents, sometimes. Now other times, that's not the case whatsoever. There are some instances where I think the parents didn't know what they were getting the kids into, and they're devastated as well."

"How do you establish a relationship with a client's parents?" I asked Rachel, another cause lawyer.

"Well," she said, "the relationship between the attorney and the child is going to be between the attorney and the child. The parent is, you know, somebody who can be useful to provide information that may be helpful to the claim. . . . And it's tempting to want to keep the parent apprised of the situation. The parent will often seem to be acting in the child's best interests, but you never know—we might discover later that there was a bad situation going on."

Unlike Rachel, who was merely suspicious of Fujianese parents, Joan explicitly dismissed them altogether: "It's hard, because parents have a really heavy Fujianese accent when they're speaking. And most of them are uneducated. It's hard to get through to them the idea of like, the legal benefit or whatever. And I feel like with them—" she paused. "This sounds bad. With the kids, I tell them as much information as they need to make a good decision. With the parents, I try to push them a little bit, to be like, 'No. This is good for [your kid]. If your kid doesn't do this legally, then . . .' There are less qualifiers that go into it. Because I think they would just get confused. They wouldn't understand."

"YOUNG SAVED ME"

Many of the documents the Young Team submitted in the course of Young's case rely on the binaries I discuss elsewhere. Young's parents are not "proper" parents, while Young is accordingly vulnerable and dependent (on the Board, the legal system, American justice). Young is resilient, courageous, educable, and a child with an American dream; his Chinese parents are mysterious and suspect. Fujianese culture is complacent and corrupt; the US is safe and just.

Still, as evidenced in conversations and case documents, the Young Team avoided any vigorous condemnation of Young's family. This likely owes to these attorneys' lack of familiarity with and limited professional commitment to—or dependence on—unaccompanied Fujianese youth as a "cause." The Young Team's conventional practice setting also matters for another reason: while every cause lawyer I interviewed expressed frustration with US immigration, their critiques were often restrained. This, of course, is not surprising. As already highlighted, most of these attorneys are generally constrained by their reliance on the funding, and therefore the management, of federal bureaucracy. The Young Team, on the other hand, had the relative luxury of being private practitioners and, accordingly, the independence to identify the opaque, exasperatingly erratic dealings of DHS—as well as the broader failings of American justice in the immigration system—as an explicit and even inspiring motivation for pro bono immigration advocacy.

This motivation is celebrated in a series entitled "The Asylum Wars: The Am Law 200's favorite pro bono cause is now a morass of arbitrary decisions, angry federal judges, and dubious policy choices" in *The American Lawyer*:

> Other lawyers say they are galvanized by the injustice they see in the system. Fulbright's John Sullivan is one of them. Since taking on Young Zheng's case, he's helped organize about two dozen lawyers at his firm to take on six more cases. And he has no plans to back down. "If anything, it's made me feel like there need to be firms with resources to go against the government," he says. . . . "[Immigration officials] wouldn't talk to us. . . . It was pretty unbelievable that the government was doing what it was doing. I'm used to dealing with professional lawyers. We may disagree, but at least they'll talk to me." (Amon 2006, 18–20)

Yet in turning from these maddening encounters with the US government, and in particular John's experiences with John Pogash, we find that Young's SIJ claim is relatively matter-of-fact, particularly as regards the establishment of parental neglect and Young's best interests. In *Zheng v. Pogash*, holding that Young was entitled to seek SIJ status, the gripping narrative of family, culture, nation, and justice is largely absent. There is some understated sympathy, but the analysis ultimately presents Young's case through an explicit, almost *simple* legal framework, tracing its successive fulfillment of the requisite elements for a preliminary injunction, including a likelihood of success in Texas family court:

> Zheng presented ample evidence supporting his father's abandonment of him, including his father's testimony from China. While a transcript

loses some of the speaker's inflection, his father's testimony is sadly unmistakable: Zheng's father has publicly disowned his son.

Zheng's father shipped him to the United States via international smugglers, arranging for Zheng to be responsible for paying his journey here. . . . It is substantially likely a state court would determine that Zheng's situation constitutes neglect.[40]

Next, Zheng must convince the state court it is not in his best interests to return to China. Zheng's father testified that he had received threats—albeit some of them veiled—about Zheng's failure to begin repayment. These threats were sufficient to cause Zheng's father to publicly disown his son. DHS argues the Snakeheads will leave Zheng alone in China because he did not successfully enter the United States, thereby never incurring a smuggling debt. However, the Court agrees with Zheng's arguments that his situation is somewhat atypical; most immigrants detained and deported do not have to repay their smuggling fee because the smugglers were not successful in securing the immigrants' entry into the country. However, after his detention, Zheng was released to his uncle's care. Zheng contends his release triggered the Snakeheads' belief that they had completed their end of the smuggling bargain . . . he will be in danger if he returns to his home country.[41]

Of course, at this point in Young's case, "fitting" the client into the statutory demands of the SIJ framework had already occurred much earlier, perhaps most compellingly and convincingly in the translated transcript of John's phone call with Young's father—"Young's father stated that he cannot return home and that Young is no longer his son." Now the issue was less about appealing to the limited language of legal relief than about *accessing* an opportunity for legal relief.

In an email he sent to me describing this intense period, John wrote with characteristic equanimity, "The judge reversed it and ordered the DHS to allow us to proceed to state family court. We had to do this before Young turned eighteen so it was a bit of a rush down the stretch but all worked out of course in the Lord's providence."

Hannah was less composed. When we talked together in Houston, she reflected, "Once we finally made it to family court, Young had a small army of Fulbright attorneys behind him!" She laughed, delighted. "There were twelve attorneys packed into the associate judge's quarters during the hearing.[42] Of course, this was when Young was about to turn eighteen, and I had heard through the grapevine that Pogash was angry and planning to move Young to adult detention. I mean, we had already prevailed; we were just waiting on a visa! John [Sullivan] had to show up at 12:00 a.m. on Young's eighteenth birthday to pick him up. Young, who came out of the shelter right at midnight, was carrying the box with everything he owned. My dad was visiting at the time, and so we surprised them with a birthday cake on the street in front of the shelter." She laughed again. As she spoke, John smiled, remembering, and shook his head. "Young was thrilled to see us, and to see the cake! And he asked right away, 'Do you have any milk?'"

"We had really good publicity and press at this point in the proceedings," John added. "Tons of letters, gifts. Lots of letters saying, 'I'll adopt Young!' People were so generous that we were able to set up a trust for Young, the money of which is paying for most of his college education."

Hannah nodded. Her expression turned pensive. "This was a really tough time for me," she stated. "I remember praying with my son at night, 'Please help Mama help Young.' My faith really faltered—my faith in law, and my faith-faith. I had gone through a divorce and stopped going to church, but this time I started going to church again. I didn't save Young; Young saved me. It was mutual."

THE REMEDY TO TRAGEDY: EXPLAINING
THE CAUSE AND THE CAUSE LAWYER

While the Young Team certainly employed the selective "scripting" of family and community I explore in Chapter 5, most overtly in their emphasis on and interpretation of Young's father's testimony, their overwhelmingly positive presentation of Young within *and beyond* the legal realm is perhaps more significant. As demonstrated above, the Young Team viewed their experience as legal—and certainly personal—advocates for Young as a sustained, meaningful, and even spiritual endeavor. In many ways, this interpretation of the case typifies cause lawyering, even as the cause itself appears to steadily evolve and surprise and, ultimately, close. Initially taken by the urgency and proximity of the case, Young's attorneys were increasingly spurred by the arbitrariness they encountered in DHS, a motivation that in some ways exceeded their service to Young (see McCann 1994; Sarat and Scheingold 2005). They also attributed their success to hard work, faith, the support of other colleagues, and, significantly, to Young himself—a clear, though in many ways equally naïve, partner in this experience (Sarat and Scheingold 1998).

In case documents and conversations, Young's attorneys recalled an intimate experience of frustration and anxiety as well as of clarity, purpose, and empathy. The story they shared was heartrending but also redemptive. Here, tense matters. Indeed, it powerfully signals a break with the cause lawyering literature, or at least reiterates that the Young Team is on the end of the "cause lawyering continuum" in which opportunities to do good are valued and taken on but still secondary to the lawyers' service to paying clients.

In other words, that story has concluded, and it ended well.

Nearly ten years after they took on his case, Young was still present in these individuals' lives. By the time I interviewed him, Young was a graduate student with citizenship—and John and the others continued to extol his ambition and self-sufficiency. This time, however, they did so as friends, mentors, a guardian. Young was as droll now as in Southwest Key, reported John, and as easy-going with the Sullivan family as when he first joined them in 2006.

How startling, then, to return to the simple, largely tragic, and ostensibly absolute version of Young's story detailed at the beginning of this chapter. "The promotion of personal narratives as 'real,'" writes Amy Shuman, "is particularly common in popular uses of local narratives that have been removed from their local contexts and that are then used to persuade or inspire distant listeners. Those uses of personal narratives make an unapologetic claim to the reality of personal experience and often *an equally unapologetic display of pathos in their invocation of others' experiences as pitiable to evoke sentimentality*" (2005, 10; emphasis added).

In many of the versions of Young's story, and most specifically those constructed and circulated by cause lawyers, we find an "unapologetic display of pathos." Notably, this tragic quality is largely absent from Young and his lawyers' (however impassioned) account of his journey to the US and, in particular, through the US immigration system. The absence of this tragedy is attributable not only to the intimately felt complexity and span of the Young Team's shared experience with Young—one in which his despair at the airport was but one of many facets of a personal narrative—but also to the fact that this grief was not *necessary* to their immediate or long-term professional goals.

As I establish above, by virtue of their practice site and the resources it provided, these attorneys did not rely on a cause for personal or professional validation. More specifically to Young's case, as conventional lawyers they had the autonomy to focus less on ambiguous understandings of age, Chinese families, and Chinese culture and to instead aggressively and explicitly challenge the erratic dealings of DHS. In contrast, immigration cause lawyers, many of whom receive funding and diffuse but often very dominating oversight from ORR, are largely unable or unwilling to contest the practices of ORR or other federal agencies. As immigration advocacy organizations vie for federal funding and private support, the tragic figure of the unaccompanied Chinese youth emerges as something of a vocation. She or he provides an opportunity for cause lawyers to establish expertise, legitimacy, and subjective jurisdiction (Abbott 1988) in an otherwise competitive "cause market."

At the same time, I am not convinced that funding limitations and professional dependence fully explain the "representative anecdote" (see Burke 1989, 153) many cause lawyers publicize of Young, one that actively downplays or dismisses the role of the government in his case and instead relies almost exclusively on a spectacular figure of Young as desperate and dependent. Consider, for instance, an account included on the website of the Young Center, the organization Maria founded and directs. At the time of this research, the organization, named in honor of Young Zheng, was unique among immigrant advocacy organizations in specifically developing and promoting the use of child advocates (guardians ad litem) to determine the best interests of unaccompanied youth in removal proceedings:[43]

> The Young Center for Immigrant Children's Rights pays tribute to
> the children we serve by naming the organization after one of our first
> clients, Young Zheng, a young man from China who was smuggled
> by ruthless traffickers at the age of 14. . . . In fear for his life, Young
> endured more than two years of detention and legal battles to remain in
> the US. All the while, his Child Advocate stood by him, advocated for
> his release and against deportation. Young Zheng has finished college,
> was granted citizenship, and has been accepted in the biotechnology
> program at Texas A&M University. He has graciously lent his name to
> this organization.[44]

Young, and a specific retelling of Young's story, clearly played a profound and meaningful role in Maria's personal and professional commitment to young migrants, even though she was relatively distanced from the actual progression of Young's legal case and his life course. As we find above, however, her *entitlement* to his story remains critical, particularly when the narrative is used to signal that a child advocate, or perhaps the organization, effects the critical transition from ruthlessness, isolation, and despair to freedom, justice, and success. In many ways, this is exemplary of the personal narrative Shuman describes, one stripped of context and intended to inspire.

A similar entitlement claim is featured on the website of another legal advocacy organization that works on behalf of unaccompanied minors. It is worth noting that the pseudonymous Mei featured here is distinct from the *other* "representative" Mei described earlier in the chapter:

> "Mei" is a young girl from China. . . . Mei's family is very poor. They told Mei that she could "help" to pay back the money by working off the debt in the US. In other words, it appears that Mei—a child with no skills and no English ability—was sent to the US for forced labor.
>
> Mei's case *is now being handled by a well-respected law firm. And, her situation has improved considerably.* . . . Mei is going to a local high school and is learning to speak English. She is very happy. . . . "I am very proud of the results that we've obtained so far," the attorney said. "I believe that KIND's efforts literally have saved a life."[45] (emphasis added)

Instead of the deeply personal, collaborative experience the Young Team described as they recalled their work on behalf of Young—"I didn't save Young; Young saved me. It was mutual"—we see in the above excerpts a different version of legal advocacy, or, more accurately, a more pronounced version of the *legal advocate*.

Undoubtedly, the narrative coupling of an endangered, unhappy, and poor child with a steadfast, prepared, and altruistic attorney certainly helps establish the worthiness of an organization for funding and public support. Yet the pathos we find highlighted in lawyers' presentations of Young's and Mei's stories also underscores the earlier critique of empathy: "Often, entitlement claims are alibis for a failure of empathy" (Shuman 2005, 4).

In this particular context, a failure of empathy is often recast as the *impossibility* of empathy: to many immigration cause lawyers, the opportunity to provide the same sort of individualized and rigorous advocacy as Young's attorneys is, or seems, foreclosed for complex structural, professional, and even moral reasons.

I devote this chapter to Young's legal case because it illuminates the most unsettling and "impossible" aspect of immigration cause lawyers' assumed empathy. However useful in its commodified form, the spectacular case remains just that: spectacular. As we find above, Young is featured in nonprofit publicity and popular press because he is meant to be representative of unaccompanied Fujianese minors: "The situation of all of the kids coming from China actually is nearly identical to Young Zheng's story," as Maria noted. A victim to his family and culture, Young demonstrates the utter despair and panic that Fujianese youth are presumed to feel about their personal lives and migration journeys, as well as their utter reliance on legal advocacy.

Yet as we move from Maria's and other media accounts to Young and the Young Team's retelling of the story, it proves entirely exceptional. Young was an unaccompanied migrant with unique and sustained legal advocacy that wasn't limited in time, resources, or autonomy or preoccupied with strategically proving itself as a "cause." And in the American imagination, Young's was also a relatively straightforward success story: he independently, or together with his lawyers, left a seemingly corrupt nation and a coercive family to achieve explicit markers of adulthood and success like education and citizenship. The majority of Fujianese youth are not like these portrayals of Young. Indeed, even *Young* may not be exactly like cause lawyers' descriptions.[46] Instead, many unaccompanied Fujianese youth tend to be more similar to Li, demonstrating an ambiguous but comfortable *and even confident* understanding of migration, legality, and labor to their attorneys.

As most of the cause lawyers I interviewed for this research acknowledged, young Fujianese migrants—including those who have successfully obtained legal status—will likely work off their smuggling debt in underground and/or exploitative work settings. Many will continue to send remittances to family members in Fuzhou, including those parents framed as "coercive and neglectful" in the legal realm. Many will not pursue an American education, choosing instead to pay off debt, save money, and someday open their own restaurants or nail salons. And perhaps most unsettling, the majority of these youth are often relatively forthright about such uneasy existences. Many identify nothing tragic about their journeys or goals.

This absence of tragedy leaves no room for empathy, for sentimentality, or for marketability. More important still, I believe it leaves immigration cause lawyers with a fraught cause—or sometimes with no cause at all. As Young's story is re/constructed by these lawyers and circulated beyond the legal realm to journalists, prospective donors, volunteers, political actors, and colleagues, it is "owned" as a mission but not a memory. It is a way in which legal advocates establish the worthiness of the cause to others and, in the face of so many "impossible," ambiguous, and far more *representative* cases, to themselves.

6 *Limited Relief*

It may also be the case that the same *lawyers simultaneously pursue different—and perhaps—competing projects. For instance, their actions may both enhance civil and political rights while undercutting economic and social ones; they may both promote access to justice through pro bono service while undermining it through practice restrictions. This duality also leaves open the possibility that individual lawyers may believe that they are advancing the cause of justice, when other observers would argue that they are in fact thwarting it. (Scott Cummings 2011, 2;* emphasis in original*)*

SUBVERTING LEGAL "SUCCESS"

That legal status matters to immigration cause lawyers is self-evident, and almost insultingly so. Yet when I pressed attorneys to articulate *why* it matters, and what it provides Fujianese clients, my questions proved uneasy and at times destabilizing. In some interviews, I received only bright, pithy responses: "As immigration attorneys, we're just protecting the child," maintained one New York lawyer. "That's really our mission." Others were more on point, though no more forthcoming: "In our world, I guess success means residency," stated an attorney. "Or it means a legal form to stay in the country where [youth] don't have to worry about being picked up."

For Lana, legal success was intrinsically connected to choice: "I think I've maybe had two successful cases, *ever*," she said coarsely. "And I've probably won a hundred. And I consider two successful. I've never lost one case. My two successful ones are my two girls who are going to college, and who are doing what they want to do with their own lives. And that's it. And, you know, it's so grand that you get a green card. It's like, great, good, you got a green card; you got a visa. I'm not helping your life. Your life is still this horrible cycle, and maybe I've alleviated one part of the pressure, and it's—to be honest, it's really hard for me to think about. It just makes me really depressed."

While Lana's definition of success interests me, so too does her unguarded admission at the end: "to be honest, it's really hard for me to think about." As my data suggest, Lana and others were reluctant to think about or discuss success for a few reasons. The first, and most simple, is time. Recall my interview with Roberta and Evelyn, two attorneys with the Children's Project in Chicago. As the number of unaccompanied youth arriving at regional shelters increased, they told me, release times correspondingly decreased. Advocacy efforts were likewise abbreviated, with uncertain conclusions.

During our conversation, I commented, "A number of the attorneys I've spoken with have implied or stated outright, 'Great, we got the kid legal status, job done.'"

Both women nodded. "It's a challenge," stated Roberta. "Some of the kids I've had successes in obtaining their legal relief, it's like you're saying, you know, a part of me is like, 'Great. Done. Next kid.'"

I understood. "And you have to be, right?"

"Right," she continued. "But then part of you as a human is like, can they survive on their own? . . . Some of these kids were fortunate and have good structure back home of adults guiding them, but I think a number of them, a large part of them might not have [that]. I don't think they're equipped to deal with adulthood here, you know, with the added challenges of not only adulthood, but you're an immigrant, you don't know the language, you don't have the skills. That's worrisome. Because a lot of these kids, while they're in custody and as soon as they're released, they're *supposed* to go to school . . ." Her voice trailed. "But if they're out there working or doing whatever they can to survive, they're so vulnerable to exploitation."

Here, Roberta introduced a more complete and uncomfortably—or even subversively—complicated reality of legal "success." Most of the attorneys I interviewed were like Lana, pleased by and proud of those rare clients who could "do what they want," namely pursue an age-appropriate marker of good citizenship like education. The majority of Fujianese clients, however, or Lana's "unsuccessful" cases, *worked*. Recall here the moral and ideological underpinnings of modern childhood I discuss in Chapter 2, specifically the deeply-felt Lockean view that children have the "natural right" to be cared for and protected but not a right to consent, which is powerfully connected to autonomy. In what follows, I extend this discussion to young people's post-release lives and in particular to their labor, the thing Lana and many others didn't want to think about.

Given the broader context of childhood and children's rights, this reluctance is not surprising, nor is it without consequence. "The moral condemnation of child labor assumes that children's place in modern society must perforce be one of dependency and passivity," writes Olga Nieuwenhuys (1996, 238). Denying young people's capacity to "*legitimately* act upon their environment by undertaking valuable work makes children altogether dependent upon entitlements guaranteed by the state"[1] (1996, 238; emphasis added). Following this, what I present here largely illuminates and confronts the limits of legally and morally circumscribed views of success, vulnerability, and age. As I demonstrate, to acknowledge and attend to—let alone esteem—a young person's needs and goals *beyond* legal relief may be an afterthought for many cause lawyers, or amid the persistent and contradictory demands of US immigration, impossible. Yet to condemn or be silent about Fujianese clients' post-release employment is of profound professional and legal significance, an often-unconsidered choice with intimate and long-term effects.

VULNERABILITY IN THE US: LABOR AND THE LIMITS OF (LEGAL) CARE

When attorneys did discuss labor, it was often in the context of identifying trafficked youth in the workplace. There is a good and ostensibly altruistic reason for this: locating unauthorized and unapprehended Chinese youth broadens the reach of cause lawyers' advocacy. Efforts to extend legal status to youth in removal proceedings as well as yet "undetected" unauthorized youth are significant, for both populations powerfully experience the persistent and stressful threat of deportation (see De Genova and Puetz 2010; Gonzales 2011).[2] "There was one young man," said Ming-Yue, the social worker featured in Chapter 3, "who came to the US from Fujian and worked on a construction crew in Michigan. He worked there for ten, fifteen years. He got married to a Fujianese girl. They had a baby. I stayed in touch with them. And then he got deported. He had worked so long, paid off his debt, had a family, and then he was sent back to China. That's happened to other people, too. You don't want anyone to have that happen to them, especially after their lives are *here*."

As it specifically pertains to labor, LPR status can offer critical protection to young migrants. It provides work authorization and, in certain circumstances, defense against workplace citizenship discrimination and employer retaliation if a workplace violation is reported. "A lot of people here who are from Fujian tend not to be high-school graduates or have [a] little bit lower educational standing," said Len. "So the work that they can do is going to be brutal, right? I mean, they're going to be working in the restaurant or factory industries, and I think in those situations, that's just . . ." He paused. "You know, especially if you don't have status. You're going to be extremely vulnerable."

Helping a young person secure a legal remedy like a T visa—and, presumably, T visa benefits—is in many ways a tangible form of "care," one that eases the vulnerability Len discussed. Yet the actual provision or procurement of these benefits is less straightforward. Individuals who are granted T visas and have a certification or eligibility letter are permitted to *apply for* benefits like TANF; SSI; Supplemental Nutrition Assistance Program (SNAP); Women, Infants, and Children (WIC); and Medicaid. Of course, the caseload for many of these services exceeds what funding and personnel resources can manage, meaning the opportunity to apply for a service does not guarantee its timely or satisfactory provision. Just as significant, my data evidence that most eligible Fujianese youth do not pursue these services. Instead, youth will often travel great distances to seek out private health care, medicine, or other daily life necessities in Chinese enclaves. As Lauren Heidbrink (2014) points out, refusing visa benefits to instead rely on kin and community networks of assistance further challenges the juridical category of "unaccompanied."

Moreover, facilitating what is often framed as the "rescue" of trafficking victims through legal relief markedly ignores the reality that most Fujianese youth with legal status still have smuggling debts and consciously *return* to exploitative work situations. "It may seem that the discussions on legality of work and freedom of movement are irrelevant for minors because, in principle, they should not be migrating as jobseekers," writes Jyoti Sanghera. "However, the reality is that minors . . . are marked most by the illegality factor because they too are an integral part of the vast pool of mobile jobseekers. Their inherent vulnerability as minors is often exacerbated severalfold by the formal and informal sanctions against child labor" (2005, 8).

Put differently, in the workplace even "legal" Fujianese youth lead "illegal" lives. A young person's age may be below the legal age of employment; workplaces may not comply with labor laws and safety regulations; employers or coworkers may be undocumented. As a result, with delayed repayment of debt[3] and in the absence of safe, secure and lawful employment, a recipient of a T visa—or any other relevant remedy, like SIJ or asylum—experiences only a limited juridical reality of membership (Ngai 2004). This is a reality with which many Fujianese youth are already markedly familiar. Throughout my fieldwork, young people often appeared less concerned with legal status as with the working conditions they encountered, including long hours and absent safety protections, health care, and, often, hourly wages.

"You commit your life to it," said Jian, a young man I met in Tennessee. "Whether you want it or not. By the time you come here, it's too late. . . . You're destined to be a third-class worker for the rest of your life. You start working in restaurants, maybe a thousand dollars a month—a lot of money for China. But no one considers living expenses in the US, even a really poor person. Ten thousand dollars to have a used car, and you're making a thousand dollars a month?" His eyes widened and he raised his eyebrows. "You're living in shitty apartments, most likely sharing an apartment with a whole bunch of strangers, also migrant workers. Most of them don't have papers. And if you're unfortunate to live in big cities like New York City, this *room* probably has six people living in it. This is your life for ten years. And then ten years later, assuming nothing goes bad, you don't get sick, you don't get injured, you don't get fired—"

"You don't get caught," I interjected.

"You don't get caught," he continued. "You might make enough money, you pay back what you owe. That's ten years later. That's assuming you're not spending anything either. So after ten years, you got to work for another five years, no, another six, seven years. At this point you're probably making two thousand dollars a month, assuming you become a chef versus just doing the dishes. Best-case scenario, you make more than two thousand, or three thousand, very rarely, in big cities. But it's fifteen, sixteen years later. You can't change anything anymore, because it's too late. It's not like you can go back, go to school, because *even if you have identification, you have legal rights to stay in the US, you're thirty or older.* You might be afraid to change anything because now it's everything you know. You might have enough money to buy a tiny apartment. But you can't change anything, you're stuck there."

Like Jian, many of the young people I spoke with seemed indifferent or almost restless around the subject of legal status, particularly when evaluated in light of their working lives. Rather than characterize LPR status as a provision of care, as did many of their attorneys, youth were frank about its social and practical benefits.

An often-mentioned advantage of having a green card was the ability to visit family members in Fujian Province and then safely return to the US. Of course, this is something youth would likely not mention to their attorneys, for it powerfully thwarts cause lawyers' assumption that youth should and presumably *want* to stay in the US, even at the cost of legally severing kin ties.[4] Youth also and more pragmatically argued that it is best to have legal status to avoid deportation, and to have it quickly. Recall Chaoxiang's frustration: "The person I was smuggled here with was twenty-one. She didn't have to go into [an ORR facility] like me. And she's been working for years. . . . I had to wait in Chicago, and now I have to wait here. *I'm losing a lot of time.*"

"I have an uncle here," another young man told me. "He's in the Midwest. I've seen him a couple of times. He's legal. His wife is here. Life sucks for him. I mean, a migrant worker with identification is not much better than a migrant worker without one. You don't speak English, you're uneducated, you come here, you don't have a future. [But] it's still better than running around without ID."

TRAFFICKED TO COMMODITY, CHINATOWN TO MIDDLE AMERICA

"They've got their green card. Our work is done, right? But they're not survivors," stated one attorney. "And that's what makes the Chinese trafficking cases the ones that people want to shy away from. It's a *giant onion*. It's the biggest onion ever. It's like, great. We get them a green card. Okay, but now they have this debt. Okay, their debt's gone. Now they're living with trauma. Now their trauma's gone, now they still see themselves as a commodity. It's just, where does it end? I think that's what's really unique in these Chinese kids' cases." Nuanced and unusually forthright, this cause lawyer reiterates the uneasy limits of legal relief, particularly as they pertain to young people's labor. To borrow from the speaker, I want to peel the onion a bit more here, to interrupt the supposedly self-evident sequence this attorney put forth—trafficking, debt, trauma, commodity—by considering the broader context around young people's working lives.

While the data I collected often appear to substantiate the relative "endlessness" of the economic and emotional challenges Chinese youth face, they also hinder attempts to ground these challenges in youths' families or "Chinese culture." Youths' reflections also introduce a concurrent reality, one in which working for pay offers young migrants opportunities for self-respect and likewise challenges a childhood ideology that places a higher value on economically "useless" work, like school (Black 1995; Fyfe 1989).

Finally, I believe attorneys' chagrin, suspicion, and even hopelessness regarding the "giant onion" of Fujianese clients illuminates a more profound trend—namely the prioritizing of the (ostensibly more straightforward) autonomous individual over family life in American law and society.[5] Made particularly clear in lawyers' interpretations of "care," this orientation disregards clients' prolonged kin and community commitments, effectively divorcing young people's "belonging" from their "becoming" (Barlett 1988). It demonstrates a shortsighted regard for Chinese families, as well as for the social embeddedness and transnational "simultaneity" (Levitt and Schiller 2004) of global youth more generally. After all, writes Deborah Boehm, "the increasingly translocal experiences of children highlight the ways that migration itself is driven by, and cannot be separated from, social and familial reproduction" (2011, 166–67).

In what follows, I consider the broader spaces of Fujianese youths' labor, with a particular focus on young people's "semi-autonomy." These sections thus explore the opportunities and identities youth make for themselves as individuals who perform valuable work and acquire valued forms of adulthood, thereby contesting notions of them as *children outside* the realm of politics and the market (Stephens 1995). At the same time, I acknowledge that many Fujianese youth are still marginalized in their communities, and often by virtue of their work. I accordingly consider how the acquisition of particular forms of adulthood is often partial and reversible (Furlong and Cartmel 1997) and how youths' social and geographic mobility is powerfully constrained by economic change and political policies.[6]

The brunt of my fieldwork focused on young people's experiences in the legal realm, a space where a youth's labor was and to an extent *had to be* separate from the self she or he presented to an attorney.[7] Accordingly, the overview I present in this chapter is just that—a broad and incomplete synopsis of Fujianese youths' intricate, dynamic, and intimately experienced realities of life and labor beyond the legal realm. However cursory, it is only by considering these contexts of work and community that we can begin to understand how youths' experiences in the legal realm powerfully shape their labor outside it. As I detail below, economic obligations are uniquely affected by the strategies of cause lawyers, as well as by the choices youth make in accordance with, and sometimes despite, their perceived "best interests."

As hinted at by Jian, Fujianese youth don't generally work—and don't always *want* to work—in major immigrant gateways: "And if you're unfortunate to live in big cities like New York City . . ." Instead, the majority travel by bus to "new destinations,"[8] communities across the South and Midwest that in recent years have experienced the greatest relative immigrant population growth (Marrow 2011, 3), even as most new immigrants continue to settle in traditional gateway cities such as New York, Los Angeles, Houston, Miami, and Chicago (Portes and Rumbaut 2006). Because primarily Mexicans, and also Central and South Americans, have driven this process, the new destinations literature tends to focus on Latinx communities (see Donato, Stainback, and Bankston 2005; Lichter and Johnson 2009; Massey and Capoferro 2008; Fennelly 2008; Millard and Chapa 2004).[9] The youth in this study are not nearly as concentrated or visible as their Latinx counterparts, yet I believe they seek or are directed to new destinations for a similar reason, namely that labor-market opportunities in the South and Midwest are more attractive than in saturated immigrant niches in gateway cities (Light 2006).[10]

Of course, for many young Fujianese, the labor journey still begins in New York. Where and how it progresses may signal a key difference between youth who are apprehended and placed in removal proceedings and those who enter the US undetected.[11] Most detained youth are like Chaoxiang, who was frustrated by the sluggish pace of his legal case, the relative lack of Mandarin-speaking staff at the detention center, and the "meaninglessness" of daily assignments and activities there. At the same time, although ORR facilities are woefully lacking in adequate social and health services (see Heidbrink 2014), they also represent a space in which young migrants share advice about legal processes and job opportunities; acquire some English, and often Spanish, skills; and are introduced by staff to the public resources that may be available to them once they are released. These youths' employment may be initiated in the same place as their undetected counterparts, but their opportunities and ability to make informed decisions are arguably broadened by the information and social networks they acquire in detention.

That "same place" is one particular street in New York, where employment is sought out amid the heavy din of city life. "You haven't been there yet?" Lana asked me during one of our conversations. I shook my head. "You've got to go," she continued. "Of the hundred kids I've worked with, maybe five actually live in New York. You know, they go to those job centers here, and they get—they pay fifty bucks and they get given a ticket, and a bus picks them up at the street corner and drives them to Arkansas and Virginia, Indiana, Illinois, North Dakota, literally everywhere. Check it out." The next day, I did. In a sense it is concealed by its obviousness, so I grew frustrated as I walked the length of the street Lana mentioned on a grey, humid afternoon. I passed fruit stands and young Chinese women holding hands, fanning themselves and chatting. Trucks rumbled by. My discomfort was heightened by both the heat and my conspicuousness.

In hindsight, I'm not sure I really wanted to find these "job shops." It was easier to talk with a lawyer *about* this phenomenon, to sit with a young person as she or he carefully, and with evident pride, pinpointed the various stops of a migration journey while I echoed the place names, shaking my head admiringly. This place, on the other hand, was gritty and loud, and to me it represented an unnervingly meaningful and distressing threshold. I currently lived in the Midwest and had already visited so many Chinese buffets. Could the young people around me imagine that *this* would lead to *that*?

"It was always 'the uncle in New York,'" Ming-Yue had told me a year earlier. "The kids think New York is equal to the US. 'Actually,' I tell them, 'It's not.' But then finally it's, 'Oh, your uncle is in *South Dakota*.' They don't know what South Dakota is. The only word for them is New York. Because anything their uncle does, he'll do it from New York." I heard her words as I walked slowly to the end of the street, shadowed by store awnings and the heavy bridge above.

Here were the job shops. Like so many tiny bus-station ticket counters, inside each open door was a long glass window with white slips taped to it. Young men stood in the neon light, crowded together and peering carefully at the pieces of paper. A group of teenagers sat on the steps of one shop, talking and smoking. One young man had his arm around a young woman; she wore short jean shorts and was laughing. A girl and an older woman walked by, arm in arm. Both looked disappointed. I passed a young man on his cell phone; his black shoes were scuffed and worn, and he carried a stiff black satchel. Another young man wore flip-flops and a navy polo shirt. The air smelled of cigarettes and ripe fruit. A tall teenage girl trudged by slowly, preoccupied, with two other young women. She was on a cellphone and held a sheet of paper with a business card clipped to it. Inside another shop was a sign advertising Internet plans and New York employment agencies. It was in English. "It was strange to be in the thick of it," I wrote in my notes later, "to know this neighborhood so well that I felt like it wasn't my first time there. It was entirely natural, but still uncomfortable and unfamiliar for anyone— myself included, or maybe just me."

The young people I observed that day now most likely work elsewhere in the US. While some may have found employment in factories or nail salons, the majority are on what one attorney termed "the restaurant circuit." They work—and sometimes live—in Chinese buffets, quitting one restaurant and securing employment at another, often through word of mouth or by returning to this stretch of city block.

While youths' experiences in broader communities of reception differed widely, their employment situations were often quite similar. In Arkansas, Hua worked from 9:30 a.m. to 10:00 p.m. six or seven days a week at Comet Buffet. She lived with her boss and the restaurant manager, a husband and wife who were also from Fujian, and their five young children. Explaining this arrangement, Hua enthusiastically held up her phone to show me photos of the children. Each time I visited Hua at Comet Buffet, the parking lot was crowded. In the front entry stood a cash register framed by fake pink and yellow flowers and faded Chinese New Year decorations. Beyond that were tables filled with local families, older couples, construction workers, and tourists. On my first visit, I felt disoriented. I was distracted by the loud noise and embarrassed to feel so surprised when I realized there was no plain rice on the long buffet, only fried rice with peas and corn. Save the hibachi cook and some Latinx men filling up the buffet, every worker was a fast-moving young Fujianese woman. Like many of the other restaurants I would visit, this felt both familiar and extraordinary—the normalcy of so many trans- national lives in passing.

In upstate New York, Dewei worked six days a week at a sushi restau- rant run by a Fujianese couple. The restaurant was considerably trendier than many of the Chinese buffets I had visited. A gleaming bar lined one side of the room, with dark tile and tapestries covering the walls. Low lights highlighted the smoky blue glass behind the sushi station where Dewei stood, expertly rolling sushi and chatting quietly with the young man next to him. Dewei lived with the restaurant owners, whom he referred to as his aunt and uncle. He was at the restaurant from 10:00 or 11:00 a.m. until 9:00 p.m. each day, "but sometimes it's 10 p.m.," he admitted, "and sometimes 11." On his days off, Dewei went swimming at a local gym.

Most of the young people I interviewed were like Hua and Dewei, insulated in and by their working lives, with long hours at a restaurant and then most spare time spent in the homes or apartments they shared with coworkers. These living situations often seemed an afterthought in our conversations. Exhausted after such long days and nights, most youth just wanted a place to sleep, "and cook, and sometimes watch Chinese videos," Dewei explained. Some had friends with cars, enabling them to go shopping or to the movies on the occasional day off. Most were like Hua, who rode to and from work with her boss and coworkers and walked everywhere else. Significantly, for Hua this "everywhere else" was considerably reduced by the hot Southern sun, the distance from her bosses' home to town, and an absence of sidewalks along the busy highways.

"Here, I'm tired," said one young man in the Midwest. "I stay in my house. If I have time off, maybe I'll go to New York." Like Hua, he mentioned New York's karaoke and Chinese food.

"I'm going to wedding [in New York] next month. Two weddings in one day!" a young woman in Illinois told me. "I take a bus. In New York, they have funeral homes, and they have weddings."

The relative ease and confidence by which many Fujianese youth travel to and from New York thwarts the image of new destination communities as isolated and remote, an assumption I held before conducting research. Of course, this is not to say that life in these small towns is easy. Indeed, the resoluteness by which youth venture to New York is most likely an indication of what is lacking, or what feels unobtainable, in the communities where they work.

Echoing what I had already heard from many Fujianese youth, an attorney in northwest Arkansas commented, "Think about this group of people. They may work in Oklahoma, and then when they need a blanket, they may take a bus all the way to New York to get a blanket. You know what I mean?" He was nonchalant.

I nodded.

"If they have needs," he continued, "They're not met in Oklahoma. Oklahoma can get them a job, because there's a Chinese restaurant. So normally, the owner will give them a place to stay. They may have laundry machines in their facilities, their so-called home, but there may be twenty people in the house. And then when they're off, they will have Chinese tapes to look at."

"It's a little bubble," I added.

"Yeah," he agreed. "But when they are talking about, okay, when you are sick? They don't know where to get a doctor in Oklahoma. Because nobody can speak their language. So they have to take a bus all the way to New York. Or if they have to send money, like some of the money they earn. Same thing."

LEGAL, WITH AN "ILLEGAL LIFE"

An even more complex interplay of labor and space emerges when we consider the above reflections in light of legal status and legal need. After I spent a number of days with Wenyun, a young woman in Alabama whose removal proceedings were ongoing, she confided that she had a terrible toothache and wasn't sure what to do about it. "Too much American candy!" she said with a quick laugh, yet it was clear the pain worried her. More worrisome was the seeming remoteness of a possible remedy. "I don't know how to talk to a dentist," she admitted, "or where to find one." She paused. "And how would I get there? And pay?"

Later that day, I reached out to some attorneys I had already interviewed in the area. They suggested a free and sliding-scale community dental clinic thirty miles away. "All they need is a proof of address and a proof of income," I told Wenyun over the phone. "I would be happy to drive you there, if you want to go." She sounded hopeful and promised to call me the next day. In the meantime, I told her, I would reach out to Amy, her attorney in Chicago. I knew Amy quite well; indeed, it was she who prompted me to visit Wenyun in Alabama. "She's a fantastic girl," she had said. "I'm sure you'll learn a lot from her."

Always warm and considerate, Amy was excited to hear I was in Alabama. She asked after Wenyun, then about my research.

"It's really different down here," I admitted. "You know, HB 56[12]—and you can feel it."

She was silent, then: "What's HB 56?"

Surprised that Amy, an attorney who heartily self-identified as an immigrant-rights advocate, had never heard of the Alabama bill, I faltered. Passed a month earlier, HB 56 represented the nation's strictest "anti-illegal immigrant" legislation; it was even tougher than Arizona's SB 1070.[13] Among its provisions, the bill prohibited undocumented immigrants from receiving any public benefits at either the state or local level and from attending public colleges or universities. It required school districts to submit annual tallies of the suspected number of undocumented K-12 students, and it prohibited landlords from renting to undocumented individuals. Though it had only been in effect for one month, many of the lawyers I interviewed had already observed changes in their communities.

"The educational provisions are fairly devastating," stated an attorney who worked for a regional civil rights advocacy organization. "There are invisible communities everywhere, of course, but it's now less easy to hide in Alabama. The law enforcement is more vindictive." She paused. "What we've learned is that the ag workers are leaving, and there's no one there to replace them. I mean, the economic repercussions of this are terrible! And they're something people talk about all the time. The crops are rotting. One of my colleagues told me he visited an Ace Hardware in Alabama, and there was a sign on the door that said, 'There are no pine straw bales' [for bedding in gardens]. We're all noticing it."

I briefly described what I had learned about the bill to Amy then mentioned the anxiety and visible pain I observed in Wenyun. "I talked to some immigration attorneys in the area, and they suggested this dental clinic. It's free or sliding scale, and run by a private nonprofit. She just needs proof of address and a pay stub, which she can get from her boss. Nothing that deals with her legal status. I'm happy to take her there."

To my surprise, Amy resisted. "There's really only a slim chance that this could be an issue for her case," she said, presumably fearful that the pending case could be affected by local attention, and perhaps suspicion, for her client. "But whatever issue might come up would be a real pain." Audibly uncomfortable, she ended the conversation abruptly.

Initially I felt ashamed. Had I exceeded the bounds of our professional relationship, or of my "freedoms" as a researcher? I would not go against Amy's wishes, but I dreaded telling Wenyun about the call. Taking notes in the dim evening light, I wrote, "Amy *cares* about Wenyun, I know." But to Amy, extending this care to a client's health simply could not be allowed to cost a legal case—or, more likely, given the bureaucratic context of Amy's work, cost the speed and efficiency of a legal case. Even more significantly, while Amy apparently felt it was "safe" for Wenyun to work eighty hours a week in a restaurant not unsusceptible to an ICE raid—labor that would help establish Wenyun's eligibility for a T visa—it was chancy, or at least not legally beneficial, for Wenyun to venture into the broader community and take advantage of available health services.[14] To many, it is perhaps unsurprising that an immigration attorney prioritized legal status over her client's other and arguably more immediate needs. Yet as a cause lawyer, Amy's response both unsettled and in many ways helped delineate the cause at hand. Here, a young migrant's access to health care proves only *conditionally* a right or, to use more familiar language, in her "best interests."

However revealing to me as a researcher, Amy's decision ultimately didn't matter. When I next spoke with Wenyun, her tone had changed. "I'm just waiting," she said, "I have to wait. It's important to go a little slowly. Because, you know, my work here? When Amy says something like, 'You have to send that to me, you have to send proof that you are sending money home,' I give her that, but my bosses—they don't like it. Because they're afraid. 'You work in my restaurant but you don't have—'" She paused.

"Documents?" I asked.

"Documents, uh-huh. So they're afraid." I wasn't surprised, given all I was learning about Alabama. "Yesterday I asked them for the [proof of] address, and they said, 'We can't give you that.'"

The matter concluded, though her pain did not.

A DIFFERENT KIND OF PRACTICE SITE

Many of the immigration attorneys I met in new destination communities knew only vaguely of meetings like the "On Their Own" conference described in Chapter 1. When I asked about these professional gatherings, individuals were often disinterested or frustrated by the disconnect between regional advocacy efforts and capabilities. "Here in Arkansas, we don't go to conferences, we don't go to trainings, we have no money!" stated one attorney.

With visible scorn, another commented, "We just don't have the money or time to go to Angelina Jolie conferences."[15]

"She didn't show," I replied.

She laughed. "Well, she's probably too busy with the UNHCR [the United Nations High Commissioner for Refugees]. I'm busy, too. For us, immigration court is five hours away in Memphis."

This disconnect matters. It is also not necessarily unproductive. As my data demonstrate, the relative professional isolation of practicing in a new destination community simultaneously offers attorneys a social proximity to young clients that colleagues elsewhere do not or cannot replicate. Overwhelmingly, the attorneys I interviewed in the Midwest and South were considerably more knowledgeable of youths' working and personal lives than those who practiced in gateway cities. Many new destination attorneys were intimately aware of and involved in local immigrant communities simply by virtue of a town's size, or what William Freudenberg (1986) calls the "high density of acquaintanceship" that tends to mark rural places.[16] Indeed, my data suggest that immigration attorneys in new destinations are better equipped, and often more willing, to extend "care" to youths' work, health, and social lives than are gateway attorneys.[17]

In many ways, this care exceeds the critical analytic of care as it is often employed by scholars of migration,[18] revealing an instance in which fetishized or actual suffering need not be the fundamental basis for advocacy or citizenship (see Ticktin 2011). The new destination attorneys I interviewed were profoundly aware of the complex challenges local migrants faced, but their responses diverged from, or in their unaffectedness transcended, the morally or politically mandated "languages of good" of humanitarianism (Ticktin 2011, 4).

These attorneys generally practiced out of small, private immigration offices, though some worked in the regional offices of national nonprofits. In their willingness to provide young migrants pro bono or "low bono" services, and in their sustained commitment to grassroots organizing around immigrant rights, this class of attorneys in many ways fits within the categorical definition of cause lawyer. Significantly, however, these lawyers appeared uninterested in establishing their "subjective jurisdiction" over a particular cause. This was most likely owing to geographic constraints that, among other things, affected exposure to the more competitive "cause market" of lawyering in gateway cities, where attorneys vie for funding, federal contracts, and publicity. The immigration attorneys I interviewed in less traditional contexts of reception were in a sense unified by their limited numbers and resources, as well as by the relative discreteness of their practice sites. Significantly, many attorneys noted that these were challenges they often shared *with their clients*.

"What is the immigration climate in Arkansas?" I asked Russell.

"It's bad from place to place," he said. "The chicken industry is big here. Tyson, Cargill, Simmons, Butterball . . . they moved to this area because labor costs were low, except there wasn't enough labor. So Mexicans and Central Americans began appearing back in the mid-90s. But towns nearby have always been bad. The police—they do road blocks and stop everybody and ask for driver's licenses. Without one they turn you over to immigration."

"No," interrupted his colleague, Maria Teresa, "they give you a ticket, and you have to appear in court."

"And then ICE is there waiting," concluded Russell.

"I know you used to practice in Chicago," I stated. Russell nodded. "How is your immigration work here different?"

"The biggest issue is just logistics," he quickly responded. "In Chicago, I was three blocks from court. Here, I'm three and a half hours from Kansas City and four and a half hours from Memphis [where EOIR courts are located], assuming the weather is good and there's not road construction. . . . So distance is a huge issue. You know, people get letters that they have to go to court in Memphis, and they don't know where Memphis is. And they don't have driver's licenses, so they have to find people to drive them who wants money, and sometimes they miss court because, you know, the car will break down or nobody will take them or they're afraid to take them."

"Or they're afraid to go," added Maria Teresa.

"Or they're afraid to go," echoed Russell.

"Because they get a lot of misadvice," she continued. "You know, like, 'Don't go to court, they'll arrest you and deport you.' So they don't go. And months pass and they—"

"Or years—" Russell interrupted.

She nodded. The room was quiet.

Sympathetic to and personally familiar with many of the logistical concerns and surveillance their clients faced, these attorneys were likewise aware of and markedly linked into the community services available to undocumented Latinx youth. This represented yet another difference with lawyers in gateway cities, many of whom reported heavy caseloads or bureaucratic constraints as impediments to connecting youth with assistance beyond legal aid. Most attorneys in new destinations were themselves members of the communities in which they worked; some had even grown up there. The familiarity and connections this positionality provided matters, permitting an extension of care beyond legal status.

"My family is from a small town nearby," Erin, a lawyer in Missouri, told me. "There are people who are like, 'Yeah, the Mexicans are running over the town.' There's definitely that. But also in that same town, I mean, the Catholic church started doing a Spanish mass years and years ago. And so you see different factions. . . . I also have met some surprisingly pro-immigrant—or at least not anti-immigrant—people who are typically kind of conservative, because they see that we need the workers. I think it's kind of schizophrenic. I think you get a lot of people who are anti-immigrant who are really loud, but I don't know that they're a majority, if that makes sense? And most of the nonprofits in the area are very aware of the immigration issue." Erin listed a number of nearby agencies and religious organizations, detailing the housing and health services and legal assistance they provided undocumented immigrants. "The community is definitely one of the biggest draws to being here," she added, "as opposed to being in a big city. I feel like I can actually make a difference."

"You don't think you'd be able to do that in a bigger area?"

"I think it would probably be a lot more difficult. I think there's a lot more red tape when you're working—you know, when I worked in DC . . ." her voice trailed. "God, I remember we had these coalitions of immigrant service providers, and it was just a huge mess because there were so many people. It's harder, I think, to make connections, and it's harder to set up systems. [Here] it was just like, I called somebody, and I said, 'We're going to do this.' . . . And then bam. It just happened. And it was super successful. I couldn't have done this in DC. . . . When you have seven different organizations doing the same thing, and then they end up fighting with each other, or like, you know, this is my turf, or this is my territory. And you're like, 'But you're all—why aren't you just one organization?" She laughed. "Why do you have to have seven?" Still laughing, she added, "You definitely don't have that here!"

Some attorneys in new destination communities also mentioned the partnerships they had initiated and developed with area law enforcement that participated in 287(g), a program through which state and local police officers are deputized by DHS to perform the functions of federal immigration agents. Allegedly intended to enforce immigration laws and locate serious criminal offenders, 287(g) agreements have proven expensive and in many ways a threat to community safety (see Weissman, Headen, and Parker 2009). In response, a number of attorneys forged collaborations with local police officers to educate them on the rights and concerns of Latinx community members, as well as the potential of 287(g) to isolate already marginalized individuals who are increasingly fearful of seeking assistance or reporting crimes.

I was surprised by the casualness with which lawyers discussed these partnerships, as they were likely unique even across new destinations. Moreover, and in light of the research I had so far conducted in gateway cities, the existence of relatively informal and arguably productive relationships between immigration advocates and immigration *agents* was astounding, at least to me. Until then, ICE had been exclusively presented by attorneys as the handy if not enigmatic "bad guy"—the trial attorney who sat on the other side of the courtroom in removal proceedings, the border-patrol agent. While I cannot speak to the success of or probable tensions within these new destination task forces, it is significant that such initiatives in many ways challenged—largely through ignoring—the oppositional stance I found elsewhere. New destination attorneys' efforts to collaborate with police officers with whom they interacted at both a professional and personal level "around town" ultimately mobilized a cause beyond legal strategizing and skepticism. However uncelebrated, here was concerted, grassroots education about the complex realities of other community members who were undocumented.

Chris, an attorney in northern Wisconsin, described a similar partnership he had developed with area schools. "A lot of the schools are really helpful. We did a pile of DACA,[19] and the schools were really great. If you're in a tiny rural school, then [migrant youth] are a significant part of the population. You work on a farm, you come to school, and you run track. You're kind of like all the other kids who go to this school."

VALUED FREEDOMS

Of course, Fujianese youth are arguably *not* like all the other kids, nor do the regional possibilities many attorneys celebrate in new destination communities necessarily translate to better or sustained advocacy on their behalf. This study in a sense documents these young people's very "adult" lives, as well as the ways in which they may be relegated to "illegal" existences by virtue of their location. Challenging the aforementioned vision of youth as *children outside* the realm of politics and the market (Stephens 1995), in this chapter I detail the ways in which Fujianese youth in new destination communities are affected by geographic remoteness, state immigration policies, local law enforcement, and a regional tendency to equate "undocumented migrant" with—and likewise direct labor advocacy and social services to—more visible Latinx populations (see Lee 2003).[20] Fujianese youth are additionally rendered *semi*-autonomous through the complicated and shifting context of local rural economies.

Though available information, linguistic isolation, and smuggling networks ostensibly shape the employment opportunities available to young Fujianese migrants,[21] these youths' propensity to work in Chinese buffets may simultaneously reflect the broader influence of both global markets and regional economic change (Jeffrey and Dyson 2008; Stadum 1995). As an example, the employment director of a Chinese mutual-aid association in Chicago shared that, in the past, meatpacking companies from Iowa and Tennessee would come to him to recruit Chinese migrants. "But these days," he said, "they've really stopped recruiting in the city. Locals there are now willing to take those jobs." In a sense, Fujianese youth are thus doubly restricted to the "restaurant circuit" as they navigate the subtle challenges wrought by demographic shifts and rural economic and industrial restructuring (see Brown and Schafft 2011).

"Fujianese youth are treated a little better, and there's less competition [in smaller communities], but they're still at the mercy of their employer," said Len. "They try different places, looking for a place they feel is safe, trying to make a living, trying to not be exploited. Life goes on; people try to make the most of it."

However apathetic—"life goes on"—Len's words also signal the choices youth make again and again as they seek safe, worthwhile employment. Often riddled with as many "stops" as their migration passages, these employment journeys are noteworthy in being largely directed by youth themselves. When I interviewed Hua in Arkansas, for instance, it was her second labor destination. Before that she was in northern Illinois, and later she worked in Ohio. By the time she received her green card, she was in Rhode Island, where her boyfriend had located two positions at a Chinese buffet outside of Providence. Hua was proud of her economic successes and excited to tell me about the plans she and her boyfriend were making together.

In presenting Hua's story, I do not wish to diminish the very real economic demands and social obligations shouldered by the youth. Nor can I gloss over the unsafe conditions in which these demands are met or the physical and emotional toll of doing so. Yet as a consideration of—and sometimes a counter to—attorneys' portrayals of youth and their families, it is important to highlight the sincerity and satisfaction many youth feel about their skills, employment, and economic achievements.

"I think people don't always understand kids' life here," shared Chengjie, a young man I first met in Chicago. "When Fujianese kids think about their future, they always—there's an old Chinese saying, like, when you are young, if you work hard you're actually saving something for the future. So we always say, you should not be afraid of working hard [*bu yao pa xinku*]." He looked at me expectantly.

"I understand," I said.

"Yeah," he nodded. "Don't be afraid of that, because that's something that's good for your future. And when you're young, you need to do some kind of—to prove yourself, like, to show that you can kind of support your family." He paused. "You are still young, it doesn't matter that you're working hard from the morning to the night. . . . And so [youth] actually make a lot of money, and maybe that's something the family had in mind—because when they are in their hometown, they cannot have a lot of chances to receive a better education. It's different from other areas. You know, maybe compared to more urban cities, you know, like Beijing or Shanghai—like, it's a different expectation. So a lot of people before they came here, they have nothing to do in their hometown. Like maybe they were working in local grocery shops, or maybe in the restaurant to learn how to be a chef. But it's much less than what they can earn in the United States."

Employment also represented something *beyond* earning power, of course. With it and in the pursuit of it, youth familiarized themselves with money transfers and management, regional and international travel, self-subsistence, local economies, other immigrant populations, and long-term planning—skills valued by youth as markers of adulthood, success, and a sort of global cosmopolitanism (see Nussbaum 2006). Describing one of her Fujianese clients, an attorney stated, "I have one awesome kid. He is *so* smart and speaks Mandarin and Cantonese and Spanish and Portuguese and is brilliant and strong, and a total punk—" She giggled. "I remember I was prepping him for court, and I was like, 'What are you going to say if the judge asks you why you aren't in school?' And he's like, 'I'm going to say, *Fuck you!*'"

I laughed.

"And I was like, great. Great. Let's rephrase that. He's hilarious. And he shows up to court with a mohawk, and I'm like, *Oh my god*. But look, he wants to work. And that's where he sees value in himself. He loves working on a construction site because he can speak to the Chinese guys, and he can speak to the Spanish guys, and he has respect."

It was the first and only time in my research that an attorney mentioned respect. Yet for many youth, the hard work Chengjie described generates a prized respect, and self-respect, in the US and in families and communities in Fujian. For a cause lawyer to acknowledge the economic and social value Fujianese youth accord to their work is significant. It also stands largely at odds with the inclination of most cause lawyers in this study, namely to abstract young people from prioritized relationships and financial obligations (see Boehm 2011).

Many of the attorneys I interviewed were like Lana, characterizing a Fujianese client's dogged pursuit of employment rather than education as an "unsuccessful case." Yet as detailed in the previous chapter, what attorneys assert to be a familial or cultural disregard for education is, in a sense, largely what makes a case *successful*. The young person's presumed inability or disinclination to seek schooling persuasively reveals the extent of their parents' ignorance, exploitation, and/or neglect. Of course, this interpretation also effectively forecloses the chance that the money a young person earns through employment may support a sibling's education in China through remittances or may be saved to support future children—"if you work hard you're actually saving something for the future."[22] So also does it deny the ways in which work confronts, and in a sense frees, young migrants from both the real and strategic "dependence" they experience in the legal realm. Indeed, little else so succinctly marks the transition from these youths' (or "children's") legally accentuated vulnerability and passivity to their actual agency, independence, and autonomy as the economic and social gains achieved through employment do (see Goździak 2008; Lancy 2008; Orellana 2009).

ABANDONED FAMILIES, ABANDONED RIGHTS

This is not to say, of course, that a young person simply *resumes* being a transnational economic actor, now with legal status, once removal proceedings are concluded. As detailed above, legal status meaningfully eases the threat of deportation and promises new freedoms and protections, even if these things are in practice not always accessible or accessed by Chinese youth. Other outcomes of legal advocacy are less straightforward—and in many ways more consequential.

A number of youth described the distress they felt upon repeatedly confronting a legal narrative that, however dialogically constructed, exclusively portrayed their parents as abusive, neglectful, coercive, and/or ignorant. While arguably constrained to legal documents, conversations with advocates, and EOIR courtrooms—indeed, only the family narratives of Young and so many pseudonymous "Meis" were publicly circulated—these portraits and the anguish they elicited powerfully illuminate the extent to which the pursuit of *one* form of status, namely legal, confronts and may even collapse others.

During their removal proceedings, many youth carefully satisfy the often-bewildering demands of legal protections as they simultaneously navigate shelter facilities, national employment networks, and full-time jobs, sending remittances home to family.[23] Yet in the legal realm, these independent accomplishments have no value. If anything, they may compromise a case. When the diminishment or denial of youths' abilities is combined with the well-intentioned chiding of attorneys—"you're too young to work"; "you need to go to school"—and attorneys' strategic disparagement of families and culture of origin, many youth are profoundly unsettled. Here, the celebrated provision of legal "membership" isolates youth from the other more valued and often intimate transnational memberships they have until now so skillfully managed.

When considering the shifting, interrelated constellation of family, labor, and legality these youth navigate, a new tension in lawyering on behalf of Fujianese youth emerges. While the youth I interviewed receive free advocacy from cause lawyers, they are uniquely positioned to accept, but never openly reject, the claims legal advocates make about their families and communities of origin. Although many youth are like Hua, who was confident and even boisterous in her description of her "bad guy" mom, they are also, like Hua, ultimately troubled by these portrayals of family members. After all, amid the loneliness and stress Hua experienced in Arkansas, her relationship with her mother represented a most valued experience of belonging. Still, this relationship was simultaneously "wrong" in the legal realm and something that had to remain secret—further compounding her loneliness and stress.

Other youth were more devastated by lawyers' claims. Confronted with the notion that his parents had abandoned him, one individual shared that his ties with his family deteriorated. "It is only now," he said, "*ten years later*, that I feel okay and want to send remittances again. I'm even starting to think about visiting my parents and sister in Fujian."

Interestingly, "abandonment" here compellingly overlaps with attorneys' understanding of "success." Establishing parental abuse, neglect, or abandonment helps an attorney successfully obtain SIJ status on behalf of a client. Yet doing so may fracture valued kin ties. And in the case of Young not meeting his father's expectations by attending school, a successful claim may also introduce the sorrowful possibility that a youth has simultaneously "abandoned" her or his family through testimony or by her or his individual economic, educational, or social choices.

There is yet another form of abandonment to consider, one that returns us to the limits of legal "success" introduced at the start of the chapter. "I feel like a lot of our Fujianese clients are definitely—not to their own faults— limited by bureaucratic restraints," shared Christine, an attorney in Chicago. "Meaning that a lot of contract funding limits their services. For example, our agency can only serve youth. And a lot of agencies working with youth can only serve them up to the age of eighteen. But I personally feel that—and this goes with the other youth who are not Fujianese that I work with, too—I still think of youth as youth even after they turn eighteen. Meaning that it's fairly obvious that they would need assistance as far as adjustment in their immigration process. And I think that we—" She caught herself. "I think *someone* could systematically abandon them [like that]. . . . I mean, through the notion that once you turn eighteen you're an adult and you don't need any more help. . . . It's sort of a timeline of experiences and the things that they would need help with, right?"

"Yes!" I couldn't hide my appreciation.

"And that doesn't end once you turn eighteen. . . . Unless we can address those issues for them, I feel we're only doing truncated work."

Between the undisputed reality of truncated work and the largely unconsidered (or unacknowledged) possibility of legal or moral abandonment are the persistent questions of age, rights, and legal success this book examines. Most of the attorneys I interviewed knew about youths' likely trajectory from "trafficking to commodity" or, more accurately, from New York to, say, North Dakota. Yet, rarely did anyone acknowledge youths' need for—and indeed *right to*—safe, secure, and lawful employment. Some attorneys identified schooling as an antidote to labor; others simply diminished the financial obligations youth still shouldered after obtaining legal status. "Do they still have to pay it?" asked one attorney. "I don't think so. I've heard that parents tell the smugglers it was a failed migration journey because the kid ended up in shelter care. That's how they get out of the debt." This of course ignores the reality that most smugglers are paid up front by community banking networks and loan sharks. Every youth I interviewed, including those even Lana would identify as "successful," intended to pay off tens of thousands of dollars of debt.

With the exception of many of the new destination attorneys I interviewed, most cause lawyers were likewise indifferent to their clients' *other* needs and rights, including access to health care, language training, and other social services. This reflects the limitations attorneys often lamented—high caseloads, insecure funding, and the bureaucratic, competitive, and inefficient "cause market" of gateway cities. At the same time, however, dismissing youths' very real need for fundamental rights and protections beyond lawful permanent residence, or *prioritizing* legal relief at the cost of other needs, as in the case with Wenyun, implicitly calls into question cause lawyers' understanding of care. This "care" is likewise destabilized when we consider the intimate consequences of the suspicion attorneys strategically cast on youths' relationships, valued identities, and social and economic successes, often in the name of "best interests."

"What does a successful case look like?" I asked during one interview.

"Well, you just hope you've made the right choice," the attorney answered. With a swift dismissal of her young clients' abilities and agency, she continued, "Because kids can say, 'This is what I want, this is what I want you to do,' but who knows if this is what they want. Or even if it really is what they want, who knows if it's the best thing for them. *You just hope you've made the right choice.*"

7 Reflections on Instability and Inconclusiveness

Long-term fieldwork is never long enough to capture everything.
One is never finished. One simply stops. In the beginning the
sense of incompleteness emerges like a self-accusation.
(Sally Falk Moore 2009, 180)

In this book's first chapter, I mention some familiar parallels between law and anthropology. At times, both lawyers and anthropologists may feel constrained by the distinct frames, institutions, and logics of our respective disciplines, even as our practices and insights are largely forged in everyday life and experiences (see, e.g., Holmes 1881, 1). Both professions involve a kind of "expert" authority, and each produces necessarily selective and compelling narratives. Recall Lisette's comment on legal strategy, noted in Chapter 1: "But that's anthropology too, right? The way you write, the framework you put something into, it completely changes the thing."

At this book's close, however, I want to center on a critical difference between lawyering and anthropology, yet one that implicates both groups. Most simply, this difference involves lawyers' aspirations of immediacy and closure and anthropologists' relative comfort with distance and inconclusiveness. As socio-legal scholars rightly point out, cause lawyers actively struggle for social justice. They try new tactics and assert their beliefs in real time; their work is daily animated by broad commitments and concerns. Anthropologists, on the other hand, often write about daily life from a distance and with considerable delay. We tend to be so mired in theoretical, methodological, and interpretive debates that the possibility of shared experiences and insights, let alone engagements, is lost (Borneman and Hammoudi 2009; Mertz 2002; Nader 2002). Moreover, whereas anthropologists typically neither aim for nor expect a neat resolution to fieldwork or its capacious foci, most lawyers, and certainly the cause lawyers in this study, concentrate largely and diligently on the ends of advocacy.

As my data suggest, these attorneys seek to offer closure in the form of legal relief; to restore order—or *reorder order*—through familial and cultural claims and best-interests determinations; and to solidify professional jurisdiction through tragic "representative anecdotes" and an emphasis on urgency. Yet as this study also evidences, the ends of advocacy are often ambiguous. Fujianese youth stress legal needs *beyond* immigration status, and their individual best interests do not always coincide with advocates' best intentions. Moreover, attorneys require a particular synthesis of time, energy, and a generalizable case or client to establish the legitimacy of a cause—and in my research, these elements prove finite, or sometimes nonexistent. While estimable and often ceremonially lauded, this cause lawyering context is simultaneously one of instability and doubt.

Enter ethnography. As with any inherently subjective, distanced, and conventionally delayed anthropological account, this book is insufficient and incomplete. This, I believe, may be its strength. Bringing together so many experiences and interpretations is not a prescriptive endeavor, and this conclusion will likely not satisfy those looking for clear-cut legal or policy recommendations. Instead, the inherent inconclusiveness of the ethnographic process is at its best a shared and familiar experience, implicitly inviting what John Borneman and Abdellah Hammoudi identify as "double-edged critiques": "mutual, intersubjective questioning rather than smug assertions of identity rights or untraversable differences" (2009, 20).

Amid the fundamental uncertainty of cause lawyering and, of course, fieldwork encounters, anthropology is poised to witness and theorize; to write with and against; to detail those ambivalent entanglements that youth and cause lawyers in their legitimate haste and preoccupations may be unable or unwilling to question. Thus, although—or because—there is always more to write and other dimensions to consider, it is arguably the very incompleteness or impossibility of a clear *end* that is most productive. Through it, we arrive at the enduring ambivalence and indeterminacy of a cause, a reality that opens into more uneven temporalities, mobilities, institutions, and ambitions.

The expansiveness of this may feel inhibiting, particularly when we situate these phenomena within a still broader and arguably intensifying context of restrictionist immigration politics, extreme material inequality wrought by global neoliberalism, and the "reterritorialization" of social relations as immigration status is reified as the sole determinant of political membership (Kawar 2015, 161; Santos 1995). Yet, in other ways, the expansiveness may be emancipatory, making space for "performance, narrative, remembrance, critique, and hope—even as [we lose] any stable referent to empirical conditions, places, persons, or predictable propriety" (Greenhouse 2002, 2). It is with this hope in mind that I conclude this book.

WHY "OTHER" YOUTH MATTER

In 2011, the US government began to record a rise in the number of unaccompanied minors arriving in the US. That year, 4,059 young people, the majority from El Salvador, Guatemala, and Honduras, were apprehended and placed in removal proceedings. In 2012, the number increased to 10,443 and in 2013, 21,537.[1] By mid-2014, as many as 10,000 young people were apprehended and designated unaccompanied *each month*. While the numbers declined sharply that winter and throughout most of 2015, the autumn again recorded some of the highest numbers of unaccompanied youth at the US-Mexico border. In November 2015, 12,091 young people were apprehended and designated unaccompanied minors (Rosenblum and Ball 2016).

Most news and policy sources cited violence and the threat of gang recruitment in home countries as explanations for these increases, along with economic necessity, a desire to reunify with parents or family members already in the US, and perceived changes in US policy that favored child immigrants (Carlson 2014; Rosenblum and Ball 2016; Semple 2014). Little attention was given to the broader historical, economic, and sociopolitical context for this migration, including the CIA's historic involvement throughout Central America, asymmetrical economic agreements such as the Dominican Republic–Central America–United States Free Trade Agreement (CAFTA-DR), and failed foreign policy in the region (see Heidbrink 2014).

In both the mainstream press and state policy reports, a hasty and familiar conclusion was drawn: these young migrants are vulnerable, and they need lawyers. Employing troublingly militaristic language, a June 16, 2014, *New York Times* editorial argued, "President Obama needs to mount a surge of humanitarian care to handle the explosion of young migrants fleeing violence in their home countries." The editorial was entitled "Innocents at the Border: Immigrant Children Need Safety, Shelter and Lawyers."

Consider also a DOJ statement regarding the 2014 creation of "justice AmeriCorps," a partnership between the Corporation for National and Community Service (CNCS) and the EOIR. The grant program would enroll approximately one hundred attorneys and paralegals as AmeriCorps members "to provide legal services to the most vulnerable of these [unaccompanied] children."[2] Significantly, vulnerability was ascribed a specific age, location, and bureaucratic positionality: justice AmeriCorps would aid young people under age sixteen who were not in the custody of ORR or DHS; who had received a notice to appear in removal proceedings before an immigration court; who had not had their cases consolidated with removal proceedings against a parent or legal guardian; and who were in an immigration court location where grants were located.[3]

Justice AmeriCorps "reaffirm[s] our allegiance to the values that have always shaped our pursuit of justice," stated Attorney General Eric Holder. "We empower new generations of aspiring attorneys and paralegals to serve their country and stand on the front lines of this fight. And we bolster both the efficacy and the efficiency of our immigration courts. . . . How we treat those in need, particularly young people who must appear in immigration proceedings—many of whom are fleeing violence, persecution, abuse or trafficking—goes to the core of who we are as a nation."[4]

While much could be written about the lauded provision of one hundred additional legal advocates to address an influx of seventy thousand unaccompanied minors, my aim is not to underscore what are often woefully limited policy solutions. Instead, I recognize this ceremonial recognition of legal advocacy—in this case as part of, if not *the* necessary "care" of unaccompanied youth—as evidence of immigration cause lawyers' successful but fraught self-promotion and public image.

This image relies largely on the figure of the "unaccompanied Fujianese child," even as the media and political interests tend to overlook this population of young migrants. That they do so is unsurprising: in fiscal year 2013, youth in the "Other" category comprised just 3 percent of total unaccompanied minors, or approximately 780 individuals.[5] Nonetheless, and as I demonstrate, the numerically insignificant "other" of Fujianese youth proves uniquely challenging to cause lawyers—*as well as necessary to the cause lawyering identity*. Indeed, what many cause lawyers describe as the frustratingly opaque or uneasy goals, family expectations, culture, and age of young Fujianese clients are at once a personal and professional advantage.

Interpreted as shadowy and desperate, the "spectacular" accounts of Fujianese youth arguably offer a more compelling and convincing cause than do those of young Central American migrants, a population believed to be known all too well as a result of nativist politics and racialized public discourse (see Lee 2003). Consider for instance the aforementioned description of an "explosion" of migrant youth. As Leo Chavez (2001, 2008) and others argue, this language taps into prevalent, deep-rooted anxieties about an invasion of Latinx "illegal aliens," no matter their childhood "innocence" (Heidbrink 2014; Rodriguez 1997). It is significant, of course, that the anti-immigrant sentiment that identifies Latinx individuals as "perpetual foreigners" reflects—and is certainly rooted in—Chinese exclusion era policies and attitudes (Lee 2003, 249; McKeown 2009; Statz 2016b).

It is perhaps no surprise, then, that immigration cause lawyers rely so heavily on "other" youth to establish the unquestioned worthiness of their work. Examples of what Greta Lynn Uehling (2008) calls a "racialized hierarchy of treatment"[6] or, perhaps in this case, a racialized hierarchy of legal advocacy, are widespread. In an introduction to the unaccompanied youth it serves (the majority of whom are Central American), the website of one advocacy organization features only an orphan from Ethiopia and a young girl from China.[7] Of the client testimonies included on another organization's "In Their Own Words" webpage, the stories of young migrants from Poland, Trinidad, China, and Guinea are featured alongside just two accounts of Central American youth—again evidencing a strategic disassociation of a cause from the majority of unaccompanied youth who need and receive legal advocacy.[8]

FROM CERTAIN CARE TO UNCERTAINTY'S POTENTIAL

As I argue in this book, the lawyers in this study maintain their subjective jurisdiction of a cause by constructing Chinese youth as uniquely vulnerable—and their parents as uniquely culpable—through normative narratives of age and morality alongside Orientalist economics and the "spectacular case." This is mutually productive, a process by which an image of Fujianese youth is established *along with* specific versions of the United States, the legal profession, and the US legal system via discourses of law (Ruskola 2013, 5). Cause lawyers further establish their obligation and, in a sense, *worthiness* to "treat" (Abbott 1988) this population of migrants through a rhetoric of care—by ambiguously conflating welfare and safety with legal status, best interests with rights, and guardianship with legal representation.

Of course, lawyers' use and understanding of "care" must be recognized as situational and also as largely divergent from Fujianese youths' own expectations and experiences of it. That the interpretations and anticipated ends of advocacy are not shared by lawyers and their clients is profoundly consequential. It also signals where the cause falls short of cause lawyering more generally. While I recognize that my engagement with these tensions is disciplinarily distanced or delayed, it is also the anthropological approach I try to maintain, one of "mutual, intersubjective questioning," that makes space for this uncertainty—and that likewise identifies the inherent potential of it in the context of cause lawyering. In what follows, I briefly retrace the uncertain rights, responsibilities, and expectations I ethnographically documented. This, I believe, is a hopeful act.

In the legal realm, immigration cause lawyers stress that their work is the "provision of care." Legal status is pursued as a form of safety and protection for children who would otherwise be unsafe in their countries or families of origin. As my data suggest, this permits lawyers to distinguish or distance themselves from the potential suspicion that they are applying for asylum, T visas, or SIJ solely for legal status and benefits. Consider the statement an attorney made at the "On Their Own" conference: "Immigration judges aren't bad people, but there's confusion among them about whether [we pursue] SIJ . . . for immigration benefits or for *the right thing*—the protection and care of the child."

Protection and care take on a different meaning outside the legal realm, perhaps most notably in the private moments when cause lawyers do not need to champion or defend their cause to audiences of funders, immigration judges, trial attorneys, or other colleagues. In our conversations, attorneys often grappled with the limitations of their advocacy, specifically the inability to extend protection to other meaningful areas of youths' lives, such as labor. In this space, care was no longer explained as safety and protection but as legal status. And legal status was, and had to be, enough.

There are compelling exceptions to this, of course, perhaps most notably in "new destination" communities, where many of the attorneys I interviewed maintained informal partnerships with local colleagues, law enforcement, educators, and others to help safeguard the rights and services available to undocumented community members. Yet while exceptional and certainly laudable, these efforts nonetheless tended to focus on more visible Latinx families. Moreover, even if a young person had a legal advocate when she moved to a new destination, as did Wenyun, it was still likely that a more expansive understanding of care—in this case, one that included dental care—would be devalued by a cause lawyer in so many ways removed in Chicago. What is lost and what is imposed in these strategic, situational interpretations of care matters. They not only signal a disregard for *other* critical rights and protections but also may additionally compromise the intimate forms of status youth themselves value.

Yet as I also evidence, implicit in these tensions is the broader and constraining context in which immigration cause lawyers work. Beyond their negotiations of the "natural rights" of children, the "inalienable rights" of immigrants, and the "rights worthiness" of unaccompanied youth who are understood as accountable but somehow lacking agency, the immigration cause lawyers in this study must navigate multiple scales of bureaucracy, time, and funding. And in the specific realm of advocacy on behalf of Fujianese youth, additional tensions emerge. As I detail in this book, the expectations, commitments, and very presence of Fujianese clients unsettle attorneys' own responsibilities and motivations. Challenging presumptions of passivity or dependency, these youth are "overtly agentful" (Coe et al. 2011) in their management of migration journeys and economic responsibilities. And in the legal realm, Fujianese minors' nuanced, creative practices complicate one-dimensional portrayals of *The Vulnerable Fujianese Child* in legal representation—even, or particularly, when youth reproduce the tragic accounts they believe their attorneys need. In this way each "using the system," attorneys and their clients emerge as strategically wielding—and powerfully encountering—vulnerability that is at once discursive, professional, and intimately felt.

As they lead and lag in their communities of origin and destination, the complex social worlds of Fujianese youth should cause us, and cause lawyers, to more critically consider the reach and possible consequences of legal advocacy on clients' relationships, obligations, and identities. Of course, while the youth in this project illuminate and implicitly unsettle the constraining choices attorneys make on behalf of a "cause," their presence also points to the constraining choices *available* to immigration lawyers. Remember Russell's description of legal advocacy: "The law forces you—the law defines the box. The lawyering task is to put [the client] in the right box."

As I demonstrate, the task of putting unaccompanied Fujianese youth "in the right box" requires a reduction of family, age, and culture in the legal realm. While certainly meaningful to this study, these routinized oversimplifications simultaneously call for more critical attention to the forms of legal relief available to immigrant youth; to contradictions in the bureaucratic management and interpretation of "care"; and to the contestations of age, agency, and rights that occur across the shifting lawscapes of the "deportation regime" (De Genova and Peutz 2010; Philippopoulos-Mihalopoulos and FitzGerald 2008). In this political context, cause lawyers' situational interpretation of protection and best interests is demanded—and perhaps even warranted. At the same time, the limited and consequential nature of this advocacy is not simply the outcome of immigration laws and policies. It also reflects lawyers' successful claims over the cause of unaccompanied Fujianese minors.

Utilizing the "spectacular case" and asserting an "expert" understanding of the cultural and kin obligations of unaccompanied Fujianese youth, cause lawyers establish their subjective jurisdiction over the rarely contextualized phenomenon of unaccompanied child migration. As my data evidence, these attorneys largely promote and rely on the power-filled appearance of intimacy with young migrants to legitimize their exclusive expertise, obligation, and indispensability to the cause at hand. The outcome of this is glaringly apparent in media and publicity campaigns, where lawyers are overwhelmingly portrayed as *the* solution to the legal needs and wellbeing of unaccompanied youth. This signals a profound impasse. Indeed, it effectively forecloses opportunities to enhance—or better, redefine—advocacy efforts by granting equal voice to child welfare authorities, social workers, researchers, parents, guardians, and most importantly, youth themselves. It also implicitly resists the notion of an uncertain or inconclusive future (Bakhtin 1981, 28) by reifying the ideal of legal status as "successful"—and ostensibly concluded—advocacy.

In a sense, then, this book calls for *more* than a recognition of the ongoing rights, responsibilities, and expectations that young migrants and cause lawyers identify as important. Indeed, it draws on anthropology's deep familiarity with doubt and ambiguity to invite a more explicit acknowledgement of the uncertainty at the root of lawyering for and around mobility. Within the questioning that arises from such an expansive acknowledgement, there abides a necessary reconsideration of profession, place, and age as fixed or "untraversable differences." It is here, I believe, that advocacy may begin to address a critically neglected component of "cause lawyering," namely a respect-filled and negotiated *partnership* with Fujianese youth to achieve more mutual, albeit never fully finished, ends.

NOTES

PREFACE

1. I utilize *Latinx* as a gender-inclusive alternative to the gender binary in Latina/o.

CHAPTER 1

1. Homeland Security Act of 2002, 6 U.S.C. § 279 (g)(2).
2. National Network for Youth, "Conference: On Their Own; Protecting the Rights of Immigrant Children." April 24–26, 2012. *www.nn4youth.org/news/ network-news/2012/03/08/conference-their-own-protecting-rights-immigrant-children-april-24-26-2.*
3. I officially registered for the "On Their Own" conference and likewise identified my status as a researcher and my research objectives to the conference organizers.
4. I have synthesized this definition from policy reports, organizational websites, fundraising promotions, and conversations with attorneys.
5. During my fieldwork, a group of immigration attorneys and an international children's rights expert who participated in this research compiled and analyzed data from the DHS Office of Immigration Statistics, recent scholarship on Chinese migration trends, and CIA testimony regarding organized crime and smuggling. They arrived at the estimation that approximately 5 percent of unauthorized Chinese migrants to the United States are unaccompanied youth, and that approximately fifteen thousand Chinese children entered the United States between 2001 and 2010, or an average of fifteen hundred per year.
6. Particularly in Chapter 4, I endeavor to highlight the unique experiences of Fuzhounese youth. While the majority of the young people I interviewed were from Fuzhou, a few migrated from elsewhere in the Province. For this reason, and because migration patterns from Fujian Province have changed over time and will continue to shift, I use the more general "Fujianese" descriptor for most of this book.
7. 2011 Fujian Statistic Bureau. n.d. Accessed August 2, 2016. *www.fujian.gov.cn/.* In 2013, Fujian had the eleventh highest GDP of China's provinces. China Statistical Database. n.d. Accessed August 19, 2014. *219.235.129.58/welcome.do.*

8. In this book, I typically utilize the term UAC only when describing the legal and political contexts in which it is most commonly enlisted. How and why a young person is determined to be "unaccompanied" and a "child" are publicly acknowledged tensions in the apprehension, detention, and release of young migrants (Heidbrink 2014). A related issue is whether or not the young person is even truly "unaccompanied." After all, many youth may be accompanied in migration by extended family or family friends, and some have parents in the United States who are reluctant to claim their child from federal authorities owing to their own unauthorized status. I am accordingly deliberate in my use of terminology, prioritizing "youth" and "global," "migrant," or "designated unaccompanied" instead of "unaccompanied child."

9. I use "legal status" to refer to someone who is a Lawful Permanent Resident (LPR, a recipient of a green card) or a US citizen.

10. United Nations, Department of Economic and Social Affairs, Population Division. 2015. "Trends in International Migrant Stock: The 2015 Revision." *www.un.org/en/development/desa/population/migration/data/estimates2/estimates15.shtml.*

11. Weiss, Debra Cassens. "Trump's travel ban 'drips with religious intolerance,' says en banc appeals court; injunction sticks." *ABA Journal,* May 25, 2017. *www.abajournal.com/news/article/trumps_travel_ban_drips_with_religious_intolerance_says_en_banc_appeals_cou/.*

12. As with the Quota Act of 1921 and the Immigration Act of 1924.

13. The 1965 Immigration Act.

14. These include "Operation Gatekeeper" in San Diego, California; "Operation Rio Grande" in Brownsville, Texas; "Operation Safeguard" in Nogales, Arizona; and "Operation Hold the Line" in El Paso, Texas.

15. Apprehended unaccompanied minors from Mexico and Canada are typically removed within seventy-two hours to their countries of origin without a hearing before an immigration judge (IJ) owing to the Contiguous Territories Agreement between Canada, the United States, and Mexico. It is thus relatively rare for young Mexican migrants to enter ORR detention centers.

16. The repatriation of Fujianese youth is rare. In the course of my research, no cause lawyer I interviewed could recall any Fujianese youth designated UAC being repatriated. In 2010 an unaccompanied Chinese minor was voluntarily returned to China, but this individual was not Fujianese and had entered the US legally and overstayed a visa. For most Fujianese youth in removal proceedings, repatriation is an option that legal advocates typically and successfully resist. This opposition reflects the uncertainty that often underlies legal advocates' and decision makers' understandings of Chinese immigration policy and, specifically, China's exit and entry administration reforms (see Liu 2009), as well as other phenomena—the age of the young person, perceptions of the Chinese family and state, and so on—discussed throughout this book.

Family reunification is another complex option for Fujianese youth and attorneys to navigate. If the child identifies someone in the US as a possible family sponsor, how the child is related to this individual is often difficult to communicate or translate, let alone prove. Only with proper documentation from family in the US *and* China and the completion of a successful home study can the child be released to a family member. To complicate things further, while many Fujianese youth do have family members in the US, often these individuals are themselves undocumented. Family reunification is technically possible in these instances, but many Fujianese youth and their relatives are not aware of or distrust this assurance. As a result, some Fujianese youth will never admit that they have family members in the US. Another complication occurs if a family member refuses sponsorship responsibilities for the youth. This may be because of financial and familial strains (cannot afford another child), distance (from school, healthcare, employment), or other concerns.

17. The US offers two forms of asylum application: affirmative and defensive. Until the 2008 passage of the William Wilberforce Trafficking Victims Protection Reauthorization Act (TVPRA), any undocumented individual who entered the US and was apprehended, including a minor, was required to file a defensive application with the IJ adjudicating her or his removal proceedings (Byrne 2008). In substantive US asylum law, youth were accordingly treated as adults and required to meet the definition of (an adult) refugee outlined in the Immigration and Nationality Act (INA): "Any person who is outside any country of such person's nationality and is unable or unwilling to avail himself or herself of the protection of that country because of persecution or a well-founded fear of persecution on account of race, religion, nationality, membership in a particular social group, or political opinion" (8 U.S.C. §1101(a)(42)(A)). This presented a profoundly consequential impediment to young asylum seekers who were unable to describe or fully comprehend the varying aspects of persecution, race, religion, nationality, political opinion, and membership in a particular social group as presented in the INA, no matter how applicable a basis one or more of these qualifications may have been for a claim.

Significant changes to asylum proceedings were introduced with the TVPRA, perhaps the most relevant being the manner in which unaccompanied minors' asylum applications should be processed. Instead of requiring an unaccompanied minor to undergo adversarial removal proceedings before an immigration judge, the TVPRA grants initial jurisdiction over UAC asylum applications to asylum officers from the US Citizenship and Immigration Services (USCIS), meaning that youth subsequently undergo non-adversarial asylum interviews (TVPRA §235(d)(7)(B)). Even those unaccompanied minors issued a "Notice to Appear" in immigration court, or minors who have not previously filed for asylum with USCIS and have a pending claim in immigration court on appeal to the Board of Immigration Appeals, can have their asylum claim heard and adjudicated by a USCIS asylum officer in an affirmative hearing in a "non-adversarial setting." This typically occurs in the asylum officer's office.

Yet if the officer denies the petition, as many attorneys report typically happens with Fujianese youth, the young person must pursue the case in immigration court through the defensive asylum process. An adversarial asylum procedure includes a trial attorney representing the government, taped proceedings, cross-examinations, and a formal courtroom set-up, often including court-provided interpreters. This is extremely frustrating for cause lawyers, who find themselves working within an adversarial setting they believe is inappropriate for young clients (see Chapter 3).

18. Intended to enhance federal activity to combat trafficking, the T visa was introduced with the 2000 passage of the Victims of Trafficking and Violence Prevention Act (VTVPA) and reauthorized in 2008 through TVPRA. To qualify for T nonimmigrant status, a person must: 1) be or have been a victim of a severe form of trafficking in persons; 2) be physically present in the US on account of trafficking; 3) comply with a request from a federal, state, or local law enforcement agency for assistance in the investigation or prosecution of human trafficking (qualifying individuals under age eighteen are not required to cooperate in order to receive immigration benefits); and 4) demonstrate that extreme hardship involving severe and unusual harm would be suffered if removed from the US. Once a T nonimmigrant visa is granted, a victim can apply for permanent residence after three years.

19. William Wilberforce Trafficking Victims Protection Reauthorization Act of 2008, §235(d)(1). It is thus a three-part process to secure SIJ: an attorney must get an SIJ predicate order from a state court, then petition for SIJ status (through USCIS, a federal agency), and finally file for lawful permanent residence with USCIS (if filing affirmatively) or federal immigration court (if filing defensively).

20. State Justice Institute. 2015:8. Accessed January 16, 2017. *www.sji.gov/wp/wp-content/uploads/15- 167_NCSC_UICGuide_FULL-web1.pdf.*

21. INA, 8 U.S.C. §1101(a)(27)(J)(iii)(II). Of equal, if not delayed, consequence, an immigration court may find an individual's petition for legal relief suspect if her or his child has earlier been declared a public ward of the state through SIJ.

22. As Lauren Heidbrink (2014, 53) demonstrates, the best interests of some children, including those who might *symbolically* warrant the state's protection—e.g., youth from Cuba or the Soviet Union—tend to matter more than that of others, often Central American and Mexican youth.

23. With the exception of this chapter's opening vignette, reference to the Undocumented Migration Project, and Chapter 6, the names of all individuals, nonprofit organizations, and some locations featured in this book have been changed or generalized to maintain anonymity. Protecting the confidentiality of research participants is something that I, following anthropological principles of professional responsibility and the ethical guidance of my university's Institutional Review Board, take very seriously. Accordingly, while I have presented the data I collected on their own terms, i.e., without ever modifying

a person's words or documented demeanor, the sources of these data have been changed via pseudonyms and generalized in order to avoid identification with places, organizations, or jurisdictions.

24. Based at the University of Michigan, the UMP is a long-term anthropological study of undocumented migration between Mexico and the United States.

25. Operation Streamline is the controversial fast-tracked, federal criminal prosecution of undocumented migrants who are apprehended at the US-Mexico border. Accessed August 1, 2016. *www.law.berkeley.edu/files/Operation_ Streamline_Policy_Brief.pdf.*

26. The Homeland Security Act of 2002 divided responsibilities for the processing and treatment of unaccompanied youth between DHS and ORR, under HHS. To DHS, the law assigned responsibility for the apprehension, transfer, and repatriation of UAC. To HHS, the law assigned responsibility for coordinating and implementing the care and placement of UAC in appropriate custody; reunifying UAC with their parents abroad if appropriate; maintaining and publishing a list of legal services available to UAC; and collecting statistical information on UAC, among other responsibilities. ORR created the Division of Unaccompanied Children's Services (DUCS) for addressing the requirements of this population.

27. Susan Terrio writes, "ORR regulations call for children to be held 'in a noninstitutional home-like atmosphere of care.' But . . . custody is not anything like home. All facilities are locked and organized on a penal model that requires controlled entry, exit and movement within the premises, as well as continuous supervision via surveillance cameras and line-of-sight checks. Children attend school inside the shelter, play sports within fenced areas and only leave the facilities for court appearances, special medical or psychiatric treatment and occasional community outings. They are subjected to rigid behavioral management programs that are both punitive and infantilizing" (2014).

28. A 2008 report from the Office of the Inspector General notes that case files from DUCS lacked documentation—"We could not determine whether lack of documentation in case files was a result of poor record keeping or failure to provide services"—and that little oversight of facilities or of methods to track the safety of youth who have been released to sponsors exists (Levinson 2008).

29. Many of the youth who invited me to their workplaces shared that they were the only "legal" (in their words) workers there.

30. These guidelines include the American Anthropological Association Code of Ethics and those put forth by the University of Washington's Institutional Review Board.

31. Within any population of unaccompanied youth, there exist individuals who enter the US to escape specific, often very private hardships including political, religious, or ethnic persecution or situations of abuse. Some youth additionally suffer trauma during their migration journeys. I did not include these individuals in my research out of respect for their privacy and well-being.

32. In this book, I only identify and excerpt from those case documents that are publicly available.
33. An obvious omission in this section, and indeed this project, is the experiences of young migrants' parents. At the time of my research, each youth I interviewed noted that her or his parents lived in Fujian Province. Then and now, I believe that the perspectives of these individuals would powerfully enhance and likely complicate the data I collected. Unfortunately, however, it was beyond the scope of my research (and ultimately, research funding) to include the experiences of Fujianese parents in a way that was necessarily rigorous, linguistically appropriate, politically and legally sensitive, and documented in Fujian Province itself.

CHAPTER 2

1. I have also found work on public-interest advocacy and street-level bureaucracies helpful and relevant (see Ashar 2007; Gordon 2005; Lipsky 2010; Tremblay 1992).
2. Accordingly, cause lawyering is generally seen as a more inclusive term than public interest law (see Albiston and Nielsen 2014; Southworth 2005a). It likewise recognizes the implicit subjectivity of a cause, whereas "to talk about public interest lawyering is to take on irresolvable disputes about what is, or is not, in the public interest. Whether the pursuit of any particular cause advances the public interest is very much in the eye of the beholder" (Scheingold and Sarat 2004, 5).
3. By "regular" I mean pro bono advocacy that is personally prioritized and/or exceeds the bounds of professional rules or recommendations for pro bono work (such as those stipulated by state bars or the American Bar Association).
4. Impact litigation refers to the use of a "leading case" such as *Brown v. Board of Education* to effect changes in the law and have broader impacts on sociopolitical conditions (see McKinley 1997).
5. Removal proceedings are civil proceedings. Undocumented youth are thus allowed to have counsel but are not entitled to it at government expense, as in criminal proceedings (INA §240(b)(4)(A); see also Haddal 2007).
6. Most of the attorneys I interviewed equated "aging out" with "turning eighteen." Under federal law, an individual is eligible to apply for SIJ status until age eighteen. However, a young person must obtain a juvenile court order and apply to USCIS for SIJ status before s/he ages out of the juvenile court's jurisdiction, usually before eighteen years of age (though in some states juvenile court jurisdiction extends beyond age twenty-one). Attorneys often rush to schedule home visits (if family reunification is a possibility) and evaluate legal remedies before a young person turns eighteen, at which point she or he is no longer eligible for certain protections and is transferred from shelter care to an adult detention center.

7. Wood and Young 2013, 1. Note that Wendy Young is President of KIND (Kids in Need of Defense, an organization that provides legal support to young migrants).
8. KIND: Kids in Need of Defense. n.d. Accessed August 1, 2014. *www. supportkind.org/en/*.
9. The Young Center for Immigrant Children's Rights. n.d. Accessed August 1, 2014. *theyoungcenter.org*.
10. UN General Assembly, UDHR supra note 3, art. 2. All thirty articles in the UDHR are age neutral except Article 16, which concerns marriage and family.
11. *Beharry v. Reno*, 183 F. Supp. 2d 584 (E.D.N.Y. 2002).
12. Somalia ratified the CRC in 2015, after this interview occurred.
13. The relevance of and relationship between child welfare and immigration law is rarely recognized. Part of this has to do with the allocation of power between state and federal courts: federal courts have authority in matters of immigration, whereas the primacy of the states in family law has long been accepted (Thronson 2008, 456; see also Frankel 2011). Likewise, undocumented youth have different, and certainly fewer, procedural rights than youth with legal status.
14. This was largely reflected in and influenced by the passage of the Child Abuse Prevention and Treatment Act (CAPTA) of 1974, in which federal grants to states were made contingent upon the provision of GAL in child protective proceedings.
15. Significantly, like deportation proceedings, delinquency proceedings are civil, not criminal, hearings.
16. This is likely the following: Mehta, Suketu. 2011. "The Asylum Seeker: For a chance at a better life, it helps to make your bad story worse." *New Yorker*, August 1, 2011. *www.newyorker.com/magazine/2011/08/01/the-asylum-seeker*.
17. Non-citizens who are present in the US or who arrive at its border may be granted asylum if they qualify as refugees, defined as "any person who is outside any country of such person's nationality or . . . any country in which such person last habitually resided, and who is unable or unwilling to return to . . . the protection of that country because of persecution or a well-founded fear of persecution on account of race, religion, nationality, membership in a particular social group, or political opinion" (INA §101(a)(42)(A)).
18. Intended to resolve legal uncertainty, a declaratory judgment is the conclusive, legally binding determination of a court. In an SIJ case, a declaratory judgment action is filed to establish that the child has been abused, abandoned, or neglected and is declared dependent upon family court.
19. Federal law requires that ORR feed, shelter, and provide medical care for unaccompanied youth until it is able to release them to safe settings with sponsors (typically family members) while they await immigration proceedings. The sponsor must agree to ensure the child's presence at all future immigration proceedings and ensure the minor reports to ICE if an IJ issues a removal order or voluntary departure order. (Office of Refugee Resettlement. 2017.

"Unaccompanied Alien Children Released to Sponsors by State." Published June 30, 2017. *www.acf.hhs.gov/orr/programs/ucs/state-by-state-uc-placed-sponsors*). Between October 2015 and April 2016, ORR released nearly 23,000 unaccompanied youth to sponsors. It released 53,515 and 27,250 in the two prior fiscal years (Schlechter 2016). Most released youth are from El Salvador, Honduras, and Guatemala.

20. The Department of Justice (DOJ) oversees the EOIR, which conducts immigration court proceedings, appellate reviews, and administrative hearings. Because the DOJ has a very strict policy regarding IJ contact with the media and public, I had only brief, informal conversations with IJs in my research.

21. In 2013, the Obama administration removed 438,000 immigrants. In the 2011 fiscal year, the administration removed 387,000 immigrants. (Gonzalez-Barrera, Ana, and Jens Manuel Krogstad. 2014. "US deportations of immigrants reach record high in 2013." *Pew Research Center*. October 2, 2014. *www.pewresearch.org/fact-tank/2014/10/02/u-s-deportations-of-immigrants-reach-record-high-in-2013/*.

22. Immigration court is not part of the US judicial branch but the DOJ, which reports to the president.

23. Section 287(g) of the INA, codified at 8 U.S.C. § 1357(g), authorizes the federal government to enter into agreements with state and local law enforcement agencies to deputize officers to perform the functions of federal immigration agents. Under 287(g), ICE provides officers with the training and authorization to identify, process, and detain immigration offenders they encounter during regular law enforcement activity. The 287(g) program has proven largely ineffective and consequential, resulting in the harassment of local residents and the isolation of increasingly marginalized im/migrant community members (see Weissman, Headen, and Parker 2009).

24. According to the EOIR Immigration Judge Benchbook, "The rules of evidence applicable to criminal proceedings do not apply to removal hearings. The Supreme Court in United States ex rel. *Bilokumsky v. Tod*, 236 U.S. 149 (1923), noted that a failure to abide by judicial rules of evidence does not render a removal hearing unfair. . . . Evidence during a removal proceeding is controlled by the Code of Federal Regulations; any type of evidence is admissible so long as it is material and relevant to the issues before the hearing. 8 C.F.R. § 1240.7(a). Regarding hearsay, the Federal Rules of Evidence define hearsay as 'a statement, other than one made by the declarant while testifying at the trial or hearing, offered in evidence to prove the truth of the matter asserted.' Fed. R. Evid. 801(c). A.) Hearsay evidence is admissible in deportation proceedings unless its use is fundamentally unfair. *Matter of Grijalva*, 19 I and N Dec. 713 (BIA 1988). Hearsay evidence may be relied on, even if contradicted by direct evidence. *Calhoun v. Bailar*, 626 F.2d 145 (9th Cir. 1980). B.) The corollary is also true" (Immigration Judge Benchbook. n.d. Accessed November 8, 2013. *www.justice.gov/eoir/vll/benchbook/resources/sfoutline/Hearsay.htm*).

CHAPTER 3

1. Typically, young research participants and I conversed using a combination of Mandarin and English. For readability, excerpts are primarily presented in English.

2. In China, primary and middle school are free, though there are fees for books, uniforms, and sometimes room and board. There is a relatively small cost to attend high school, and some parents pay money for private tutors, particularly to help young people prepare for *gaokao*, the National Higher Education Entrance Examination.

3. China Statistical Yearbook. 2016. *www.stats.gov.cn/tjsj/ndsj/2016/indexeh.htm*.

4. O'Shaughnessy, Patrice. 2008. "The Golden Venture Tragedy: From hell at sea to the American Dream." *New York Daily News*, June 8, 2008. *www.nydailynews.com/news/golden-venture-tragedy-hell-sea-american-dream-article-1.294299*; Peter Cohn, dir. 2006. *Golden Venture: A Journey into the US Immigration Nightmare*. Hillcrest Films. *www.goldenventuremovie.com/*; Hyland, Julie. 2000. "58 Chinese migrants found dead in lorry at Dover, Britain." World Socialist Web Site. June 21, 2000. *www.wsws.org/en/articles/2000/06/immi-j21.html*.

5. Ross, Ben. 2007. "Coming to America . . . Fuzhou's Main Export is People." *Ben Ross' Blog*. May 22, 2007. *benross.net/wordpress/illegal-immigration/2007/05/22/*.

6. See also Gonçalo dos Santos' work on the "orthodoxy of the lineage paradigm" (2006). Largely developed by anthropologists in the 1960s, the lineage paradigm puts forth a male-centric, politico-jural model of the "Confucian family." It is founded on shared norms (such as patriarchy and filial piety), shared resources, and a common ritual base of ancestral duties and obligations (Fei [1947] 1992; Freedman 1958, 1966; Watson 1982). Though subtly challenged by Wolf's "uterine family" (1972), R. Watson's attention to social inequality (1985), and Judd's emphasis on women's relationships within natal families (1989), the lineage paradigm put forth an influential, arguably static understanding of "Chinese Culture," one that persists today.

7. I have fully translated all interview excerpts with Fujianese youth into English, with the exception of my conversations with Hua. Here, Hua's words are presented with no translation or adjustment for proper grammar, tense, etc. This is a deliberate choice, made to highlight Hua's enthusiastic command of English and, accordingly, the efforts and skills of which she was particularly proud. Doing so also underscores those broader concepts and realities (including illegality and her relatively young age) to which Hua responded with both linguistic and emotional reticence.

8. As in other populations of clandestine migrants, there are some Fujianese minors who suffer trauma during their migration journeys. I thus draw only on narratives like that of Hua and others, youth with whom I had sufficient rapport and who exhibited comfort and candor as they reflected on their experiences. This decision arises from my personal concern for individuals'

privacy and well-being, as well as my ethical responsibilities as a researcher. Yet, I also believe that the youth I consider in this book are fairly representative of their counterparts around the US, including those unaccompanied Fujianese who arrived in the US with similar goals and responsibilities but were never apprehended.

9. The most obvious, if cynical, explanation for this is the relative impossibility of gaining legal relief for a young adult who maintains she or he independently chose to come to the US.

10. In interviews with youth and attorneys from 2010 to 2013, I was repeatedly told that $80,000 was the typical fee for youth to be smuggled from China to the US (See also Liu 2007).

CHAPTER 4

1. In the US, this is evidenced through the 2000 passage of the VTVPA, the 2008 reauthorization of the T visa, and the ongoing allocation of state and NGO resources to anti-trafficking campaigns and counter-trafficking activities.

2. In an effort to identify the "inadequacies and service gaps" in the US' treatment of undocumented youth designated as victims of trafficking, Elzbieta Gozdziak and Margaret MacDonnell write: "The particular vulnerability of child [trafficking] victims, related to biophysiological, social, behavioral, and cognitive phases of the maturity process, distinguishes them from adult victims and underscores the necessity of special attention to their particular needs" (2007, 171). The authors also place a specific emphasis on sex trafficking: "Human trafficking for sexual exploitation and forced labor is believed to be one of the fastest growing areas of criminal activity. The vast majority of victims of severe forms of trafficking are women and children."

3. While there has been a marked increase in federal prosecutions of cases involving the trafficking of young people for sex (TRAC 2013), there is also, significantly, a well-documented tendency among state and nonprofit agencies to focus uncritically on the sexual exploitation of "women and children" in reports and publicity efforts rather than the more prevalent, though arguably less sensational, trafficking for labor. The United Nations Office on Drugs and Crime's (UNODC) "Factsheet on Human Trafficking" likewise acknowledges: "Human trafficking has many faces: forced or bonded labor; domestic servitude and forced marriage; organ removal; and the exploitation of children. . . . However, *probably due to statistical bias and national legislation*, sexual exploitation (79 percent) is by far the most commonly identified form of trafficking in persons" (UNODC 2010; emphasis added).

4. While I believe anti-trafficking discourses deserve critical attention, I also recognize the tenuous identification that may emerge from this position, namely being "anti-anti-trafficking." One suggested response is to follow Clifford Geertz's (1984) stance on anti-relativism, i.e., a rejection of anti-relativism but

not a commitment to or defense of relativism (see also Engle 2001), though I find this insufficient. For now, I view nascent research on the doubt and irony, as well as the expansiveness and hope, inherent in anti-trafficking initiatives and policy-making a critical and promising direction (see, e.g., Marcus and Curtis 2014).

5.   As Sanghera and others point out, the factors to which the growth of global trafficking has been attributed—poverty, lack of sustainable livelihoods, structural inequities, gender discrimination, armed conflict, natural disasters—are not in themselves the causes of trafficking. Rather, they simply exacerbate the vulnerability of marginalized and disadvantaged groups (Sanghera 2005, 8; see also Ruggerio 2003) already rendered precarious through more complex global economic policies that call for free trade and large transnational corporations' unqualified access to natural resources and raw materials (Kempadoo 2005; see also Hill 2014; Jones 2016). These are policies that significantly "guarantee, and defend, the rights of social powerful elites . . . while they limit the access, movement, and rights of [others]" (Kempadoo 2005, xiv–xv). Thus, despite offering focused, highly-publicized advocacy efforts on behalf of the world's "most vulnerable," presumably poor women and children of the Global South, the framework of international anti-trafficking organizations like the UNODC implicitly supports the economic interests of corporations, multilateral agencies, and national governments. It is accordingly unsurprising that the majority of anti-trafficking interventions continue to emphasize the rescue, repatriation, and rehabilitation of victims and target the supply side of trafficking. Rarely, if ever, do these efforts recognize the trafficking of persons as a demand-driven phenomenon.

6.   22 U.S.C. § 7102(9)(b) (2000).

7.   While attorneys largely appeal to the labor or services category rather than prostitution, my data suggest it is often more important to establish *that* a young person has been trafficked as opposed to *why* s/he was trafficked. Accordingly, this section largely traces the efforts attorneys take to clarify that parents sent a young person to the US against her or his volition, thereby establishing that the youth was trafficked and not smuggled.

8.   When presenting aspects of my research at scholarly conferences, my project was often reframed by audience members as *actually* being about "the dysfunctional US immigration system." While I found this interpretation frustratingly superficial, it is also relevant given the confusing nature of immigration law and the pervasive view of the US immigration system as chaotic, inconsistent, and, ultimately, dysfunctional.

9.   While I was initially reluctant to rely so heavily on *one* document, "It Was(n't) My Choice" was at the time of my research representative of, and a trusted resource for, many attorneys' trafficking claims on behalf of Fujianese minors in removal proceedings. (See Chapter 6 for cultural interpretations and legal strategies similar to those Burke provides.)

10. Another VTVPA remedy, the U visa was designed for undocumented victims of violent crimes who, as with T nonimmigrant status, collaborate with US law enforcement in the investigation and/or prosecution of the crimes they experienced (22 U.S.C. 7101§1513(b)(3)(iii) 2000).

11. The 1994 Violence Against Women Act (VAWA) provides immigration relief to family members abused by their citizen or LPR spouse or parent.

12. A common argument is that this process simply reflects the accepted professional commitments of lawyers. "Lawyers," one law professor stated flatly, "are obligated under ethical rules to make the best argument possible."

13. A "legal fiction" is most commonly understood as an assumption of fact made by the court as a basis for deciding a legal question. While ultimately an ad hoc remedy to meet an unforeseen situation, many legal fictions are nonetheless institutionalized, preserved to advance public policy and the rights of certain individuals and groups. "Legal fiction" has a complex and often contested history in jurisprudence, but at the risk of oversimplifying things, I draw on a common example of legal fiction—the granting of personhood to a corporation—to extend the term to this research, where the law and legal practitioners understand a group as a unit, strategically disregarding the group's individual members. Thus, while I do not view the Fujianese migration narrative as a legal fiction, particularly since it may be disputed by trial attorneys or judges, the static category of "Chinese UACS" and assertions of childhood as an "immutable status" are arguable fictions (see also Barskey 2006).

14. ORR assumed this role on March 1, 2003, and subsequently created the Division of Unaccompanied Children's Services (DUCS). Between then and 2005, ORR began to focus on options for legal services, eventually contracting with the Vera Institute of Justice (see Byrne and Miller 2012; Haddal 2007).

15. *Ayi* translates as "maternal aunt," but it is also a designation for a paid helper, like a housekeeper or nanny, and also a common term children use to address adult women. Attorneys often suspect the person a youth describes as an *ayi* is affiliated with snakehead smugglers and only posing as an aunt.

16. INA §101(a)(27)(J) (1952) and TVPRA §235(d)(1) (2008).

17. A spiritual discipline of meditation, qigong exercises, and moral philosophy, Falun Gong has also been described as a religion, a cult, and a dissident spiritual movement (see Porter 2003; Lum 2006). In the 2005 Report on International Religious Freedom, the US State Department designated China a "country of particular concern" (CPC) owing to the continued arrest, detention, and imprisonment of Falun Gong practitioners (*www.state.gov/j/drl/rls/irf/2005/*). A popular and often suspect asylum claim, a number of attorneys referenced Falun Gong as another instance of "the jig is up."

18. A petition for U nonimmigrant status must contain a certification of helpfulness from a certifying agency. That means the victim must provide a U Nonimmigrant Status Certification from a US law enforcement agency that demonstrates the petitioner "has been helpful, is being helpful, or is likely

to be helpful" in the investigation or prosecution of the criminal activity. In the case of T nonimmigrant status, if the victim is under the age of eighteen, he or she is eligible for certain benefits without the requirement of certification (USCIS. 2017. "Victims of Criminal Activity: U Nonimmigrant Status." Last updated August 25, 2017. *www.uscis.gov/humanitarian/victims-human-trafficking-other-crimes/victims-criminal-activity-u-nonimmigrant-status/victims-criminal-activity-u-nonimmigrant-status*).

19. I evaluate various interpretations of "care" in more detail in Chapter 7. For now, it is important to note that no attorney ever explicitly connected "care" to tangible immigration benefits like the permission to apply for Temporary Assistance for Needy Families (TANF); Supplemental Security Income (SSI); Medical Screening; One-Stop Career Center System; Housing Choice Vouchers; and so on.

CHAPTER 5

1. In this chapter I draw on media reports, firm profiles, case documents, and formal interviews and informal conversations with Young Sullivan, Audrey Hendricks, Hannah Sibiski, John Sullivan, and Maria Woltjen. Because of the public nature of the documents I rely on, and indeed, of the case itself, the individuals featured in this chapter are not assigned pseudonyms. To ensure I accurately captured their words and sentiments, I asked Young, John, Maria, and Hannah to read through and approve those chapter excerpts that directly feature and identify their reflections. I also systematically checked the public accessibility of the court documents I cite. My deep appreciation goes to these individuals for sharing so much legal, and often very personal, information with me.

2. In this section I re-present Young's story by juxtaposing the multiple retellings of it I encountered throughout my research. These include interviews and informal conversations with Maria as well as news stories, fundraising campaigns, and organizational promotions in which she—and sometimes Young—recounted his migration and legal journey. I also include excerpts from relevant case files and news articles detailing Young's case. These citations are footnoted.

3. Maria Woltjen as featured in the WBEZ program *Afternoon Shift*, "Number of Unaccompanied Immigrant Youth Coming to the US Rises," June 4, 2013. *soundcloud.com/afternoonshiftwbez/immigrant-minors-beyond-the*.

4. In 2014 the DHS estimated that more than sixty thousand unaccompanied minors would enter the United States that year. The majority of these youth arrived from El Salvador, Guatemala, and Honduras (see Millman and Jordan 2014).

5. WBEZ *Afternoon Shift*, "Number of Unaccompanied Immigrant Youth Coming to the US Rises," June 4, 2013. *soundcloud.com/afternoonshiftwbez/immigrant-minors-beyond-the*.

6. By "practice site," I mean the specific setting in which lawyers practice, such as a large private firm or a small, regional nonprofit that relies on state and federal

funding. "Practice sites help shape cause lawyering by providing different opportunities while imposing different costs. They make certain strategic decisions possible, while foreclosing others" (Sarat and Sheingold 2005, 11).

7. Blumenthal 2005.

8. Immigration Reform and Control Act of 1986, 8 USC § 1101(a)(27)(J)(iii)(l) (1986).

9. *Zheng v. Pogash*, 416 F. 2d 550 (S.D. Tex. 2006).

10. An injunction is a prohibitive, equitable remedy (a court order) issued or granted by a court that prohibits someone from doing some specified act or commands someone to undo some wrong or injury. A preliminary injunction is an injunction entered by a court prior to a final determination of the merits of a legal case in order to prohibit a party from moving—or compel a party to move—forward with a course of conduct until the case has been decided.

11. A key procedural question in this case was whether the REAL ID Act of 2005 (L. No. 109-13, 119 Stat. 231 (2005)) precluded a district court's jurisdiction to review the DHS's decision to deny consent. DHS argued that the REAL ID Act furthered congressional intent that discretionary decisions like Pogash's remain within the exclusive purview of the Attorney General and the Secretary of DHS. Young's counsel argued that the provision of the statute DHS highlighted did not apply to the process of obtaining SIJ status. Instead, the provision only limited judicial review of the executive decisions arising under Subchapter 2 of the INA, whereas a decision regarding specific consent arose from Subchapter 1 of the INA. The Court agreed with Young's counsel. Another procedural question raised in *Zheng v. Pogash* was whether DHS's decision was reviewable under the Administrative Procedure Act. Judge Hittner held that it was reviewable (*Zheng v. Pogash*, 416 F.2d 550 (S.D. Tex. 2006)).

12. Fulbright and Jaworski, the firm where John and Hannah worked when they took on Young's case.

13. My thanks to Heather Turcotte for this phrasing.

14. Maria attributed this closure to bad shelter conditions. The *New York Times* article about Young also mentions a child-abuse scandal (Blumenthal 2005).

15. In this section I rely almost exclusively on publicly available court documents and media reports.

16. Blumenthal 2005.

17. UN General Assembly, Convention Against Torture and Other Cruel, Inhuman or Degrading Treatment or Punishment, December 10, 1984, U.N.T.S. 1465.

18. *Young v. Ashcroft*, Petition for Review of Decision of the Board of Immigration Appeals (3d Cir. Dec. 22, 2003).

19. In re C-Y-Z-, 21 I. and N. Dec. 915 (BIA 1997).

20. Discussed in *Young v. Ashcroft*, Petition for Review of Decision of the Board of Immigration Appeals (3d Cir. Dec. 22, 2003).

21. *Young v. Ashcroft*.

22. Citing *Li v. INS*, in which an individual's claim of a well-founded fear of future persecution based on unauthorized departure from China was rejected by

relying in part on documentation that 118 undocumented migrants repatriated to Fujian were only detained "for initial screening and a fine" (*Li v. INS*, 92 F.3d 985 (9th Cir. 1996)).

23. Affidavit by Young Zheng, May 24, 2005, included in Motion to Stay Appeal Pending Resolution of Motion to Re-Open and Remand and Motion to Stay Removal, submitted by Sullivan et al. on May 26, 2005.

24. Remand here refers to a court procedure, an action by an appellate court in which a case is sent back to the trial court or lower appellate court for further action.

25. *Young Zheng v. Alberto Gonzales*. 2005. Brief of Young Zheng, Petitioner, on Petition for Review of a Final Order of the Board of Immigration Appeals. July 6, 2005.

26. Submitted letter of support written by Ruby Roman, Southwest Key, May 24, 2005.

27. Submitted letter of support written by Maria Woltjen, May 11, 2005.

28. Blumenthal 2006.

29. Submitted letter of support written by Ruby Roman, Southwest Key, May 24, 2005.

30. Submitted letter of support written by Adriana Macias Chamorro, Southwest Key Clinician, May 20, 2005.

31. Family commitment to education in China is, of course, overlooked in these statements, and is arguably a more pervasive and strongly held social value than in the United States (see Fong 2004; Kipnis 2011). My thanks to Stevan Harrell for this reminder.

32. Telephonic Statement and Answers of Yu Ping Zheng, transcribed by John Sullivan, June 11, 2005.

33. Of course, higher education is also a marker of adulthood and success in China, just as there are distinct but arguably parallel expectations and con-structions of childhood/youth as a sacrilized educational stage. What is sig-nificant here is the belief put forth by cause lawyers and advocates that higher education is a particularly "Western" marker of success and that China doesn't value education.

34. A particularly scathing description of Young's father is found in an amicus brief filed by Thomas H. Burton on August 2, 2005: "Young's father volun-tarily allowed his son to be transported to the United States by murderous smuggling gangs. . . . Young's father's conduct would also classify as *criminal* abandonment because *no reasonable adult* (with any regard for his child's safety) would refuse all contact with their son when the son is facing torture and death threats from others. . . . Young has been traumatized by his father's conduct" (emphasis added).

35. Brief in Support of Respondent's Motion to Re-open and Remand and Motion to Stay Removal (May 25, 2005).

36. Following Ian Tyrrell (1991), I recognize the theory of American exceptionalism not as based on one particular narrative but rather as a composite of claims about

American national identity that are used for a variety of purposes. The version I utilize here can be traced in part to Alexis de Tocqueville, who identifies America as different from Europe largely because of its revolutionary and Puritanical origins, its relative equality, and, relevant to the following excerpt, its dominant ethic of *hard work* (Tocqueville [1835 and 1840] 2000).

37. Email correspondence, April 12, 2017.

38. An amicus brief is filed by an *amicus curiae* (lit. "friend of the court"), someone who is not party to a case but has been solicited by a party to assist a court. This assistance typically takes the form of a legal opinion, testimony, or learned treatise (the amicus brief, a text that is sufficiently authoritative to be considered admissible evidence). It is a way to introduce the possibly broad legal effects of a court decision and is often particularly helpful in appeals, as appellate cases are normally limited to the factual record and arguments coming from the lower court under appeal.

39. Brief of Justice for Children, Amicus Curiae, Filed on Behalf of Petitioner Young Zheng (Young Zheng v. Alberto Gonzales, in the US Court of Appeals for the Third Circuit, on Petition for Review of a Final Order of the Board of Immigration Appeals). August 2, 2005.

40. This satisfies one of the requisite elements for a preliminary injunction, namely a substantial likelihood of success upon merits.

41. *Zheng v. Pogash*, 416 F. 2d 550 (S.D. Tex. 2006).

42. On April 7, 2006, Young was found neglected and abandoned and a dependent on a Texas family court, and that it was not in his best interests to return to China (Case No. 2006-14477).

43. "The Young Center's goal is to change the immigration system to ensure that all decisions made on behalf of immigrant children are made in consideration of the child's best interests, safety and well-being. . . . We serve as Child Advocates (guardians *ad litem*) and promote change by advocating for the best interests of individual immigrant children." The Young Center for Immigrant Children's Rights. n.d. Accessed May 5, 2017. *theyoungcenter.org/about/the-organization*.

44. The Young Center for Immigrant Children's Rights. n.d. Accessed March 19, 2014. *theyoungcenter.org*.

45. Zuno, Ariana. n.d. "Escaping the Traffickers' Grasp." KIND (Kids In Need of Defense). "Success Stories." Accessed March 19, 2014. *www.supportkind.org/en/kind-in-action/success-stories/in-their-own-words/108-escaping-the-traffickers-grasp*.

46. Much of what Young shared with me was done so off the record or incorporated elsewhere in this book under a pseudonym.

CHAPTER 6

1. Nieuwenhuys's argument is relevant here, though in other contexts it might be fairly critiqued for overlooking young people's dependence on the labor of parents, relatives, and/or guardians in addition to—or instead of—state entitlements. Moreover, even though Fujianese youth without the capacity for

"legitimate" work are ostensibly now reliant upon the state, the young people in this study rarely sought out these supposed entitlements.

2. In addition to alleviating this stress, legal status through a green card ensures freedom of mobility, and it permits individuals to apply for financial aid, Social Security benefits, and driver's licenses. Only citizens have the right to vote.

3. As youth reported, most loan sharks or community banking networks charge interest on smuggling debts, sometimes as much as fifteen thousand dollars.

4. By declaring a youth a ward of the state, as in SIJ. See Chapter 1.

5. Taking natural rights as its premise, US constitutional doctrine reflects this individualistic approach. Yet as Hafen (1983, 3) points out, the concepts embodied in the Bill of Rights were originally intended to define the political relationship between individual citizens and the state—not the domestic and personal relationships among citizens themselves. Indeed, Hafen (1991) later argues that American laws and judicial decisions remained largely premised on the family through the 1950s, even as economic and political thought were more grounded in individualistic self-interest. He links the relatively recent reorientation in family law toward the individual to the social movements of the 1960s and 1970s, in which the family was viewed as an authoritarian and role-oriented tradition (see also Adams 1971; Hamilton 2006). Glendon (1989) likewise highlights this shift as situated in family law's simultaneous recognition of the nation's heterogeneity and a declining confidence in the "ideal family patterns" in which so few families appeared to fit.

6. Of course, the context I detail here hardly captures the complexities of a community, a workplace, or a young person's negotiations within the two. To do so would require attending to the multifaceted interface of local and global markets, demographic shifts, economic restructuring, federal immigration policy, and regional histories. Moreover, neither local populations nor immigrant groups are ever homogenous. Indeed, the newcomer–local resident interplay is made all the more complex by divisions within these populations along ethnic and class lines (Zuniga and Hernandez-Leon 2005).

7. Consider, for instance, that many youth in removal proceedings denied or never disclosed to their attorneys that they still worked and sent remittances home to family members—and specifically to parents now termed abusive, neglectful, etc. in the legal realm.

8. While it is certainly a helpful term, I employ "new destinations" with some reluctance, as it problematically overlooks complex and *extended* regional histories of immigration.

9. One exception is Griffith (2008), who also considers the experiences of Somalis and Hmong migrants.

10. Though some authors have attended to the labor of unaccompanied Fujianese youth or Fujianese migrants more broadly (Kotlowitz 2006; Kwong 1996, 1997), their work has generally focused on urban spaces, primarily Chinatowns. Indicating a frustratingly familiar urbanormative bias (Pruitt and Showman 2014; Boso 2013), the relative dearth of knowledge about young

Chinese migrants' lives in "new destinations" demands more rigorous scholarly and public attention.

11. This is a suggested argument. For participant safety, I only informally interacted with youth I assumed were undocumented. Most of the information I collected on their experience in the US was anecdotal, shared by friends and peers who participated in my research and who had been apprehended.

12. Alabama House Bill 56, or the Beason-Hammon Alabama Taxpayer and Citizen Protection Act, additionally mandated that police, in the course of any lawful "stop, detention, or arrest," should attempt to determine a person's citizenship and immigration status ("Act No. 2011-535." 2011. Immigration.alabama.gov. *immigration.alabama.gov/docs/Immigration-AL-Law-2011.pdf*). Later in 2011, significant portions of the law were blocked or invalidated following legal actions taken by the Obama administration and religious and immigrant-rights organizations.

13. The Support Our Law Enforcement and Safe Neighborhoods Act, introduced in 2010 as Arizona Senate Bill 1070, was until HB 56 the broadest anti-undocumented immigration measure in US history. It included an incredibly controversial provision requiring immigration status checks during law enforcement stops.

14. While less rare than raids on factories and poultry processing plants, ICE has in the past targeted Chinese buffets, particularly in the South (see Draper 2013). In addition, many attorneys rely on exploitative workplace conditions—and the notion that no one would ever *consent* to these conditions—to indicate that a Fujianese client is a victim of trafficking (e.g., Burke 2011, 16–18).

15. Angelina Jolie is a founder and co-chair of KIND (Kids in Need of Defense), an advocacy organization for unaccompanied minors based in New York City. There is often inter-agency tension with KIND due in part to its relatively large budget as well as its prominent organizational publicity efforts.

16. See also Pruitt (2006), who highlights both the positive and negative aspects of the closeness of community among rural residents while also illuminating the presence of these popular "close-knit" stereotypes in judicial opinions.

17. A notable exception to this argument is Lana, a cause lawyer who deliberately pursued work at an organization that offers legal assistance *alongside* counseling services. Another compelling example of "holistic" legal advocacy is the Bronx Defenders (The Bronx Defenders. 2015. "Who We Are." *www.bronxdefenders. org/who-we-are/*).

18. Other relevant considerations of care in the context of migration include global chains of care or reciprocities of care as meaningful and necessarily sustained strategies of obligation, connectedness, social capital, and security across diverse social fields, as via remittances (Boehm 2012; Coe 2016).

19. Deferred Action for Childhood Arrivals. In 2012, the Secretary of Homeland Security announced that certain individuals who came to the United States as children and meet several guidelines may request consideration of deferred

action (a use of prosecutorial discretion to defer removal action against an individual) for a period of two years, subject to renewal. They are also eligible for work authorization. Deferred action does not provide lawful status (Department of Homeland Security. n.d. "Consideration of Deferred Action for Childhood Arrivals." Accessed July 1, 2014. *www.uscis.gov/humanitarian/ consideration-deferred-action-childhood-arrivals-daca*).

20. In my research, I did seek out the availability—or even existence—of human services and labor rights' advocacy directed to Chinese youth, both in gateway cities and in "new destinations." There was an obvious disparity in services available to urban documented and undocumented (or unprotected laboring) immigrant communities, and even more so between urban and rural populations.

21. Many attorneys suspected snakehead involvement in the "job shops" and transport of youth to job sites.

22. My thanks to Steve Harrell for noting the significance of this tension.

23. Recall that exploitative labor conditions and proof of remittances establish qualifications for a T visa (a more successful remedy in New York), as in Wenyun's case. Yet exploitative labor conditions and proof of remittances would have no value to, and may even thwart, another youth's eligibility for SIJ status in Chicago (where a T visa is less of an option).

CHAPTER 7

1. These figures do not include unaccompanied Mexican youth, whose numbers are likewise substantial: In 2011, approximately 13,000 Mexican children were apprehended. In 2012 there were 15,709, and in 2013 the number reached 18,754. Unlike unaccompanied youth arriving from nations non-contiguous to the US, most of these young people were immediately returned to Mexico. Though the TVPRA established that the Border Patrol must screen unaccompanied children from Mexico to determine that a youth is not a trafficking victim and has no claim to asylum, only a small number of Mexican children are transferred to ORR. Prior to passage of TVPRA, unaccompanied minors from Mexico were nearly always automatically given voluntary return (Chishti and Hipsman 2014).

2. Department of Justice Office of Public Affairs. 2014. "Justice Department and CNCS Announce New Partnership to Enhance Immigration Courts and Provide Critical Legal Assistance to Unaccompanied Minors." Press release. June 6, 2014. *www.justice.gov/opa/pr/2014/June/14-ag-609.html*. Significantly, as of July 2016 there were just forty-six justice AmeriCorps positions available. Almost a year later, this number remained the same. Equal Justice Works. n.d. "justice Americorps." Accessed November 15, 2017. *joinjusticeamericorps.wordpress.com/*.

3. Corporation for National and Community Service. n.d. "justice AmeriCorps." Accessed November 15, 2017. *www.nationalservice.gov/special-initiatives/ task-force-expanding-national-service/justice-americorps*.

4. Department of Justice Office of Public Affairs. 2014. "Justice Department and CNCS Announce New Partnership to Enhance Immigration Courts and Provide Critical Legal Assistance to Unaccompanied Minors." Press release. June 6, 2014. *www.justice.gov/opa/pr/2014/June/14-ag-609.html.*

5. My thanks to Perla Trevizo, border reporter at the *Arizona Daily Star*, for sharing these statistics with me.

6. According to Uehling (2008, 839), Latin American youth must often meet multiple criteria (risk of being trafficked, complex medical or mental health concerns, severe trauma) in order to be placed in ORR custody and receive assessments and follow-up care. Youth who fall in the "Other" category, including young people from China and India, receive a higher and almost "automatic" standard of legal and welfare protection.

7. The Young Center for Immigrant Children's Rights. n.d. Accessed August 16, 2014. *theyoungcenter.org/learn/child-migrants/.*

8. KIND: Kids in Need of Defense. n.d. Accessed August 16, 2014. *www.supportkind.org/en/kind-in-action/success-stories/in-their-own-words.*

REFERENCES

Abbott, Andrew. 1988. *The System of Professions: An Essay on the Division of Expert Labor*. Chicago: University of Chicago Press.

Adams, Paul. 1971. *Children's Rights: Toward the Liberation of the Child*. Santa Barbara, CA: Praeger Publishing.

Agamben, Giorgio.1998. *Homo Sacer: Sovereign Power and Bare Life*. Stanford, CA: Stanford University Press.

Albiston, Catherine, and Laura Beth Nielsen. 2014. "Funding the Cause: How Public Interest Law Organizations Fund Their Activities and Why It Matters for Social Change." *Law & Social Inquiry* 39 (1): 62–95.

Amon, Elizabeth. 2002. "The Snakehead Lawyers." *National Law Journal*, July 27, 2002.

———. 2006. "Winning Asylum Has Never Been so Difficult: As More Firms Take on Cases, Can Their Zealous Advocacy Overcome the Obstacles?" *American Lawyer* 28:13–21.

Appell, Annette. 2004. "Uneasy Tensions between Children's Rights and Civil Rights." *Nevada Law Journal* 5:141–70.

———. 2006. "Children's Voice and Justice: Lawyering for Children in the 21st Century." *Nevada Law Journal* 6:692–723.

———. 2009. "The Pre-political Child of Child-Centered Jurisprudence." *Houston Law Review* 46:703–56.

Archard, David. 2004. *Children: Rights and Childhood*. New York: Routledge.

Arendt, Hannah. 1973. *The Origins of Totalitarianism*. Vol. 244. New York: Houghton Mifflin Harcourt.

Arnett, Jeffrey. 2000. "Emerging Adulthood: A Theory of Development from Late Teens through the Twenties." *American Psychologist* 55 (5): 469–80.

Arnold, David, and Stuart Blackburn. 2005. *Telling Lives*. Bloomington: Indiana University Press.

Ashar, Sameer M. 2007. "Public Interest Lawyers and Resistance Movements." *California Law Review* 95 (5): 1879–1925.

Atkins, Marc, Angela Kim, Stephanie Pituc, and Christine Yeh. 2008. "Poverty, Loss, and Resilience: The Story of Chinese Immigrant Youth." *Journal of Counseling Psychology.* 55 (1): 34–48.

Bakhtin, Mikhail. 1981. *The Dialogic Imagination: Four Essays*. Translated by Caryl Emerson and Michael Holquist. Austin: University of Texas Press.

Bamo, Ayi, Stevan Harrell, and Ma Lunzy. 2007. *Fieldwork Connections: The Fabric of Ethnographic Collaboration in China and America*. Seattle: University of Washington Press.

Barclay, Scott, and Anna-Maria Marshall. 2005. "Supporting a Cause, Developing a Movement, and Consolidating a Practice: Cause Lawyers and Sexual Orientation Litigation in Vermont." In *The Worlds Cause Lawyers Make: Structure and Agency in Legal Practice*, edited by Austin Sarat and Stuart Scheingold, 171–202. Stanford, CA: Stanford University Press.

Barsky, Robert. 1994. *Constructing a Productive Other: Discourse Theory and the Convention Refugee Hearing*. Amsterdam: John Benjamins Publishing Company.

———. 2006. "From Discretion to Fictional Law." *SubStance*, Special Issue 109: Law and Literature 35 (1): 116–45.

———. 2016. *Undocumented Immigrants in an Era of Arbitrary Law: The Flight and the Plight of People Deemed "Illegal."* New York: Routledge.

Bartlett, Katharine. 1988. "Re-expressing Parenthood." *Yale Law Journal* 98:293–340.

Beck, Ulrich, and Elisabeth Beck-Gernsheim. 2002. *Individualization: Institutionalized Individualism and Its Social and Political Consequences*. London: Sage.

Behar, Ruth. 1992. "A Life Story to Take across the Border: Notes on an Exchange." In *Storied Lives: The Cultural Politics of Self-Understanding*, edited by George Rosenwald and Richard Ochberg, 108–23. New Haven, CT: Yale University Press.

Berger, Susan. 2009. "(Un)Worthy: Latina Battered Immigrants under VAWA and the Construction of Neoliberal Subjects." *Citizenship Studies* 13 (3): 201–17.

Bernstein, Elizabeth. 2010. "Militarized Humanitarianism Meets Carceral Feminism: The Politics of Sex, Rights, and Freedom in Contemporary Antitrafficking Campaigns." *Signs: Journal of Women in Culture and Society* 36 (1): 45–71.

Bernstein, Nina. 2000. "Press Coverage and Public Perception: In Child Welfare Reporting, Even Good Daily Coverage Can Be Distorting." *Nieman Reports* 54 (4): 82–84.

Best, Amy, ed. 2007. *Representing Youth: Methodological Issues in Critical Youth Studies*. New York: New York University Press.

Best, Joel. 1993. *Threatened Children: Rhetoric and Concern about Child-Victims*. Chicago: University of Chicago Press.

Bhabha, Jacqueline. 2009. "Arendt's Children: Do Today's Migrant Children Have a Right to Have Rights?" *Human Rights Quarterly* 31:410–51.

Bhabha, Jacqueline, and Mary Crock. 2006. *Seeking Asylum Alone: A Comparative Study. Unaccompanied and Separated Children and Refugee Protection in Australia, the UK and the US*. Sydney: Themis Press.

Bhabha, Jacqueline, and Susan Schmidt. 2006. *Seeking Asylum Alone: Unaccompanied and Separated Children and Refugee Protection in the United States*. Cambridge, MA: President and Fellows of Harvard College.

Black, Maggie. 1995. *In the Twilight Zone: Child Workers in the Hotel, Tourism and Catering Industry*. Geneva: International Labor Organization.

Blumenthal, Ralph. 2005. "Chinese Boy Asks for Stay of Deportation, Citing Fear." *New York Times*, June 8, 2005. *www.nytimes.com/2005/06/08/national/08deport.html*.

———. 2006. "After 3-Year Battle, Chinese Teenager Is on Road to US Citizenship." *New York Times*, April 11, 2006. *www.nytimes.com/2006/04/11/us/11smuggle.html*.

Boehm, Deborah. 2011. "Here/Not Here: Contingent Citizenship and Transnational Mexican Children." In *Everyday Ruptures: Children, Youth, and Migration in Global Perspective*, edited by Cati Coe, Rachel R. Reynolds, Deborah A. Boehm, Julia Meredith Hess, and Heather Rae-Espinoza, 161–73. Nashville, TN: Vanderbilt University Press.

———. 2012. *Intimate Migrations: Gender, Family, and Illegality among Transnational Migrants*. New York: New York University Press.

Borneman, John, and Abdellah Hammoudi. 2009. "The Fieldwork Encounter, Experience, and the Making of Truth." In *Being There: The Fieldwork Encounter and the Making of Truth: An Introduction*, edited by John Borneman and Abdellah Hammoudi, 1–24. Berkeley: University of California Press.

Boso, Luke. 2013. "Urban Bias, Rural Sexual Minorities, and the Courts." *UCLA Law Review* 60 (3): 562–637.

Brewer, Holly. 2005. *By Birth or Consent: Children, Law and the Anglo-American Revolution in Authority*. Chapel Hill: University of North Carolina Press.

Brown, David, and Kai Schafft. 2011. *Rural People and Communities in the 21st Century: Resilience and Transformation*. Cambridge, UK: Polity Press.

Burke, Kenneth. 1989. *On Symbols and Society*. Edited by Joseph R. Gusfield. Chicago: University of Chicago Press.

Burke, Lauren. 2011. "It Was(n't) My Choice: Identifying Human Trafficking in the Unaccompanied Chinese Youth Population." Practice advisory commissioned by the Unaccompanied Children Program at the Vera Institute of Justice.

Byrne, Olga. 2008. *Unaccompanied Children in the United States: A Literature Review*. New York: Vera Institute of Justice.

Byrne, Olga, and Elise Miller. 2012. *The Flow of Unaccompanied Children through the Immigration System: A Resource for Practitioners, Policy Makers, and Researchers*. New York: Center for Immigration and Justice.

Calavita, Kitty. 1998. "Immigration, Law, and Marginalization in a Global Economy: Notes from Spain." *Law and Society Review* 32 (3): 529–66.

———. 2005. "Law, Citizenship, and the Construction of (Some) Immigrant 'Others.'" *Law and Social Inquiry* 30 (2): 401–20.

Caneva, Elana. 2015. "Children's Agency and Migration: Constructing Kinship in Latin American and East European Families Living in Italy." *Childhood* 22 (2): 278–92.

Carlson, Laura. 2014. "US Mainstream Press Notices Child Migrants, Tells Half the Story." *Americas Mexico* (blog). June 9, 2014. *americasmexico.blogspot. mx/2014/06/us-mainstream-press-notices-child.html.*

Carr, Bridgette. 2009. "Incorporating a 'Best Interests of the Child' Approach into Immigration Law and Procedure." *Yale Human Rights and Development Journal* 12 (1): 120–59.

Chanock, Martin. 2000. "'Culture' and Human Rights: Orientalising, Occidentalising and Authenticity." In *Beyond Rights Talk and Culture Talk: Comparative Essays on the Politics of Rights and Culture,* edited by Mahmood Mamdani, 15–36. Cape Town, South Africa: Rustica Press.

Chavez, Leo. 2001. *Covering Immigration: Popular Images and the Politics of the Nation.* Berkeley: University of California Press.

——. 2008. *The Latino Threat: Constructing Immigrants, Citizens, and the Nation.* Stanford, CA: Stanford University Press.

Cheney, Kristen. 2007. *Pillars of the Nation: Child Citizens and Ugandan National Development.* Chicago: University of Chicago Press.

Chin, Elizabeth. 2001. *Purchasing Power: Black Kids and American Consumer Culture.* Minneapolis: University of Minnesota Press.

Chin, Ko-Lin. 1999. *Smuggled Chinese: Clandestine Immigration to the United States.* Philadelphia, PA: Temple University Press.

——. 2001. "The Social Organization of Chinese Human Smuggling." In *Global Human Smuggling: Comparative Perspectives,* edited by David Kyle and Rey Koslowski, 216–35. Baltimore, MD: Johns Hopkins University Press.

Chishti, Muzaffar, and Faye Hipsman. 2014. "Dramatic Surge in the Arrival of Unaccompanied Children Has Deep Roots and No Simple Solutions." *Migration Policy Institute,* June 13, 2014. *www.migrationpolicy.org/article/ dramatic-surge-arrival-unaccompanied-children-has-deep-roots-and-no-simple- solutions.*

Chu, Julie. 2006. "To Be 'Emplaced': Fuzhounese Migration and the Politics of Destination." *Identities: Global Studies in Culture and Power.* 13:395–425.

——. 2010. *Cosmologies of Credit: Transnational Mobility and the Politics of Destination in China.* Durham, NC: Duke University Press.

Chung, Hoewook. 2013. "Korean Temporary Migrant Mothers' Conceptualization of Parent Involvement in the United States." *Asia Pacific Journal of Education* 33 (4): 461–75.

Clifford, James. 1988. *The Predicament of Culture: Twentieth-Century Ethnography, Literature, and Art.* Cambridge, MA: Harvard University Press.

Coe, Cati. 2016. "Orchestrating Care in Time: Ghanaian Migrant Women, Family, and Reciprocity." *American Anthropologist* 118 (1): 37–48.

Coe, Cati, Rachel Reynolds, Deborah Boehm, Julia Meredith Hess, and Heather Rae-Espinoza, eds. 2011. *Everyday Ruptures: Children, Youth, and Migration in Global Perspective.* Nashville, TN: Vanderbilt University Press.

Comaroff, John. 1995. "The Discourse of Rights in Colonial South Africa: Subjectivity, Sovereignty, Modernity." In *Identities, Politics, and Rights*, edited by Austin Sarat and Thomas R. Kearns, 193–236. Ann Arbor: University of Michigan Press.

Coombe, Rosemary. 1995. "The Cultural Life of Things: Anthropological Approaches to Law and Society in Conditions of Globalization." *American University International Law Review* 10 (2): 791–835.

Coutin, Susan. 2000. *Legalizing Moves Salvadoran Immigrants' Struggle for US Residency.* Ann Arbor: University of Michigan Press.

Coutin, Susan. 2001. "Cause Lawyering in the Shadow of the State: A US Immigration Example." In *Cause Lawyering and the State in a Global Era*, edited by Austin Sarat and Stuart Scheingold, 117–40. New York: Oxford University Press.

———. 2005. "Being En Route." *American Anthropologist* 107 (2): 195–206.

———. 2011. "Falling Outside: Excavating the History of Central American Asylum Seekers." *Law and Social Inquiry* 36 (3): 569–96.

Cresswell, Timothy. 2006. *On the Move: Mobility in the Modern Western World.* New York: Taylor and Francis.

Cummings, Scott, ed. 2011. *The Paradox of Professionalism: Lawyers and the Possibility of Justice.* Cambridge, UK: Cambridge University Press.

Das, Veena. 1989. "Voices of Children." *Daedalus* 118 (4): 262–94.

Dawes, James R. 1999. "Language, Violence, and Human Rights Law." *Yale Journal of Law and the Humanities* 11 (2): 215–50.

De Genova, Nicholas, and Nathalie Peutz, eds. 2010. *The Deportation Regime: Sovereignty, Space, and the Freedom of Movement.* Durham, NC: Duke University Press.

De Leon, Jason, and Michael Wells. 2015. *The Land of Open Graves: Living and Dying on the Migrant Trail.* Berkeley: University of California Press.

De Jong, Sara. 2011. "False Binaries: Altruism and Selfishness in NGO Work." In *Inside the Everyday Lives of Development Workers: The Challenges and Futures of Aidland*, edited by Anne-Meike Fechter and Heather Hindman, 21–40. Sterling, VA: Kumarian Press.

Deleuze, Gilles, and Félix Guattari. 1987. *A Thousand Plateaus: Capitalism and Schizophrenia.* Translated by Brian Massumi. Minneapolis: University of Minnesota Press.

Donato, Katharine, Melissa Stainback, and Carl Bankston III. 2005. "The Economic Incorporation of Mexican Immigrants in Southern Louisiana: A Tale of Two Cities." In *New Destinations: Mexican Immigration in the United States*, edited by Victor Zuniga and Ruben Hernandez-Leon, 76–100. New York: Russell Sage Foundation.

Dos Santos, Gonçalo Duro. 2006. "The Anthropology of Chinese Kinship: A Critical Overview." *EGEAS* 5 (2): 275–333.

Draper, Bill. 2013. "Charges against Restaurant Owners Part of Crackdown on Illegal Immigration: US Attorney Working to Target Businesses That Employ Undocumented Workers." *Topeka Capital Journal*, November 9, 2013. *cjonline.com/news/business/2013-11-09/charges-against-restaurant-owners-part-crackdown-illegal-immigration.*

Dreby, Joanna. 2007. "Children and Power in Mexican Transnational Families." *Journal of Marriage and Family* 69:1050–64.

Durham, Deborah. 2000. "Youth and the Social Imagination in Africa: Introduction to Parts 1 and 2." *Anthropological Quarterly* 73:113–20.

Engle, Karen. 2001. "From Skepticism to Embrace: Human Rights and the American Anthropological Association from 1947–1999." *Human Rights Quarterly* 23 (3): 536–59.

Fairbank, John King. 1969. *Trade and Diplomacy on the China Coast: The Opening of the Treaty Ports, 1842–1854.* Stanford, CA: Stanford University Press.

Fei, Xiaotong. (1947) 1992. *From the Soil, the Foundations of Chinese Society: A Translation of Fei Xiaotong's Xiangtu Zhongguo.* Translated by Gary G. Hamilton and Wang Zheng. Berkeley: University of California Press.

Fennelly, Katherine. 2008. "Prejudice toward Immigrants in the Midwest." In *New Faces in New Places: The Changing Geography of American Immigration*, edited by Douglas Massey, 151–78. New York: Russell Sage Foundation.

Fitzpatrick, Peter. 1992. *The Mythology of Modern Law.* London: Routledge.

Fong, Vanessa. 2004. *Only Hope: Coming of Age under China's One-Child Policy.* Stanford, CA: Stanford University Press.

Foucault, Michel. 1984. "What Is Enlightenment?" In *The Foucault Reader*, edited by Paul Rabinow, 32–50. New York: Random House.

———. 1991. "Governmentality." In *The Foucault Effect: Studies in Governmentality*, edited by Graham Burchell, Colin Gordon, and Peter Miller, 87–104. Chicago: University of Chicago Press.

———. 1994. *The Order of Things: An Archaeology of the Human Sciences.* New York: Vintage Books.

Fraidin, Matthew. 2010. "Stories Told and Untold: Confidentiality Laws and the Master Narrative of Child Welfare." *Maine Law Review* 63 (1): 2–59.

———. 2012. "Changing the Narrative of Child Welfare." *Georgetown Journal on Poverty Law and Policy* 19 (1): 97–109.

Frankel, Elizabeth. 2011. "Detention and Deportation with Inadequate Due Process: The Devastating Consequences of Juvenile Involvement with Law Enforcement for Immigrant Youth." *Duke Forum for Law and Social Change* 3:63–107.

Freedman, M. 1958. *Lineage Organisation in Southeastern China.* London: Athlone Press.

———. 1966. *Chinese Lineage and Society: Fukien and Kwangtung.* London: Athlone Press.

Freudenburg, William. 1986. "The Density of Acquaintanceship: An Overlooked Variable in Community Research?" *American Journal of Sociology* 92 (1): 27–63.

Furlong, Andy, and Fred Cartmel. 1997. *Young People and Social Change: New Perspectives.* New York: Open University Press.

Fyfe, Alec. 1989. *Child Labour.* Cambridge, UK: Polity Press.

Gans, Herbert. 1995. *The War against the Poor.* New York: Basic Books.

Gao, Yang, Liping Li, Jean Kim, and Sian Griffiths. 2010. "The Impact of Parental Migration on Health Status and Health Behaviours among Left Behind Adolescent School Children in China." *BioMed Central Public Health* 10 (1): 1–10.

Geertz, Clifford. 1984. "Distinguished Lecture: Anti Anti-Relativism." *American Anthropologist* 86 (2): 263–78.

Gleeson, Shannon, and Roberto Gonzales. 2012. "When Do Papers Matter? An Institutional Analysis of Undocumented Life in the United States." *International Migration* 50:1–19.

Glendon, Mary Ann. 1989. *The Transformation of Family Law.* Chicago: University of Chicago Press.

Gonzales, Roberto. 2011. "Learning to be Illegal: Undocumented Youth and Shifting Legal Contexts in the Transition to Adulthood." *American Sociological Review* 76 (4): 602–19.

———. 2015. *Lives in Limbo: Undocumented and Coming of Age in America.* Berkeley: University of California Press.

Gonzales, Roberto, and Leo Chavez. 2012. "'Awakening to a Nightmare': Abjectivity and Illegality in the Lives of Undocumented 1.5–Generation Latino Immigrants in the United States. *Current Anthropology* 53 (3): 255–81.

Goodwin, Charles. 1994. "Professional Vision." *American Anthropologist* 96 (3): 606–33.

Gordon, Jennifer. 2005. *Suburban Sweatshops: The Fight for Immigrant Rights.* Cambridge, MA: Harvard University Press.

Goździak, Elżbieta. 2008. "On Challenges, Dilemmas, and Opportunities in Studying Trafficked Children." *Anthropological Quarterly* 81 (4): 903–23.

Goździak, Elżbieta, and Margaret MacDonnell. 2007. "Closing the Gaps: The Need to Improve Identification and Services to Child Victims of Trafficking." *Human Organization* 66 (2): 171–84.

Goździak, Elżbieta, and Micah Bump. 2008. *Data and Research on Human Trafficking: Bibliography of Research-Based Literature.* Report prepared for the Institute for the Study of International Migration, Walsh School of Foreign Service, Georgetown University, September–October 2008. *isim.georgetown.edu/sites/isim/files/files/upload/2.23.2015%20Trafficking%20Bibliography.pdf.*

Green, Bruce, and Bernardine Dohrn. 1996. "Recommendations of the Conference on Ethical Issues in the Legal Representation of Children." *Fordham Law Review* 64 (4): 1301–23.

Greenhalgh, Susan. 1994. "De-Orientalizing the Chinese Family Firm." *American Ethnologist* 21 (4): 746–75.

Greenhouse, Carole. 2002. "Introduction: Altered States, Altered Lives." In *Ethnography in Unstable Places: Everyday Lives in Contexts of Dramatic Political Change*, edited by Carole Greenhouse, Elizabeth Mertz, and Kay Warren, 1–36. Durham, NC: Duke University Press.

Griffith, David. 2008. "New Midwesterners, New Southerners: Immigration Experiences in Four Rural American Settings." In *New Faces in New Places: The Changing Geography of American Immigration*, edited by Douglas Massey, 179–210. New York: Russell Sage Foundation.

Guest, Kenneth. 2004. "Liminal Youth among Fuzhou Chinese Undocumented Workers." In *Asian American Religions: The Making and Remaking of Borders and Boundaries*, edited by Tony Carnes and Genggang Yang, 55–75. New York: New York University Press.

Guggenheim, Martin. 1980. *The Rights of Parents*. New York: Bantam Books.

———. 1984. "The Right to be Represented but Not Heard: Reflections on Legal Representation for Children." *New York University Law Review* 59:76–156.

———. 1985. *The Rights of Young People*. New York: Bantam Books.

———. 1998. "Reconsidering the Need for Counsel for Children in Custody, Visitation, and Child Protection Proceedings." *Loyola University Chicago Law Journal* 29:299– 352.

———. 2005. *What's Wrong with Children's Rights*. Cambridge, MA: Harvard University Press.

Gusterson, Hugh. 1997. "Studying Up Revisited." *PoLAR* 20 (1): 115–19.

Haddal, Chad. 2007. *Unaccompanied Alien Children: Policies and Issues*. Washington, DC: Congressional Research Service Report (RL33896).

Hafen, Bruce. 1983. "The Constitutional Status of Marriage, Kinship, and Sexual Privacy: Balancing the Individual and Social Interests." *Michigan Law Review* 81 (3): 463–574.

———. 1991. "Individualism and Autonomy in Family Law: The Waning of Belonging." *Brigham Young University Law Review* 3 (1): 1–42.

Hamilton, Vivian. 2006. "Principles of US Family Law." *Fordham Law Review* 75 (1): 31–73.

Haraway, Donna. 1988. "Situated Knowledges: The Science Question in Feminism and the Privilege of Partial Perspective." *Feminist Studies* 14:575–99.

Hashim, Iman. 2010. *The Positives and Negatives of Children's Independent Migration*. Brighton: Development Research Centre on Migration, Globalisation and Poverty.

Heidbrink, Lauren. 2014. *Migrant Youth, Transnational Families, and the State: Care and Contested Interests*. Philadelphia: University of Pennsylvania Press.

Heidbrink, Lauren, and Michele Statz. 2017. "Parents of Global Youth: Contesting Debt and Belonging." *Children's Geographies* 15 (5): 545–57. dx.doi.org/10.108 0/14733285.2017.1284645.

Heimer, Carol, and Lisa Staffen. 1998. *For the Sake of the Children: The Social Organization of Responsibility in the Hospital and the Home.* Chicago: University of Chicago Press.

Henken, Louis. 1990. *The Age of Rights.* New York: Columbia University Press.

Hill, Annie. 2014. "Demanding Victims: The Sympathetic Shift in British Prostitution Policy." In *Negotiating Sex Work: Unintended Consequences of Policy and Activism,* edited by Carisa R. Showden and Samantha Majic, 77–98. Minneapolis: University of Minnesota Press.

Hilbink, Thomas. 2004. "You Know the Type . . . : Categories of Cause Lawyering." *Law and Social Inquiry* 29 (3): 657–98.

Hobbes, Thomas. (1651) 2010. *Leviathan: Or, The Matter, Forme, and Power of a Common-Wealth Ecclesiasticall and Civill.* Edited by Ian Shapiro. New Haven, CT: Yale University Press.

Holmes, Oliver Wendell. 1881. *The Common Law.* Boston: Little, Brown.

Holquist, Michael. (1990) 2002. *Dialogism: Bakhtin and his World.* 2nd ed. London: Routledge.

Honwana, Alcinda. 2011. *Child Soldiers in Africa.* Philadelphia: University of Pennsylvania Press.

Horton, Sarah. 2004 "Different Subjects: The Health Care System's Participation in the Differential Construction of the Cultural Citizenship of Cuban Refugees and Mexican Immigrants." *Medical Anthropology Quarterly* 18 (4): 472–89.

Hsu, Immanuel C.Y. 2000. *The Rise of Modern China.* 6th ed. Oxford, UK: Oxford University Press.

Hsu, Spencer, and Andrew Becker. 2010. "ICE Officials Set Quotas to Deport More Illegal Immigrants." *Washington Post,* March 27, 2010. *www.washingtonpost.com/wp-dyn/content/article/2010/03/26/AR2010032604891.html.*

Ignatiev, Noel. 1995. *How the Irish Became White.* Milton Park, UK: Routledge.

Ikels, Charlotte, ed. 2004. *Filial Piety: Practice and Discourse in Contemporary East Asia.* Stanford, CA: Stanford University Press.

Jefferson, Thomas. (1788) 1954. *Notes on the State of Virginia.* Edited by William Peden. Chapel Hill: University of North Carolina Press.

Jeffrey, Craig, and Jane Dyson, eds. 2008. *Telling Young Lives: Portraits of Global Youth.* Philadelphia: Temple University Press.

Jones, Reese. 2016. *Violent Borders: Refugees and the Right to Move.* London: Verso Press.

Judd, Ellen. 1989. "*Niangjia*: Chinese Women and Their Natal Families." *Journal of Asian Studies* 48 (3): 525–44.

Kawar, Leila. 2015. *Contesting Immigration Policy in Court: Legal Activism and Its Radiating Effects in the United States and France.* Cambridge, UK: Cambridge University Press.

Kell, William. 1998. "Ties that Bind?: Children's Attorneys, Children's Agency, and the Dilemma of Parental Affiliation." *Loyola University Chicago Law Journal* 29:353–76.

Kelly, Michael. 1994. *Lives of Lawyers: Journeys in the Organization of Practice*. Ann Arbor: University of Michigan Press.

Kempadoo, Kamala. 2005. "From Moral Panic to Global Justice: Changing Perspectives on Trafficking." In *Trafficking and Prostitution Reconsidered: New Perspectives on Migration, Sex Work, and Human Rights*, edited by Kamala Kempadoo, Jyoti Sanghera, and Bandana Pattanaik, 3–24. Boulder, CO: Paradigm Publishers.

Kennedy, Elizabeth. 2013. "Unnecessary Suffering: Potential Unmet Health Needs of Unaccompanied Alien Children." *JAMA Pediatrics* 167 (4): 319–20.

Kilwein, John. 1998. "Still Trying: Cause Lawyering for the Poor and Disadvantaged in Pittsburgh, Pennsylvania." In *Cause Lawyering: Political Commitments and Professional Responsibilities*, edited by Austin Sarat and Stuart Scheingold, 181–200. Oxford, UK: Oxford University Press.

Kipnis, Andrew. 2011. *Governing Educational Desire: Culture, Politics, and Schooling in China*. Chicago: University of Chicago Press.

Koh Peters, Jean. 1996. "The Roles and Content of Best Interests in Client Directed Lawyering for Children in Child Protective Proceedings." *Fordham Law Review* 64 (4): 1505–70.

———. 2001. *Representing Children in Child Protective Proceedings: Ethical and Practical Dimensions*. Newark, NJ: LexisNexus.

Kotlowitz, Alex. 2006. "The Smugglers' Due." *New York Times Magazine*, May 11, 2006. *www.nytimes.com/2006/06/11/magazine/11chinese.html*.

Kuper, Adam. 1999. *Culture: The Anthropologists' Account*. Cambridge, MA: Harvard University Press.

Kwong, Peter. 1996. *The New Chinatown*. New York: Hill and Wang.

———. 1997. *Forbidden Workers: Illegal Chinese Immigrants and American Labor*. New York: New Press.

———. 2001. "Impact of Chinese Human Smuggling on the American Labor Market." In *Global Human Smuggling: Comparative Perspectives*, edited by David Kyle and Rey Koslowski, 235–56. Baltimore, MD: Johns Hopkins University Press.

Laerke, Anna. 1998. "By Means of Re-membering: Notes on a Fieldwork with English Children." *Anthropology Today* 14:3–7.

Lai, Him Mark. 2004. *Becoming Chinese American: A History of Communities and Institutions*. Walnut Creek, CA: AltaMira Press.

Lancy, David. 2008. *The Anthropology of Childhood: Cherubs, Chattel, Changelings*. Cambridge, UK: Cambridge University Press.

Lee, Erika. 2003. *At America's Gates: Chinese Immigration During the Exclusion Era, 1882–1943*. Chapel Hill: University of North Carolina Press.

Leong, Karen. 2000. "A Distant and Antagonistic Race: Constructions of Chinese Manhood in the Exclusionist Debates, 1869–1878." In *Across the Great Divide: Cultures of Manhood in the American West*, edited by Laura McCall, Matthew Basso, and Dee Garceau, 131–48. New York: Routledge.

Lev, Daniel. 1998. "Lawyers' Causes in Indonesia and Malaysia." In *Cause Lawyering: Political Commitments and Professional Responsibilities*, edited by Austin Sarat and Stuart Scheingold, 431–52. Oxford: Oxford University Press.

Levinson, Daniel. 2008. *Division of Unaccompanied Children's Services: Efforts to Serve Children*. Department of Health and Human Services Report, March: OEI-07-06-00290.

Levitt, Peggy, and Nina Glick Schiller. 2004. "Conceptualizing Simultaneity: A Transnational Social Field Perspective on Society." *International Migration Review* 38 (145): 595–629.

Liang, Zai, and Wenzhen Ye. 2001. "From Fujian to New York: Understanding the New Chinese Immigration." In *Global Human Smuggling: Comparative Perspectives*, edited by David Kyle and Rey Koslowski, 187–215. Baltimore, MD: Johns Hopkins University Press.

Lichter, Daniel, and Kenneth Johnson. 2009. "Immigrant Gateways and Hispanic Migration to New Destinations." *International Migration Review* 43 (3): 496–518.

Light, Ivan. 2006. *Deflecting Immigration: Networks, Markets, and Regulation in Los Angeles*. New York: Russell Sage Foundation.

Lipsky, Michael. 2010. *Street-Level Bureaucracy, 30th Anniversary Edition: Dilemmas of the Individual in Public Service*. New York: Russell Sage Foundation.

Liu, Guofu. 2009. "Changing Chinese Migration Law: From Restriction to Relaxation." *International Migration & Integration* 10(3):311-333.

Liu, Irene Jay 2007. "Smuggled Chinese Travel Circuitously to the US." *National Public Radio Morning Edition*, November 20, 2007. *www.npr.org/templates/story/story.php?storyId=16422719*.

Liu, Shao-hua. 2011. *Passage to Manhood: Youth Migration, Heroin, and AIDS in Southwest China*. Stanford, CA: Stanford University Press.

Locke, John. (1689) 1988. *Two Treatises of Government*. Edited by Peter Laslett. Cambridge, UK: Cambridge University Press.

Lopez, Gerold. 1992. *Rebellious Lawyering: One Chicano's Vision of Progressive Law Practice*. Boulder, CO: Westview Press.

Lovell, George. 2012. "The Myth of the Myth of Rights." *Studies in Law, Politics, and Society* 59:1–30.

Luban, David. 1988. *Lawyers and Justice: An Ethical Study*. Princeton, NJ: Princeton University Press.

Lum, Thomas. 2006. *China and Falun Gong*. Congressional Research Service Report for Congress: RL33437.

Lustig, Stuart, Niranjian Karnik, Kevin Delucchi, Lakshika Tennakoon, Brent Kaul, Dana Leigh Marks, and Denise Slavin. 2008. "Inside the Judges' Chambers: Narrative Responses from the National Association of Immigration Judges Stress and Burnout Survey." *Georgetown Immigration Law Journal* 23:57–83.

Malkki, Liisa. 1996. "Speechless Emissaries: Refugees, Humanitarianism, and Dehistoricization." *Cultural Anthropology* 11 (3): 377–404.

Macpherson, C. B., 1962. *The Political Theory of Possessive Individualism: Hobbes to Locke*. Oxford: Oxford University Press.

Maine, Henry. (1861) 1969. *Ancient Law*. New York: Dutton.

Maloney, Sarah. 2002. "TransAtlantic Workshop on 'Unaccompanied/Separated Children': Comparative Policies and Practices in North America and Europe." *Journal of Refugee Studies* 15 (2002): 102–19.

Mann, Kenneth. 1999. "Beyond the Law of Evidence: Facts and Inequality in Criminal Defense." In *Social Science, Social Policy, and the Law*, edited by Patricia Ewick, Robert Kagan, and Austin Sarat, 101–36. New York: Russell Sage Foundation.

Marcus, Anthony, and Ric Curtis. 2014. "Implementing Policy for Invisible Populations: Social Work and Social Policy in a Federal Anti-Trafficking Taskforce in the United States. *Social Policy and Society* 13 (4): 481–92.

Marrow, Helen. 2011. *New Destination Dreaming: Immigration, Race, and Legal Status in the Rural American South*. Stanford, CA: Stanford University Press.

Martinez, Michel Angela, and Alison Dundes Renteln. 2017. "The Human Right to Photograph." In *Images and Human Rights: Local and Global Perspectives*, edited by Nancy Lipkin Stein and Alison Dundes Renteln, 11–40. Cambridge, UK: Cambridge University Press.

Massey, Doreen. 1993. "Power-Geometry and a Progressive Sense of Place." In *Mapping the Future: Local Cultures, Global Change*, edited by Jon Bird, Barry Curtis, Tim Putnam, George Robertson, and Lisa Tickner, 59–69. New York: Routledge.

Massey, Douglas, and Chiara Capoferro. 2008. "The Geographic Diversification of American Immigration." In *New Faces in New Places: The Changing Geography of American Immigration*, edited by Douglas Massey, 25–50. New York: Russell Sage Foundation.

Mather, Lynn, and Barbara Yngvesson. 1980–1981. "Language, Audience, and the Transformation of Disputes." *Law and Society Review* 15:3–4.

Mayer, Tamar. 2004. "Embodied Nationalisms." In *Mapping Women, Making Politics: Feminist Perspectives on Political Geography*, edited by Lynn Staeheli, Eleonore Kofman, and Linda Peake, 154–68. New York: Routledge.

McCann, Michael. 1994. *Rights at Work: Pay Equity Reform and the Politics of Legal Mobilization*. Chicago: University of Chicago Press.

McKeown, Adam. *Melancholy Order: Asian Migration and the Globalization of Borders*. New York: Columbia University Press.

McKinley, Michelle. 1997. "Life Stories, Disclosure and the Law." *PoLAR: Political and Legal Anthropology Review* 20 (2): 70–82.

Menjivar, Cecilia. 2011. "The Power of the Law: Central Americans' Legality and Everyday Life in Phoenix, Arizona." *Latino Studies* 9 (4): 999–1037.

Menkel-Meadow, Carrie. 1998. "The Causes of Cause Lawyering: Toward an Understanding of the Motivation and Commitment of Social Justice Lawyers." In *Cause Lawyering: Political Commitments and Professional Responsibilities*, edited by Austin Sarat and Stuart Scheingold, 31–68. Oxford: Oxford University Press.

Merry, Sally Engle. 2000. *Colonizing Hawai'i: The Cultural Power of Law.* Princeton, NJ: Princeton University Press.

———. 2003. "Human Rights Law and the Demonization of Culture (and Anthropology along the Way)." *PoLAR: Political and Legal Anthropology Review* 26 (1): 55–76.

———. 2007. "Introduction: Conditions of Vulnerability." In *The Practice of Human Rights: Tracking Law Between the Global and the Local,* edited by Mark Goodale and Sally Engle Merry, 195–203. Cambridge, UK: Cambridge University Press.

Mertz, Elizabeth. 2002. "The Perfidy of Gaze and the Pain of Uncertainty: Anthropological Theory and the Search for Culture." In *Ethnography in Unstable Places: Everyday Lives in Contexts of Dramatic Political Change,* edited by Carole Greenhouse, Elizabeth Mertz, and Kay Warren, 355–78. Durham, NC: Duke University Press.

Millard, Ann, and Jorge Chapa. 2004. *Apple Pie and Enchiladas: Latino Newcomers in the Rural Midwest.* Austin: University of Texas Press.

Millman, Joel, and Miriam Jordan. 2014. "Flow of Unaccompanied Minors Tests US Immigration Agencies." *Wall Street Journal,* January 29, 2014. *www.wsj.com/articles/flow-of-unaccompanied-minors-tests-us-immigration-agencies-1391042404.*

Miner, Casey. 2010. "Judges on the Verge of a Nervous Breakdown." *Mother Jones,* November/December, 2010. *www.motherjones.com/politics/2010/11/immigration-judge-case-overload.*

Moore, Sally Falk. 2009. "Encounter and Suspicion in Tanzania." In *Being There: The Fieldwork Encounter and the Making of Truth,* edited by John Borneman and Abdellah Hammoudi, 151–82. Berkeley: University of California Press.

Morando Lakhani, Sarah. 2013. "Protecting Immigrant Victims' 'Right' to Legal Status and the Management of Legal Uncertainty." *Law and Social Inquiry* 38 (2): 442–73.

Moskal, Marta, and Naomi Tyrrell. 2015. "Family Migration Decision-Making, Step-Migration and Separation: Children's Experiences in European Migrant Worker Families." *Children's Geographies* 14 (4): 453–67.

Mummert, Gail. 2009. "Siblings by Telephone: Experiences of Mexican Children in Long-Distance Childrearing Arrangements." *Journal of the Southwest* 51 (4): 503–21.

Nader, Laura. (1969) 1974. "Up the Anthropologist: Perspectives Gained from Studying Up." In *Reinventing Anthropology,* edited by Dell Hymes, 284–311. New York: Vintage Books.

———. 2002. *The Life of the Law: Anthropological Projects.* Berkeley: University of California Press.

————. 2010. *Controlling Processes Reader*. Course reader printed in Berkeley: Zee Zee Copy.

Newman, Katherine. 1999. *No Shame in My Game: The Working Poor in the Inner City*. New York: Russell Sage Foundation.

Ngai, Mae. 2004. *Impossible Subjects: Illegal Aliens and the Making of Modern America*. Princeton, NJ: Princeton University Press.

Nieuwenhuys, Olga. 1996. "The Paradox of Child Labor and Anthropology." *Annual Review of Anthropology* 25:237–51.

Nugent, Christopher. 2006. "Whose Children Are These? Towards Ensuring the Best Interests and Empowerment of Unaccompanied Alien Children." *Boston University Public Interest Law Journal* 15:219–35.

Nugent, Christopher, and Steven Schulman. 2003. "A New Era in the Legal Treatment of Alien Children: The Homeland Security and Child Status Protection Acts." *Interpreter Releases* 80 (7): 233–36.

Nussbaum, Martha. 2006. "Patriotism and Cosmopolitanism." In *For Love of Country: Debating the Limits of Patriotism*, edited by Joshua Cohen, 155–62. Boston: Beacon Press.

O'Brien, Erin. 2013. "Ideal Victims in Trafficking Awareness Campaigns." In *Crime, Justice and Social Democracy*, edited by Kerry Carrington, Matthew Ball, Erin O'Brien, and Juan Marcellus Tauri, 315–26. London: Palgrave Macmillan UK.

Ong, Aiwha. 1996. "Immigrants Negotiate Racial and Cultural Boundaries in the United States." *Current Anthropology* 37 (5): 737–62.

Orellana, Marjorie Faulstich. 2009. *Translating Childhoods: Immigrant Youth, Language, and Culture*. New Brunswick, NJ: Rutgers University Press.

Osanloo, Arzoo. 2006. "Islamico-Civil 'Rights Talk': Women, Subjectivity, and Law in Iranian Family Court." *American Ethnologist*. 33 (2): 191–209.

————. 2009. *The Politics of Women's Rights in Iran*. Princeton, NJ: Princeton University Press.

Ozer, Emily. 2016. "Youth-Led Participatory Action Research: Developmental and Equity Perspectives." In *Handbook of Methodological Approaches to Community-Based Research: Qualitative, Quantitative, and Mixed Methods*, edited by Leonard Jason and David Glenwick, 263–72. New York: Oxford University Press.

Panter Brick, Catherine. 2002. "Street Children, Human Rights, and Public Health: A Critique and Future Directions." *Annual Review of Anthropology* 31:147–71.

Perez, William. 2015. *Americans by Heart: Undocumented Latino Students and the Promise of Higher Education*. New York: Teachers College Press.

Peters, Michael. 2001. "Education, Enterprise Culture and the Entrepreneurial Self: A Foucauldian Perspective." *Journal of Educational Enquiry* 2 (2): 58–71.

Philippopoulos-Mihalopoulos, Andreas, and Sharron FitzGerald. 2008. "From Space Immaterial: The Invisibility of the Lawscape." *Griffith Law Review* 17 (2): 438–53.

Polikoff, Nancy. 1996. "Am I My Client?: The Role Confusion of a Lawyer Activist." *Harvard Civil Rights–Civil Liberties Law Review* 31:458.

Porter, Noah. 2003. "Falun Gong in the United States: An Ethnographic Study." Master's thesis, University of South Florida.

Portes, Alejandro, and Ruben Rumbaut. 2006. *Immigrant America: A Portrait*. Berkeley: University of California Press.

Pratt, Mary Louise. 1992. *Imperial Eyes: Travel Writing and Transculturation*. New York: Routledge.

Preston, Julia. 2009. "Immigration Judges Found Under Strain." *New York Times*, July 11, 2009.

Pribilsky, Jason. 2001. "Nervios and 'Modern Childhood'–Migration and Shifting Contexts of Child Life in the Ecuadorian Andes." *Childhood* 8 (2): 251–273.

Pruitt, Lisa. 2006. "Rural Rhetoric." *Connecticut Law Review* 39 (1) 159–240.

Pruitt, Lisa, and Bradley Showman. 2014. "Law Stretched Thin: Access to Justice in Rural America." *South Dakota Law Review* 59:466–528.

Pupavac, Vanessa. 2006. "Humanitarian Politics and the Rise of International Disaster Psychology." In *The Handbook of International Disaster Psychology: Fundamentals and Overview*, edited by Gilbert Reyes and Gerard Jacobs, 15–34. Westport, CT: Praeger.

Quesada, James. 2009. "The Vicissitudes of Structural Violence: Nicaragua at the turn of the 21st Century." In *Global Health in Times of Violence*, edited by Barbara Rylko-Bauer, Linda Whiteford, and Paul Farmer, 157–80. Santa Fe, NM: School for Advanced Research.

Qvortrup, Jens. 1999. "Childhood and Societal Macrostructures." Working Paper No. 9. Odense: Department of Contemporary Cultural Studies, University of Southern Denmark.

Rae-Espinoza, Heather. 2016. "Transnational Ties: Children's Reactions to Parental Emigration in Guayaquil, Ecuador." *Ethos* 44 (1): 32–49.

Rhode, Deborah. 1982. "Class Conflicts in Class Actions." *Stanford Law Review* 34:1183–262.

Rodriguez, Clara. 1997. *Latin Looks: Images of Latinas and Latinos in the US Media*. Boulder: Westview Press.

Rosenblum, Marc, and Isabel Ball. 2016. "Trends in Unaccompanied Child and Family Migration from Central America." Migration Policy Institute Fact Sheets. January 2016. *www.migrationpolicy.org/research/trends-unaccompanied-child-and-family-migration-central-america*.

Rosenwald, George, and Richard Ochberg, eds. 1992. *Storied Lives: The Cultural Politics of Self-Understanding*. New Haven, CT: Yale University Press.

Ruggerio, Vicenzo. 2003. "Global Markets and Crime." In *Critical Reflections on Transnational Organized Crime, Money Laundering, and Corruption*, edited by Margaret Beare, 171–82. Toronto: University of Toronto Press.

Rumbaut, Rubén. 2005. "Turning Points in the Transition to Adulthood: Determinants of Educational Attainment, Incarceration, and Early

Childbearing among Children of Immigrants." *Ethnic and Racial Studies* 28 (6): 1041–86.

Rumbaut, Ruben, and Golnaz Komaie. 2010. "Immigration and Adult Transitions." *Future of Children* 20 (1): 39–63.

Ruskola, Teemu. 2013. *Legal Orientalism: China, the United States, and Modern Law.* Cambridge, MA: Harvard University Press.

Saler, Benson. 2003. "The Ethnographer as Pontifex." In *Translating Cultures: Perspectives on Translation and Anthropology,* edited by Paula G. Rubel and Abraham Rosman, 197–212. New York: Berg.

Sanghera, Jyoti. 2005. "Unpacking the Trafficking Discourse." In *Trafficking and Prostitution Reconsidered: New Perspectives on Migration, Sex Work, and Human Rights,* edited by Kamala Kempadoo, Jyoti Sanghera, and Bandana Pattanaik, 3–24. Boulder, CO: Paradigm Publishers.

Santos, Boaventura de Sousa. 1995. "Beyond Neoliberal Governance: The World Social Forum as Subaltern Cosmopolitan Politics and Legality." In *Law and Globalization from Below: Towards a Cosmopolitan Legality,* edited by Boaventura de Sousa Santos and Cesar A. Rodriguez-Garavito, 29–63. Cambridge, UK: Cambridge University Press.

Sarat, Austin. 1998. "Between (the Presence of) Violence and (the Possibility of) Justice: Lawyering against Capital Punishment." In *Cause Lawyering: Political Commitments and Professional Responsibilities,* edited by Austin Sarat and Stuart Scheingold, 317–46. Oxford: Oxford University Press.

Sarat, Austin, and Stuart Scheingold. 1998. "Cause Lawyering and the Reproduction of Professional Authority: An Introduction." In *Cause Lawyering: Political Commitments and Professional Responsibilities,* edited by Austin Sarat and Stuart Scheingold, 3–28. Oxford: Oxford University Press.

———. 2001. "State Transformation, Globalization, and the Possibilities of Cause Lawyering: An Introduction." In *Cause Lawyering and the State in a Global Era,* edited by Austin Sarat and Stuart Scheingold, 3–31. New York: Oxford University Press.

———. 2005. "The Dynamics of Cause Lawyering: Constraints and Opportunities." In *The Worlds Cause Lawyers Make: Structure and Agency in Legal Practice,* edited by Austin Sarat and Stuart Scheingold, 1–34. Stanford, CA: Stanford University Press.

———. 2008. *The Cultural Lives of Cause Lawyers.* Cambridge, UK: Cambridge University Press.

Scheingold, Stuart. 2004. *The Politics of Rights.* Ann Arbor: University of Michigan Press.

Scheingold, Stuart, and Austin Sarat, eds. 2004. *Something to Believe In: Politics, Professionalism, and Cause Lawyering.* Stanford, CA: Stanford University Press.

Schlechter, Katie. 2016. "Reunification with Family in the US is Bittersweet for Child Migrants." April 19, 2016. *latinousa.org/2016/04/19/reunification-family-us-bittersweet-child-migrants.*

Schuck, Peter H. 1998. *Citizens, Strangers, and In-Betweens: Essays on Immigration and Citizenship*. Boulder: Westview Press.

Scott, James C. 1998. *Seeing Like a State: How Certain Schemes to Improve the Human Condition Have Failed*. New Haven, CT: Yale University Press.

Semple, Kirk. 2014. "Surge in Child Migrants Reaches New York, Overwhelming Advocates." *New York Times*, June 17, 2014. *www.nytimes.com/2014/06/18/nyregion/immigration-child-migrant-surge-in-New-York-City.html*.

Shamir, Ronan, and Sara Chinski. 1998. "Destruction of Houses and Construction of a Cause: Lawyers and Bedouins in Israeli Courts." In *Cause Lawyering: Political Commitments and Professional Responsibilities*, edited by Austin Sarat and Stuart Scheingold, 227–57. Oxford: Oxford University Press.

Shdaimah, Corey. 2005. "Dilemmas of Progressive Lawyering: Empowerment and Hierarchy." In *The Worlds Cause Lawyers Make: Structure and Agency in Legal Practice*, edited by Austin Sarat and Stuart Scheingold, 239–73. Stanford, CA: Stanford University Press.

———. 2009. *Negotiating Justice: Progressive Lawyering, Low-Income Clients, and the Quest for Social Change*. New York: New York University Press.

Showden, Carisa. 2011. *Choices Women Make: Agency in Domestic Violence, Assisted Reproduction, and Sex Work*. Minneapolis: University of Minnesota Press.

Shuman, Amy. 2005. *Other People's Stories: Entitlement Claims and the Critique of Empathy*. Urbana: University of Illinois Press.

Sime, Daniela, and Rachael Fox. 2015. "Migrant Children, Social Capital and Access to Services Post-Migration: Transitions, Negotiations and Complex Agencies." *Children and Society* 29 (6): 524–34.

———. 1984. "Visions of Practice in Legal Thought." *Stanford Law Review* 36:469–507.

Southworth, Ann. 2005a. "Conservative Lawyers and the Contest over the Meaning of Public Interest Law." *UCLA Law Review* 52:1223–78.

———. 2005b. "Professional Identity and Political Commitment among Lawyers for Conservative Causes." In *The Worlds Cause Lawyers Make: Structure and Agency in Legal Practice*, edited by Austin Sarat and Stuart Scheingold, 83–111. Stanford, CA: Stanford University Press.

Spence, Jonathan. 1999. *The Search for Modern China*. New York: W. W. Norton.

Stadum, Beverly. 1995. "The Dilemma in Saving Children from Child Labor: Reform and Casework at Odds with Families' Needs." *Child Welfare* 74 (1): 20–33.

Statz, Michele. 2016a. "Between Children and Transnational Economic Actors: The Discounted 'Belongings' of Young Chinese Migrants." *PoLAR: Political and Legal Anthropology Review* 39 (S1): 4–18.

———. 2016b. "Chinese Difference and Deservingness: The Paper Lives of Young Migrants." *American Behavioral Scientist* 60 (13): 1629–48.

———. 2018. "Transnational Migration and the Construction of Vulnerability." In *Routledge Handbook on Ethics and International Relations*, edited by Brent Steel and Eric Heinze. New York: Routledge.

Stephens, Sharon. 1995. *Children and the Politics of Culture*. Princeton, NJ: Princeton University Press.

Stepick, Alex, and Carol Dutton Stepick. 2002. "Becoming American, Constructing Ethnicity: Immigrant Youth and Civic Engagement." *Applied Developmental Science*, 6 (4): 246–57.

Sterett, Susan. 1998. "Caring about Individual Cases: Immigration Lawyering in Britain." In *Cause Lawyering: Political and Professional Responsibilities*, edited by Austin Sarat and Stuart Scheingold, 293–316. New York: Oxford University Press.

Suarez-Orozco, Carola, and Marcelo Suarez-Orozco. 2001. *Children of Immigration*. Cambridge, MA: Harvard University Press.

Terrio, Susan. 2014. "Life Ended There: Rare Interviews with the Children of America's Border Disaster." *Politico Magazine*, July 10, 2014. *www.politico.com/magazine/story/2014/07/children-border-detention-108788*.

———. 2015. *Whose Child Am I?: Unaccompanied, Undocumented Children in US Immigration Custody*. Berkeley: University of California Press.

Thronson, David. 2002. "Kids Will Be Kids?: Reconsidering Conceptions of Children's Rights Underlying Immigration Law." *Ohio State Law Journal* 63:979–1016.

———. 2005. "Of Borders and Best Interests: Examining the Experiences of Undocumented Immigrants in US Family Courts." *Texas Hispanic Journal of Law and Policy* 11:45–73.

———. 2008. "Custody and Contradictions: Exploring Immigration Law as Federal Family Law in the Context of Child Custody." *Hastings Law Journal* 59:453–513.

Ticktin, Miriam. 2006. "Where Ethics and Politics Meet: The Violence of Humanitarianism in France." *American Ethnologist* 33 (1): 33–49.

———. 2011. *Casualties of Care: Immigration and the Politics of Humanitarianism in France*. Berkeley: University of California Press.

———. 2014. "Transnational Humanitarianism." *Annual Review of Anthropology* 43:273–89.

Timmer, Andria. 2010. "Constructing the 'Needy Subject': NGO Discourses of Roma Need." *PoLAR: Political and Legal Anthropology Review* 33 (2): 264–81.

Tocqueville, Alexis de. (1835 and 1840) 2000. *Democracy in America*. Edited by Harvey Mansfield and Delba Winthrop. Chicago: University of Chicago Press.

Toor, Rachel. 2017. "Scholars Talk Writing: Ruth Behar." *Chronicle of Higher Education*, April 23, 2017. *www.chronicle.com/article/Scholars-Talk-Writing-Ruth/239847*.

TRAC (Transactional Records Action Clearinghouse). 2013. "Fourfold Increase in Prosecutions of Child Sex Trafficking Crimes Since 2008." August 21, 2013. *trac.syr.edu/tracreports/crim/328*.

Tremblay, Paul R. 1992. "Rebellious Lawyering, Regnant Lawyering, and Street-level Bureaucracy." *Hastings Law Journal* 43:947–70.

Tyrrell, Ian. 1991. "American Exceptionalism in an Age of International History." *American Historical Review* 96 (4): 1031–55.

Uehling, Greta Lynn. 2008. "The International Smuggling of Children: Coyotes, Snakeheads, and the Politics of Compassion." *Anthropological Quarterly* 81 (4): 833–71.

UN General Assembly. 1948. Universal Declaration of Human Rights (UDHR). Resolution 217 A (3) of December 10, 1948. *www.refworld.org/docid/ 3ae6b3712c.html.*

UNODC (United Nations Office on Drugs and Crime). 2010. "Factsheet on Human Trafficking." Accessed April 15, 2017. *www.unodc.org/documents/ human-trafficking/UNVTF_fs_HT_EN.pdf.*

USCIS. 2013. "Questions and Answers: Updated Procedures for Determination of Initial Jurisdiction over Asylum Applications Filed by Unaccompanied Alien Children." June 10, 2013. *www.uscis.gov/sites/default/files/USCIS/Refugee% 2C%20Asylum%2C%20and%20Int%27l%20Ops/Asylum/ra-qanda-determine- jurisdiction-uac.pdf.*

Watson, James. 1982. "Chinese Kinship Reconsidered: Anthropological Perspectives on Historical Research." *Chinese Quarterly* 92:589–622.

Watson, Rubie. 1985. *Inequality among Brothers: Class and Kinship in South China.* Cambridge, UK: Cambridge University Press.

Weissman, Deborah, Rebecca C. Headen, and Katherine Lewis Parker. 2009. *The Policies and Politics of Local Immigration Enforcement Laws: 287(g) Program in North Carolina.* Chapel Hill: American Civil Liberties Union of North Carolina Legal Foundation and University of North Carolina at Chapel Hill Legal Immigration and Human Rights Policy Clinic.

White, Allen, Caitriona Ní Laoire, Naomi Tyrrell, and Fina Carpena-Mendez. 2011. "Children's Roles in Transnational Migration." *Journal of Ethnic and Migration Studies* 37 (8): 1159–70.

White, James Boyd. 1990. *Justice as Translation: An Essay in Cultural and Legal Criticism.* Chicago: University of Chicago Press.

White, Lucie. 2001. "Two Worlds of Ghanaian Cause Lawyers." In *Cause Lawyering and the State in a Global Era,* edited by Austin Sarat and Stuart Scheingold, 35–67. New York: Oxford University Press.

Willen, Sarah. 2007. "Toward a Critical Phenomenology of 'Illegality': State Power, Criminalization, and Abjectivity among Undocumented Migrant Workers in Tel Aviv, Israel." *International Migration* 45 (3): 8–38.

———. 2012. "Migration, 'Illegality,' and Health: Mapping Embodied Vulnerability and Debating Health-Related Deservingness." *Social Science and Medicine* 74 (6): 805–11.

———. 2015. "Lightning Rods in the Local Moral Economy: Debating Unauthorized Migrants' Deservingness in Israel." *International Migration* 53 (3): 70–86.

Wolf, Marjorie. 1972. *Women and the Family in Rural Taiwan.* Stanford, CA: Stanford University Press.

Wollstonecraft, Mary. (1792) 1975. *A Vindication of the Rights of Woman*, edited by Miriam Brody Kramnick. London: Penguin Books.

Wood, Julie Myers, and Wendy Young. 2013. "Children Alone and Lawyerless in a Strange Land." *Wall Street Journal*, September 23, 2013.

Yan, Yunxiang. 2003. *Private Life Under Socialism: Love, Intimacy, and Family Change in a Chinese Village*. Stanford, CA: Stanford University Press.

Yarris, Kristin. 2014. "'Quiero ir y no quiero ir' (I Want to Go and I Don't Want to Go): Nicaraguan Children's Ambivalent Experiences of Transnational Family Life." *Journal of Latin American and Caribbean Anthropology* 19 (2): 284–309.

Yarris, Kristin, and Heide Casteneda. 2015. "Discourses of Displacement and Deservingness: Interrogating Distinctions between 'Economic' and 'Forced' Migration." *International Migration* 53 (3): 64–69.

Yngvesson, Barbara, and Susan Coutin. 2008. "Schrodinger's Cat and the Ethnography of Law." *PoLAR: Political and Legal Anthropology Review* 31 (1): 61–78.

Young, Lorraine. 2004. "Journeys to the Street: The Complex Migration Geographies of Ugandan Street Children," *Geoforum* 35 (4): 471–88.

Yousef, Odette. 2013. "Sharp Rise in Young, Unaccompanied Illegal Immigrants Tests US." *WBEZ News*. June 4, 2013. *www.wbez.org/shows/wbez-news/sharp-rise-in-young-unaccompanied-illegal-immigrants-tests-us/ef1a5c89-75d7-4ba3-ab69-c8424755dc9e*.

Zatz, Marjorie S., and Nancy Rodriguez. 2015. *Dreams and Nightmares: Immigration Policy, Youth, and Families*. Berkeley: University of California Press.

Zelizer, Viviana. 1985. *Pricing the Priceless Child: The Changing Social Value of Children*. Princeton, NJ: Princeton University Press.

Zetter, Roger. 1991. "Labeling Refugees: Forming and Transforming a Bureaucratic Identity." *Journal of Refugee Studies* 4 (1): 39–62.

Zhu, Guohong. 1990. "A Probe into Reasons for International Migration in Fujian Province." *Chinese Journal of Population Science* 2 (3): 229.

Zuniga, Victor, and Ruben Hernandez-Leon, eds. 2005. *New Destinations: Mexican Immigration in the United States*. New York: Russell Sage Foundation.

INDEX

John (attorney). *See* Sullivan, John
Jolie, Angelina, 169
Judd, Ellen, 197n6
June (attorney), 61–62
justice AmeriCorps, 183

Kempadoo, Kamala, 199n5
Kim (attorney), 106–7
KIND (Kids in Need of Defense),
    195n7, 206n15
Kwong, Peter, 72–73, 95–96

Lana (attorney)
    on cause lawyering, 60, 62, 63
    counseling services and, 206n17
    on Fujianese migrants, 91, 109–10,
        176
    on "job shops," 164
    on legal "success," 156, 176
Law on the Control of Exit and Entry
    of Citizens (1985), 71–72
Lawful Permanent Resident (LPR)
    status, 12, 120, 159, 161
Len (immigration law professor),
    79–81, 111, 114–15, 159, 174
Li (migrant), 126
Li v. INS (1996), 201–2n22
Lisette (attorney), 31, 110–11, 113,
    180
Liu, Shao-hua, 90
Lixue (migrant), 117–18
Locke, John, 36, 40, 157–58
Lustig, Stuart, 58

MacDonnell, Margaret, 198n2
Maine, Henry, 36–37, 40
Malkki, Liisa, 99
Margaret (cause lawyer), 79–80
Maria (attorney). *See* Woltjen, Maria
Maria Teresa (attorney), 171
Marsha (attorney), 109
McKinley, Michelle, 106, 127
Mei (migrant), 145, 153

Mexican youth migrants, 190n15,
    207n1
Michael (legal scholar), 100
migrant workers, 5
Miner, Casey, 58
Ming Dynasty (1368–1644), 70
Ming-Yue (social worker), 94, 95–97,
    158–59, 164
modern attitude, 117
Morando Lakhani, Sarah, 105–6
mutual-aid associations, 93–97

Nader, Laura, 28, 29–30
Nanjing Treaty (1842), 70
National Child Welfare, Juvenile, and
    Family Law Conference, 27
Nelson (attorney), 111–12
New York Times (newspaper), 182
Nieuwenhuys, Olga, 158
nonprofit organizations, 27, 34–35,
    43

O'Brien, Erin, 101
Office of Refugee Resettlement (ORR)
    cause lawyers and, 43
    fieldwork and, 21
    role of, 43, 56, 61, 62, 107,
        193n26
    "On Their Own" conference and, 2
"On Their Own: Protecting the Rights
    of Immigrant Children" conference
    (Washington, DC, 2012), 1–4, 47,
    49, 51, 120, 185
"one child policy," 75–77
Ong, Aiwha, 106
Operation Streamline, 17
Opium War (1839–1842), 70
Organization of American States
    (OAS), 1

Painter v. Bannister (1966), 13–14
People's Republic of China (PRC). *See*
    China

www.ingramcontent.com/pod-product-compliance
Lightning Source LLC
Chambersburg PA
CBHW030647270326
41929CB00007B/242